OXFORD WORLD'

LETTERS CON
THE ENGLISH

VOLTAIRE was the assumed name of François-Marie Arouet (1694–1778). Born into a well-to-do Parisian family, he was educated at the leading Jesuit college in Paris. Having refused to follow his father and elder brother into the legal profession he soon won widespread acclaim for *Œdipe* (1718), the first of some fifty tragedies which he continued to write until the end of his life. His national epic *La Henriade* (1723) confirmed his reputation as the leading French literary figure of his generation. Following a quarrel with the worthless but influential aristocrat, the chevalier de Rohan, he travelled to England. This period (1726–8) was particularly formative, and his *Letters concerning the English Nation* (1733) constitute the first major expression of Voltaire's deism and his subsequent lifelong opposition to religious and political oppression. Following the happy years (1734–43) spent at Cirey with his mistress Mme Du Châtelet in the shared pursuit of several intellectual enthusiasms, notably the work of Isaac Newton, he enjoyed a brief interval of favour at court during which he was appointed Historiographer to the King. After the death of Mme Du Châtelet in 1749 he finally accepted an invitation to the court of Frederick of Prussia, but left in 1753 when life with this particular enlightened despot became intolerable. In 1755, after temporary sojourn in Colmar, he settled at Les Délices on the outskirts of Geneva. He then moved to nearby Ferney in 1759, the year *Candide* was published. Thereafter a spate of tragedies, stories, philosophical works, and polemical tracts, not to mention a huge number of letters, poured from his pen. The writer of competent tragedies had become the militant embodiment of the Age of Enlightenment. After the death of Louis XV in 1774 he eventually returned to Paris in 1778 for the performance of his last tragedy *Irène*. He was acclaimed and fêted by the entire capital as the greatest living Frenchman and as one of the most effective champions of freedom, tolerance, and common sense the world has ever seen. He died there on 30 May 1778.

NICHOLAS CRONK is Director of the Voltaire Foundation and General Editor of *The Complete Works of Voltaire*, and Fellow of St Edmund Hall, Oxford. He has edited Rostand, *Cyrano de Bergerac* and Diderot, *Rameau's Nephew and First Satire* for Oxford World's Classics.

OXFORD WORLD'S CLASSICS

*For over 100 years Oxford World's Classics have brought
readers closer to the world's great literature. Now with over 700
titles—from the 4,000-year-old myths of Mesopotamia to the
twentieth century's greatest novels—the series makes available
lesser-known as well as celebrated writing.*

*The pocket-sized hardbacks of the early years contained
introductions by Virginia Woolf, T. S. Eliot, Graham Greene,
and other literary figures which enriched the experience of reading.
Today the series is recognized for its fine scholarship and
reliability in texts that span world literature, drama and poetry,
religion, philosophy and politics. Each edition includes perceptive
commentary and essential background information to meet the
changing needs of readers.*

OXFORD WORLD'S CLASSICS

═══

VOLTAIRE

Letters concerning the English Nation

═══

Edited with an Introduction and Notes by
NICHOLAS CRONK

OXFORD
UNIVERSITY PRESS

OXFORD

UNIVERSITY PRESS

Great Clarendon Street, Oxford OX2 6DP

Oxford University Press is a department of the University of Oxford.
It furthers the University's objective of excellence in research, scholarship,
and education by publishing worldwide in

Oxford New York

Athens Auckland Bangkok Bogotá Buenos Aires Calcutta
Cape Town Chennai Dar es Salaam Delhi Florence Hong Kong Istanbul
Karachi Kuala Lumpur Madrid Melbourne Mexico City Mumbai
Nairobi Paris São Paulo Shanghai Singapore Taipei Tokyo Toronto Warsaw

with associated companies in Berlin Ibadan

Oxford is a registered trade mark of Oxford University Press
in the UK and in certain other countries

Published in the United States
by Oxford University Press Inc., New York

Editorial material © Nicholas Cronk 1994

The moral rights of the author have been asserted

Database right Oxford University Press (maker)

First published as a World's Classics paperback 1994
Reissued as an Oxford World's Classics paperback 1999
Reissued 2009

British Library Cataloguing in Publication Data

Data available

Library of Congress Cataloging in Publication Data

Voltaire, 1694–1778.
[Lettres philosophiques. English]
Letters concerning the English nation/Voltaire: edited with an
introduction by Nicholas Cronk.
p.   cm.—(Oxford world's classics)
1. Imaginery letters. 2. Philosophy, Modern—18th century.
3. Great Britain—Civilization—18th century. I. Cronk, Nicholas.
II. Title. III. Series
942.07—dc20   PQ2086.L4E5   1994   93–38332

ISBN 978–0–19–955532–1

12

Printed in Great Britain by
Clays Ltd, Elcograf S.p.A.

CONTENTS

ACKNOWLEDGEMENTS

I am extremely grateful to William Barber for his comments on the Introduction and Notes, and to Nicholas John for awakening my interest in Rolli; Giles Barber, Andrew Brown, and Charles Wirz have been generous with help and advice on bibliographical matters. The errors which remain are my unique contribution. Richard Fargher has been teaching me about this text since I was an undergraduate: to him this volume is affectionately dedicated.

INTRODUCTION

VOLTAIRE: AN AUGUSTAN AUTHOR

A perfect Judge will *read* each Work of Wit
With the same Spirit that its Author *writ*.
(Pope, *An Essay on Criticism*)

Oliver Goldsmith in 1760 described Voltaire as 'the poet and philosopher of Europe'.[1] By then in his mid-sixties, Voltaire was the most famous living author, and his estate at Ferney, close to Geneva, was becoming a place of pilgrimage for travellers on the Grand Tour. British visitors were especially favoured: he joked to one group that 'if ever I smell of a Resurrection, or come a second time on Earth, I will pray God to make me be born in England, the Land of Liberty'.[2] The reported remark has all the more savour for being framed in Voltaire's own English. 'I addressed him in English . . . which he spoke with tolerable fluency,' wrote one visitor, while another recorded that: 'He affected to talk chiefly in English (which he speaks very tolerably).'[3] Two visitors from the American colonies were more precise in their assessment of his linguistic abilities:

Although at a loss sometimes for an english Word, and that he used many Gallecisms, yet he took pains to articulate his words properly and accent them fully. In this he succeeded beyond what one might expect from his having been but only twelve Month in england and that so many years past as in 1726. We meet with few French men who pronounce english better.[4]

In fact, Voltaire had spent two-and-a-half years in England, and forty years later at Ferney he was still quoting Dryden

---

[1] *The Citizen of the World*, Letter 43. (For full details of works cited in the notes, see the Select Bibliography.)

[2] G. de Beer and A.-M. Rousseau, *Voltaire's British Visitors*, 73.

[3] Ibid. 130, 153.

[4] Ibid. 71.

by heart to impress his visitors. He could still swear in English, too, as James Boswell discovered:

I got [Voltaire] to speak English, which he does in a degree that made me now and then start up and cry, 'Upon my soul this is astonishing!' When he talked our language he was animated with the soul of a Briton. He had bold flights. He had humour. He had an extravagance; he had a forcible oddity of style that the most comical of our *dramatis personae* could not have exceeded. He swore bloodily, as was the fashion when he was in England . . .[5]

Voltaire was a lifelong actor, and Boswell not the only visitor to be subjected to this display of outmoded Augustan oaths. After his arrival in England in 1726, Voltaire had apparently learned his English largely in the theatre, and so his English never quite lost its theatrical tang. William Chetwood, who worked at Drury Lane, later recalled Voltaire's visits:

This noted Author, about twenty Years past, resided in *London*. His Acquaintance with the *Laureat* brought him frequently to the Theatre, where (he confess'd) he improved in the *English* Orthography more in a Week, than he should otherwise have done by labour'd Study in a Month. I furnish'd him every Evening with the Play of the Night, which he took with him into the *Orchestre* (his accustomed Seat): In four or five Months, he not only convers'd in elegant *English*, but wrote it with exact Propriety.[6]

Voltaire also understood the need to put into practice what he heard and read: in a letter to his French friend Thiriot, written in English after less than six months in England, Voltaire reflects on the death of his own sister: 'Life is but a dream full of starts of folly, and of fancied, and true miseries. Death awakes us from this painful dream, and gives us, either a better existence or no existence at all' (D303).[7] Thiriot must surely have been impressed by Voltaire's fluency of style, though he may not have recog-

[5] *Journals*, 28 Dec. 1764.

[6] W. R. Chetwood, *A General History of the Stage, from its Origin in Greece down to the Present Time* (London: Owen, 1749), 46–7.

[7] References throughout to Voltaire's correspondence are to Besterman's 'definitive' edition.

nized the pastiche of Hamlet's soliloquy. Voltaire's grasp of literary register in his newly acquired language was not, however, always so assured. His relationship with Alexander Pope never quite recovered from a supper at Twickenham when, in response to a polite enquiry from Pope's mother about his poor health, Voltaire explained to her that 'those damned Jesuits, when I was a boy, buggered me to such a degree that I shall never get over it as long as I live'. Thomas Gray, to whom we owe this report, adds that: 'This was said in English aloud before the servants.'[8]

Many Continental thinkers and writers came to England in search of Enlightenment—the abbé Prévost and Montesquieu both followed Voltaire in the late 1720s—but it was rare for such visitors to make much effort to master English (Prévost, later to translate Richardson into French, is an exception, but he had the incentive of wanting to seduce the actress Anne Oldfield). Voltaire from the start made a determined effort to acquire English, keeping a notebook in which he recorded comments and observations in English. While in England, he wrote letters in English, not only to English acquaintances (including Pope and Swift) but also, more surprisingly, to French friends in France; his claim that this was for reasons of confidentiality is not convincing: these English letters to France show Voltaire experimenting with a new *persona*, that of the English author. Thus, in the two-and-a-half years which he spent in England, he published a pair of essays in English, began a play intended for the English stage and, most importantly, wrote over half of the *Letters concerning the English Nation*. Voltaire nurtured the extraordinary ambition not just to write in English but to write as an English author.

The story of Voltaire's precipitate departure for England is well known: the young and impetuous poet, beaten by the servants of an aristocrat for supposed insolence and incarcerated in the Bastille by the authorities to prevent a duel,

---

[8] A.-M. Rousseau, *L'Angleterre et Voltaire*, i. 113.

flees the humiliation and oppression of *ancien régime*
France and seeks exile and freedom in England. It is a good
story, a kind of Enlightenment morality tale, and it is
very largely a fiction. In a letter which Voltaire wrote to
George I on 6 October 1725[9] (D250) requesting royal
patronage for the poem later known as *La Henriade*, he
declares his wish to travel to London. Thus the journey was
evidently in his mind well before he became embroiled in
the quarrel with the chevalier de Rohan-Chabot—which, in
the event, did not cause his departure from France but did
cause its delay. The true reason for his journey to England
is stated explicitly in two letters of recommendation which
the British ambassador to Paris, Horatio Walpole, wrote in
May 1726 to the Duke of Newcastle (D296) and to George
Bubb Dodington: 'Mr Voltaire, a French poet, who has
wrote several pieces with great success here, being gone for
England in order to print by subscription an excellent
poem, called *Henry IV*, which, on account of some bold
strokes in it against persecution and the priests, cannot be
printed here' (D295).

Voltaire's decision to publish *La Henriade* in London is
not surprising. He was surely attracted to the image of
England as a land of freedom (a cliché of contemporary
travel writing), and there were English friends, such as
Bolingbroke and Fawkener, whose acquaintance he had
already made in Paris. Voltaire's primary reason for wish-
ing to visit England, however, was purely professional;
he was extremely ambitious—a letter written as early as
1721 (D101) talks of his hopes of entering the Académie
française—and the summit of this youthful ambition seems
to have been a desire to excel in the two genres canonized by
Aristotle. His first major literary success, *Œdipe*, in 1718,
had established him as a master of classical tragedy, and he
then sought to consolidate his literary reputation by com-

---

[9] Dates, like this one, referring to France are given in New Style; dates
referring to Britain are given in Old Style. Britain remained eleven days
behind the rest of Europe until 1752, when it finally adopted the Gregorian
calendar.

posing an epic poem. The subject of the siege of Paris by the future Henry IV during the religious wars of the late sixteenth century gave him ample opportunity to depict religious fanaticism and to dwell on the virtues of toleration; under the title *La Ligue*, the poem was published surreptitiously in 1723, and it enjoyed an enormous success. No other work had brought him such acclaim, and Voltaire considered it the major achievement of his career so far (an autobiography written in the 1770s would be entitled *Commentaire historique sur les œuvres de l'auteur de la Henriade*); he continued work on his epic, adding a sixth book, and it was natural that he should wish to oversee a definitive and handsome edition of the enlarged poem. Given the criticisms of Catholicism expressed in the work (notably in a full-dress description of the St Bartholomew's Eve massacre of Protestants in 1572), Voltaire knew that it would not be possible to publish the new edition in France, and London, with its large community of French Huguenot printers and booksellers, was therefore an obvious choice. As he later wrote in his third-person autobiography (quoted here in the English translation published in 1777)— it is the only comment on his English visit he makes in this work—'These continual mortifications determined him to print the *Henriade* in England, as he could neither obtain privilege nor patronage for it in France.'[10]

Once in England, Voltaire studiously sought all those who could assist him in his project, and he enlisted the help of friends to set up a subscription for the first edition of *La Henriade* (as the poem was now called). That this was his principal concern after arriving in England is clear from a letter which John Gay wrote on 22 November 1726 to his friend James Dormer, then abroad:

We have a famous French Author in town, who upon a Quarrell with the Chevalier de Rohan is banish'd his Country. He hath been here about half a year, and begins to speak English very well.

[10] *Historical memoirs*, 548. At an earlier stage, Voltaire had hesitated between London, Amsterdam, and Geneva as places to publish *La Henriade* (see D259).

His name is Voltaire, the Author of Oedipe. He hath finish'd his Poem of the Ligue, which he intends to publish in England in Quarto with very fine copper plates which he hath got already grav'd by the best Gravers in Paris.[11]

A year later Voltaire had made sufficient progress in his new language to be able to write two essays in English, *An Essay upon the Civil Wars of France and also upon the Epick Poetry of the European Nations from Homer down to Milton*, which he published in one volume in December 1727; the work enjoyed some success, and there were several further editions. To write a book in a language he had been studying for little more than a year was an extraordinary feat—as he himself pointed out:

It is to be hoped, [the Reader] will look with some Indulgence on the Diction of this Essay, and pardon the Failings of one who has learn'd *English* but this Year, of one who has drawn most of his Observations from Books written in *England*, and who pays to this Country but Part of what he owes to her. A Nurse is not displeased with the stammering Articulations of a Child, who delivers to her with much ado his first undigested Thoughts.[12]

Paolo Rolli, an Italian who published a reply to the *Essay on Epic Poetry*, grudgingly acknowledged Voltaire's achievement:

As for his having learned *English* so soon, I only admire his Vanity, and his pretty Simile of the *Nurse* who *was not displeased with the stammering Articulations of a Child*, particularly when she help'd him. I have been now twelve Years in *England*, and have apply'd me self to the understanding of so opulent a Language; wherefore I thought myself obliged to answer M. *V.* in the very Language he has writ his Essay; but I do own I have been corrected by my Learned Friends; and tho' corrected, I am sensible that my Reader will immediately find me out for a Foreigner.[13]

---

[11] *The Letters of John Gay*, ed. C. F. Burgess (Oxford, 1966), 63.

[12] *An Essay upon the Civil Wars of France, and also upon the Epick Poetry of the European Nations from Homer down to Milton* (London: Jallasson, 1727), 47.

[13] Paul Rolli, *Remarks upon M. Voltaire's Essay on the Epick Poetry of the European Nations* (London: Edlin, 1728), 24.

Voltaire's purpose in publishing the two *Essays* was clear. By writing first on the historical background of *La Henriade*, and then on the generic tradition to which it belonged, he was preparing his English readership for the edition of the French poem which by then was imminent. The great work finally appeared in March 1728, almost two years after he had first set foot in England, and with a dedication 'To the Queen': 'YOUR MAJESTY will find in this Book, bold impartial Truths, Morality unstained with Superstition, a Spirit of Liberty, equally abhorrent of Rebellion and of Tiranny, the Rights of Kings always asserted, and those of Mankind never laid aside.'

Perhaps the most surprising aspect of Voltaire's stay in England is that he did not return to France at this point. He had achieved all that he had come to do, and it seems that he could have obtained permission to return to France if he had so wished; instead, he chose to remain in London. He decided, in other words, to become an English author. In 1728 Paolo Rolli published in London his *Remarks upon M. Voltaire's Essay on the Epick Poetry of the European Nations* (in which he takes Voltaire to task for, among other things, his ignorance of *Macbeth*, *The Tempest*, and Spenser's *Faerie Queen*), and later, in 1741, Josiah Martin would publish *A Letter from one of the People call'd Quakers to Francis de Voltaire, occasioned by his remarks on that People in his Letters concerning the English Nation*; these two responses to Voltaire's English publications are of course a great compliment: they acknowledge and confirm his position as a figure in London's literary world.

It had been twelve years since he had begun work on his epic poem, and it belonged to a phase of his literary career which by now was closed. With *La Henriade* finally in print, Voltaire was free to turn his mind to new projects, and in April 1728 he writes to a French friend—in English—that 'I think and write like a free englishman' (D330). And so he did, embarking on two works in English, in addition to an important work of history, the *Histoire de Charles XII*, which he wrote in French. The two English

works were both considerably more ambitious than the pair
of essays which he had written in English the previous year.
The first, a response both to English government and to
Shakespearean theatre, was a play, *Brutus*, on the theme of
political freedom. When Voltaire left abruptly for France
later in the year, the first act was written; the English text
has not survived, apart from a fragment preserved in Oliver
Goldsmith's memoir of Voltaire.[14] The play was later completed in French and published in 1731 with an important
prefatory discourse on tragedy dedicated to Bolingbroke,
from which it is clear that the work had originally been
intended for the English stage:

Your Lordship knows that the Tragedy of *Brutus* was struck out
in *Great Britain*. You may remember that whilst I was in *Wandsworth* with my excellent friend Mr. *Faulkener*, I amused myself
with writing the first act of the following Tragedy in *English* prose,
which I have since work'd up in *French* verse, with little alteration.
I used to mention it to you sometimes, and we both wonder'd that
no *English* poet had yet attempted to raise a Tragedy upon this
subject, which, of all others, is perhaps the best adapted to the
English stage.[15]

Voltaire's other English project was even more ambitious: a book about the English, written in English, and
aimed therefore, at least initially, at an English readership.
As early as October 1726 he had written to Thiriot: 'One
day I will acquaint you with the character of this strange
people' (D303); the thought was still in his mind later that
year when he wrote the preface to his two English *Essays*:
'I am ordered to give an Account of my Journey into
England.'[16] Voltaire now turned his mind to this project,
the work which was to become the *Letters concerning the
English Nation*, and over half the book was finished (all the

---

[14] See Appendix C.

[15] 'A Discourse on Tragedy', *An Essay upon the Civil Wars and also
upon Epick Poetry*, fourth edition (London: Prevost, 1731), 1–2. This
English translation of the French preface to *Brutus* was added to the *Essays*
in 1731. Voltaire had earlier sketched out some notes for this preface in
English (*Notebooks*, i. 104–5).

[16] 'Advertisement to the Reader' (see Appendix B).

letters on religion and some of those on politics and literature) when in October or November work on it came to an abrupt standstill.

Voltaire's unexpected departure from England was suspiciously sudden, and the reasons for it remain unclear. (Thomas Gray—who admittedly disliked him—would later write that: 'If Voltaire had stayed longer in England, he would have been *hanged* for forging banknotes.')[17] Reintegration into France and into French literary life was not easy, and for a while 'my english letters', as Voltaire referred to the work (D502), were put on one side. In the preface to *Brutus*, he addresses Bolingbroke with the dilemma:

I will own to your Lordship, that at my return from *England*, where I had closely studied the *English* language for two years together, 'twas with some diffidence that I attempted to write a Tragedy in *French*. I had almost accustomed myself to think in *English*, and I found that the expressions of my own tongue were not now so familiar to me; 'twas like a river, whose course having been diverted, both time and pains were required to bring it back to its own bed.[18]

Brutus was first performed in December 1730, and the following year appeared the *Histoire de Charles XII*. 'As to the english letters, be sure I'll put the last hand to them in a very short time' (D488), writes Voltaire to Thiriot (then in England) in May 1732, and in December that year he tells another friend (in French this time): 'I am finally determined to publish these English letters, and because of that I have had to reread Newton' (D542). It is at this stage, 1732–3, that Voltaire found time to research and write the letters on Locke and Newton; they are different in tone from the letters which he had written in England, more soberly narrative and less brilliantly satirical; and he composed them in French—he was using French source materials and, since he had now been back in France for four years, his English was probably starting to get rusty.

[17] Rousseau, *L'Angleterre et Voltaire*, i. 153.
[18] 'A Discourse on Tragedy', 2.

But Voltaire was still writing with an English as well as a French audience in mind, for early in 1733 he dispatched to London a manuscript containing the letters which he had originally written in English in 1727–8, supplemented by the letters written in French in 1732–3, and asked his friend Thiriot (the fictive addressee of the letters), then in London, to see the work through the press. A translator in London was put to work to turn the French letters into English, and at the end of April, perhaps before the translation was even finished, the printer William Bowyer began work on the text. The first edition of 2,000 copies was ready by August, and the work was advertised in the press.

Not until the following year, 1734, did the same London printer produce a French version of the work, with the title *Lettres écrites de Londres sur les Anglois.* Voltaire was evidently nervous about publishing the book in France but he continued to rework the French text, and eventually entrusted a third version to a printer in Rouen, where it appeared clandestinely in 1734 as the *Lettres philosophiques.* For the first time the text included a twenty-fifth letter on Pascal (see Appendix A), and it is this enlarged French edition of the 'English Letters' which is now the best- (or only) known version of the work; it has so totally eclipsed the earlier London editions that the status and importance of the original English text have been consistently overlooked.[19]

There survives a sketch (in French) of a letter in which Voltaire describes a French traveller's arrival in England;[20] it is written very much in the style of earlier travel writers to England, using the commonplaces then current about the English, such as their predilection for suicide. That Voltaire decided at some point to discard the letter from the final volume (and also a more philosophical treatment of suicide, of which a fragment survives in French) is a revealing indication of the work's genesis: the *Letters* may have begun as

[19] For more detail on this point, see Note on the Text.
[20] See *Lettres philosophiques*, ed. Lanson, ii. 256–77.

one more travel narrative, but they grew into the portrait and critique of a civilization. If he had no obvious model to follow, there was one which he was eager to avoid, and he is dismissive of the superficial and often facetious accounts of certain authors:

I will leave to others the Care of describing with Accuracy, *Paul*'s Church, the *Monument*, *Westminster*, *Stonehenge*, etc. I consider *England* in another View; it strikes my Eyes as it is the Land which hath produced a *Newton*, a *Lock*, a *Tillotson*, a *Milton*, a *Boyle*, and many great Men either dead or alive, whose Glory in War, in State-Affairs, or in Letters, will not be confined to the Bounds of this Island.[21]

This is more than just a rejection of a certain style of travel writing; it is a manifesto for a new form of cultural history. William Kent's 'Temple of British Worthies' (1735) at Stowe is an iconographical lesson in Whig history, with busts of, among others, Bacon, Locke, Newton, Shakespeare, Milton, and Sir Thomas Gresham (representing 'the honourable profession of a merchant'). The *Letters concerning the English Nation* constitute a similar pantheon of Whig heroes. (Milton's absence from the *Letters*, apart from the reference to his daughter in Letter XI, may be due to the fact that Voltaire had already discussed him at length in the *Essay on Epic Poetry*.)[22]

In their attack on religious and political intolerance and in their defence of empirical thought and the experimental method, the *Letters* constitute one of the earliest expressions of Enlightenment thinking. More than that, this is a book which helped create for the Enlightenment a self-image. By describing the rise of empiricism from Bacon to Locke as an English phenomenon in opposition to the French tradition of rationalism as exemplified by Descartes (a view which conveniently ignores French empiricists such as Gassendi), Voltaire was able to invent an intellectual prehistory for the Enlightenment which proved hugely influential—for example, on d'Alembert's 'Discours pré-

---

[21] 'Advertisement to the Reader' (see Appendix B).
[22] See Appendix B.

liminaire' (1751) to the *Encyclopédie*—and which continues to this day to shape our view of the movement of ideas in the eighteenth century. Voltaire was not the first to recognize the importance of Locke and Newton, but he was one of the first to be able to convey a sense of the importance of their ideas to a wide public: his achievement is more literary than philosophical.

A simple example of his technique is provided by Newton's apple. The story of how the great scientist, seated beneath a tree, was moved to muse upon gravity after the chance fall of an apple, is a piece of popular mythology which has figured on postage stamps and pub signs: we owe it entirely to Voltaire that the story has survived. He apparently learned of the anecdote on a visit to Catherine Conduitt, Newton's niece, and grasping instantly its potential as an exemplar, he recounted it in his very next work, the *Essay on Epic Poetry* (where it was of no relevance at all), then again, and to greater effect, in the *Letters* (Letter XV), and yet again—Voltaire never being one to underplay a good idea—a few years later in the *Eléments de la philosophie de Neuton*. Francesco Algarotti, who produced a popularizing work on Newton for the Italian public (*Il newtonianismo per le dame*, 1737), had been the guest of Voltaire at Cirey and must have known the 'English Letters'—but he did not seize on the literary potential of the apple, and his book is much less memorable than Voltaire's.

Voltaire's polemical technique is seen to good advantage in the use he makes, in the penultimate paragraph of Letter VI, of the Royal Exchange (not to be confused with the Stock Exchange, founded later in the century: the image is often misunderstood because of a mistranslation back into English of the French 'Bourse'). The Royal Exchange, where merchants then met and transacted business, is situated between Cornhill and Threadneedle Street, in the heart of the City. The original sixteenth-century building had been destroyed in the Great Fire, and its replacement, dating from 1669, is described by Defoe as 'the greatest and finest of the kind in the world'. The Royal Exchange was a potent image of the benefits of trade, and is so used by Pope in *The Rape of the Lock*: 'The Merchant from th'*Exchange* returns in Peace'. Voltaire extends the image by introducing a comparison with religion, an idea which had occurred to him some time before, as we see from an ungrammatical sentence in the earliest of the surviving English notebooks: 'England is meeting of all religions, as the Royal exchange is the rendez vous of all foreigners.'[23] This sketch is developed in Letter VI, where he describes trade not merely as a parallel to religion but as a substitute for it. Whereas, in the preceding letters, religion manifestly divides, here trade unites and the Royal Exchange, described as a 'pacific and free assembly' where differences are submerged for 'the benefit of mankind', is invested with the full metaphorical weight of a church. In his *Tour Through the Whole Island of Great Britain* (1724–6), Daniel Defoe had taken three volumes to draw a portrait of a country at a time of rapid commercial expansion; Voltaire attempts it in a paragraph (to be followed by Letter X on trade). Voltaire's symbolic use of the Royal Exchange is succinct and immensely potent. *Infidel* is defined in Johnson's *Dictionary* as 'a pagan, one who rejects Christianity', so when Voltaire writes that merchants 'give the name of Infidel to none but bankrupts', the language of religion is assimilated to (and so subverted by) the language of trade. The discussion of the benefits of trade is metaphorically inextricable from the attack on religious intolerance.

Gustave Lanson, the first modern editor of the *Lettres philosophiques*, memorably, and misleadingly, described the work as 'the first bomb thrown at the *ancien régime*'. Critics continue to take it for granted that Voltaire was writing with a French audience in mind, and that he was really using England as a foil to talk about France. It is certainly true that praise of England often (though not always) implies criticism of France; thus, the success of inoculation among the English described in Letter XI shows by contrast the French mistrust not just of inoculation but of the experimental method in general. Even the criticisms made of cer-

---

[23] *Notebooks*, i. 51.

tain English authors in the later letters are part of a complex strategy which allows the French reader to feel superior to at least some aspects of English civilization, and perhaps therefore more inclined to engage with the narrator in complicit criticism of French religion, politics, philosophy, and science. For the French reader of the book, France, whether mentioned explicitly or not, is present in every letter.

But this is not the whole story. Lanson had assumed—wrongly, as we now know—that Voltaire wrote this book in French. Now that it is understood that he began writing it in English, and that he took care that it should be published in English and in England, we need to think again about the audience for whom Voltaire was writing. The English language had no obvious currency on the Continent: French, not English, was the lingua franca of the eighteenth century. Voltaire and Frederick II corresponded in French, as later did Diderot and Catherine the Great; Edward Gibbon wrote his first essay in French. A Voltaire text in English was not likely to be read much outside the British Isles—Germans, for example, seem to have read the 'English Letters' in the French edition published in London—and the *Letters concerning the English Nation* were therefore targeted specifically at a British readership. The preface of the first French edition, published in London after the English one, remarks that the English edition 'sold prodigiously', and the *Letters concerning the English Nation* certainly rank as an eighteenth-century best-seller in the British Isles: in the course of the century there followed fourteen further editions, more than the number of separate French editions published in the same period. For the eighteenth century, the 'English Letters' were as much an English text as a French one.

An example of how the *Letters* spoke directly to an English audience is provided by the book's treatment of politics. Voltaire arrived in England at a moment of keen debate about the concept of mixed government and the proper balance of power between monarchy, aristocracy, and democracy. His remark that: 'The house of Lords and that of the Commons divide the legislative power under the

King, but the *Romans* had no such balance' (Letter VIII) treads a careful line between the views of the Tories (who accused Walpole's government of 'ministerial despotism') and those of the Whigs (who preferred the monarch's powers to be circumscribed). English readers of either party would have placed Voltaire's comment in the context of the contemporary constitutional debate. French readers of the later French text would have read (virtually) the same sentence but understood something different; unversed in the niceties of Hanoverian politics, they would have read into this comment on the British constitution an implicit attack on the unbridled power of the French monarch (Voltaire had already described the British constitution, with a similar strategy of indirect criticism, in some verses which he added to *La Henriade*).

The knowledge that Voltaire's intended audience was English as well as French has unexpected consequences for the manner in which we respond to the satire. What are we to make of the statement in Letter VIII that 'there is in *London* a Senate, some of the members whereof are accus'd, (doubtless very unjustly) of selling their voices on certain occasions'? A French reader, lacking any information to the contrary, might be forgiven for taking this at face value; an English reader, on the other hand, would most certainly have read the parenthetical aside as irony. Walpole was notorious for his control of Parliament through patronage, and Opposition newspapers made the charge repeatedly. The *Craftsman*, for example, in an issue published when Voltaire was in London, likens the Commons to a monster called Polyglott who 'had above *five hundred Mouths* and as many *Tongues*', whose 'favourite Diet was *Gold* and *Silver*', and whose master (Walpole) 'could make more than *three hundred* of his Tongues, at once, lick his Foot, or any other part about him'.[24] Voltaire subscribed to the *Craftsman*, and was on close terms with its founder Bolingbroke; he could not have been unaware of Walpole's reputation, and his comment in the *Letters* has to be ironic—for an

[24] No. 55 (22 July 1727).

English reader.[25] Most of the leading literary figures of the period—Pope, Swift, Gay—attacked Walpole for venality, and Voltaire evidently aspired to be counted among their number. Only his tactic was different, and his status as foreign visitor enabled him to assume the role of the *faux naïf*, rather in the manner of one of Montesquieu's Persians.[26]

In the treatment of religion, too, Voltaire can be seen to be writing with an English audience in mind. Religious toleration is a central theme of the book: 'If one religion only were allowed in *England*, the government would very possibly become arbitrary; if there were but two, the people wou'd cut one another's throats; but as there are such a multitude, they all live happy and in peace' (Letter VI). As Voltaire does not discuss the position of Catholics in England, and makes only facetious and fleeting reference to the loss of privileges suffered by the Dissenters (Letter V), a reader in France might reasonably take this at face value as a statement about England, and see in this passage a reference to France and to the harm caused by the Revocation of the Edict of Nantes (1685). A reader in England, on the other hand, would surely read irony in this passage. Catholics in England (whose absolute numbers, unlike those of the Dissenters, rose in the eighteenth century) were prevented by the Corporation and Test Acts from holding either local or national office, and they were subject to double taxation; in the wake of the rebellion of 1715 and of the Atterbury plot of 1722, the Catholic community, suspected of Jacobite sympathies, was certainly not perceived as living 'in peace' with the Hanoverian regime. (At the time of the 1745 rebellion Voltaire was part of the pro-Jacobite party at Versailles, and he drafted on behalf of the French King a manifesto in support of Prince Charles

---

[25] Voltaire's engagement with English politics is further discussed by D. Fletcher, *Lettres philosophiques*, 21–7.

[26] The heading 'Answer to the Persian letters' in one of Voltaire's English notebooks (*Notebooks*, i. 104) suggests that he contemplated some form of response to Montesquieu's *Lettres persanes* (1721) while he was in England: the 'English Letters' are perhaps that reply. Compare the remark about Persian travellers in the 'Advertisement to the Reader' (Appendix B).

and the Stuart monarchy—which he himself translated into English.) England was appreciably more tolerant in religious matters than France at this time, but discrimination of a sort existed in both countries, and Voltaire contrives to write in such a way that his plea for toleration can hit home on both sides of the Channel.

After blatantly controversial letters on religion, politics, and philosophy, the final letters concerned with literature may seem anti-climactic. For French readers, they serve the obvious purpose of introducing writers who were scarcely known. But what is the point of telling the English about their own literature? Voltaire may have wished to lecture the English on the virtues of French classical restraint, a quality lacking in Shakespeare but all-too prominent in Addison's *Cato*, here lavishly praised. His translation of Waller in Letter XXI may be read as a demonstration of how French can tame the excesses of English verse. This does not, however, explain the puzzle of the other translations: there are altogether five English passages quoted together with a French version, one French version with no English original, and one French passage (Boileau) with an imitation by John Oldham. (The French editions of the 'English Letters' do not concern us here, but they are significantly simpler in this respect.) How and why are these intended to interest the English reader?

The English who could read French with ease—and Fawkener, Bolingbroke, and Hervey were all in this category—would not fail to pick up the anti-clerical bias of Voltaire's renderings of Shakespeare, Rochester, Pope, and Hervey, though the case of Hervey is problematic because on this occasion Voltaire uniquely gives the French translation without the original, leaving us to guess about the probable infidelity of the translation. This attack on religious extremism adds a further twist to a theme which has been developed all through the book; but it occurs in only four of the seven passages, and so cannot be the sole reason for their inclusion.

The anti-clerical slant of some of the French renderings certainly alerts us to the instability of translation, all translation, and even of language in general; every linguistic utterance presupposes a viewpoint, as Voltaire remorselessly reminds us: 'Pardon the Blemishes of the Translation for the Sake of the Orig-inal...'; 'Woe to the Writer who gives a literal Version...'; 'The Translation... is so inexpressive of the Strength and delicate Humour of the Original...'; 'I must first desire you always to remember, that the Versions... are written with Freedom and Latitude...'; 'Here is an Extract... translated with the Latitude I usually take on these Occasions...' Such repeated pleas have, to say the least, a disorienting and corrosive effect: as we face up to this vertiginous state of ever-shifting values, we are challenged to engage critically with the language before us. In this respect, the impact of the translations is identical to that of previous letters. Throughout the work, alternative views of reality jostle with each other, and not only in the fundamental contrast between England and France: the *plenum* of Paris versus the *vacuum* of London, Descartes's passion versus Newton's virginity, Turkish inoculation versus French smallpox, the London Parliament versus the Roman Senate, and so forth. The opening of the book sets the tone, a confrontation between a bare-headed and simpering representative of the *ancien régime* and a behatted speaker of plain home truths; as *you* answers *thou*, the reader sits in judgement of a quarrel between two languages, two views of truth. The book concludes in the same way, with a firework display of mismatched translations, and with truth as elusive as ever; but there is a difference, for by the end it is the reader who is directly challenged to engage with these rival languages. The narrator at the start of Letter I announces that he has come in quest of truth; the reader at the end of the book is invited to carry on the search. As Voltaire writes in the preface to his *Dictionnaire philosophique*: 'The most useful books are those in which the readers themselves supply half the meaning.'

The bilingual aspect of the *Letters* makes them unique in Enlightenment literature, and the consequent complexity of the irony in the work is unprecedented. The works which

Voltaire wrote before his time in England are both more and less ambitious: they strive to give expression to the idea of religious toleration, but in verse, and in the genres, epic and tragedy, of classical antiquity. Inevitably, the mismatch of form and content inhibits the radicalism of the writing. In England Voltaire discovered new writers—he wrote of Pope in 1726 that he was 'the best poet of England, and at present, of all the world' (D303)—and found himself exposed to a range of sharply satirical works, *Gulliver's Travels*, *The Beggar's Opera*, newspapers like the *Craftsman*, which had no immediate parallel in French literary culture of the period. Memories of the authors whom he discovered in England were still vivid forty years later: 'He says he admires Swift, and loved Gay vastly,' reported one visitor to Ferney in 1765. 'He said that Swift had a great deal of the *ridiculum acre* . . .'[27] Satire, after all, is the principal mode of Augustan literature, and it is in the literary climate of Walpole's London that Voltaire conceives the *Letters concerning the English Nation*.[28] The *Letters* represent one of Voltaire's first attempts (the other is the *Histoire de Charles XII*) to write an extended work in prose; and it is with the *Letters*, as he creates a form of satire which is an appropriate vehicle for his ideas, that he finds for the first time his true satirical voice. (The major short stories, for which he is nowadays best remembered, are written later in his career.)

Voltaire achieves this breakthrough not despite, but because of, writing in a foreign language: freedom from the constraints of the French language was as significant as freedom from France itself. A passage in one of his English notebooks, inspired by an article by Addison he must have read in the *Spectator* (No. 135, 4 August 1711), gives some insight into Voltaire's thinking on this matter—despite his

---

[27] de Beer and Rousseau, *Voltaire's British Visitors*, 94.

[28] The *Letters* are also the first of the English Lucianic satires inspired by Montesquieu's *Lettres persanes* (1721), translated into English in 1722; later examples include George Lyttelton's *Letters from a Persian in England* (1735); Horace Walpole's *A Letter from Xo Ho, a Chinese Philosopher at London, to his friend Lien Chi at Peking* (1757); and Oliver Goldsmith's *Citizen of the World* (1762).

syntax and spelling, which at this early stage were still rather individual:

An English man is full of taughts, French all in miens, compliments, sweet words and curious of engaging outside, overflowing in words, obsequious with pride, and very much self concerned under the appearance of a pleasant modesty. The English is sparing of words, openly proud and unconcerned. He gives the most quick birth, as he can, to his taughts, for fear of loosing his time.[29]

Perhaps the only other author who has so relished moving between French and English is Samuel Beckett, of whom it has been said that he switched from English to French because he viewed French 'as a way to strip his language to the bare essentials of his vision'.[30] Voltaire's decision to switch from French to English is equally momentous, and has a similarly emboldening effect on his powers of expression in prose.

In July 1728 Voltaire wrote to Richard Towne, who had embarked on a translation of *La Henriade* into English:

You do me the greatest honour I could ever boast of, in bestowing an English dress upon my French child. I receive the best reward of all my labours if you go on in the generous design of translating my undeserving work into a language which gives life and strength to all the subjects it touches. The *Henriade* has at least in itself a spirit of liberty which is not very common in France; the language of a free nation as yours is the only one that can vigorously express what I have but faintly drawn in my native tongue: the work will grow under your hands, worthy of the British nation, and that tree transplanted in your soil and grafted by you will bear a new and a better sort of fruit. (D340)

Voltaire returned to France with his views on religious toleration reaffirmed, and with a deepened understanding of Lockean empiricism and Newtonian physics. When, in 1743, Voltaire was made a Fellow of the Royal Society (largely on account of his *Eléments de la philosophie de Neuton*, which he published in 1738), he wrote to the president:

One of my strongest desires was to be naturaliz'd in England; the royal society, prompted be you vouschafes [*sic*] to honour me with the best letters of naturalisation. My first masters in your free and learned country, were Shakespear, Adisson, Dryden, Pope; I made some steps afterwards in the temple of philosophy towards the altar of Newton. I was even so bold as to introduce into France some of his discoveries; but I was not only a confessor to his faith, I became a martir. (D2890)

English philosophy and science had clearly marked Voltaire's thought, as the *Letters* testify. But as the *Letters* also testify, the English language had marked his style *and* his thought. After being in England only a few months, Voltaire told Thiriot in a letter (in French) that England was a country where he could 'learn to think' (D299). In 1733, back in France, Voltaire wrote (in French) to a friend: 'If you had spent two years in England as I did, I am sure that you would have been so touched by the energy of the language that you would have written something in English' (D681). He began by wanting to learn to think, and finished up learning to write prose. Energy of language and energy of thought are inseparable, and the *Letters concerning the English Nation* are more than just the fruit of Voltaire's stay in England; they are, more importantly, the fruit of Voltaire's encounter with the English language, and the product of his two-and-a-half-year apprenticeship as an Augustan author.

NOTE ON THE TEXT

The genesis of this text is one of unparalleled complexity. The work which Voltaire refers to in his correspondence as the 'English Letters' has not one, but three, 'first' editions, one in English and two in French; both French editions have a false imprint. The three different titles are, in order of publication:

(1) *Letters concerning the English Nation* (London: Davis and Lyon, 1733);
(2) *Lettres écrites de Londres sur les Anglois et autres sujets* ('Basle' [London], 1734);
(3) *Lettres philosophiques* ('Amsterdam: Lucas' [Rouen: Jore], 1734).

The three texts are each different in detail; the most important difference is that the *Lettres philosophiques* are enlarged by the addition of a twenty-fifth letter, on Pascal.

The condemnation of the *Lettres philosophiques* by the Parlement of Paris in 1734 (Voltaire was forbidden even to use the title of the work) limited the number of further editions of the French versions of the text in separate form (there were ten in the 1730s. Voltaire managed to rescue most of the work, at the expense of sacrificing the integrity of the whole, by breaking it up into separate essays which he inserted into the *Mélanges de littérature*, and which later reappeared in the *Dictionnaire philosophique*. It was in this unrecognizable and fragmented form that the French text was generally known from 1739 until 1828, when the Beuchot edition reassembled the first twenty-four letters (though in an unreliable version). In Britain and Ireland, meanwhile, the *Letters concerning the English Nation* had acquired a literary life of their own, and the book had become a best-seller: there were fourteen further editions in the course of the eighteenth century, published variously in London, Glasgow, and Dublin.[1]

The first ever critical edition of the 'English Letters' was published by Gustave Lanson at the beginning of this century. Faced with three base texts, Lanson decided to edit the *Lettres philosophiques*, and ignore the other two. The *Letters concerning the English Nation* he discarded (wrongly, but understandably) as a mere translation; and of the two French versions, he chose the *Lettres philosophiques* in preference to the *Lettres écrites de Londres* as being more complete (it has the twenty-fifth letter), and—in Lanson's view—as exemplifying Voltaire's polemical project in its most developed form. Lanson's editorial decision has decisively shaped our view of the 'English letters': every subsequent editor has similarly adopted the text of the *Lettres philosophiques*, and has set aside the other two versions. For modern readers and critics, the 'English letters' *are* the *Lettres philosophiques*.

In 1967 Harcourt Brown first drew attention to the importance of the *Letters concerning the English Nation*, demonstrating on the basis of internal evidence that over half of the English text must be Voltaire's original.[2] Certain discrepancies between the English and French versions suggest that the French was loosely reworked from the English, but in a manner far freer than any translator would have permitted himself. If we compare 'a hale ruddy complexion'd old man' with 'un vieillard frais' (Letter I), 'our giggling rural vicar Rabelais' with 'notre curé de Meudon' (Letter XXII), the description of Clark as 'the most sanguine stickler for Arianism' and as 'le plus ferme patron de la doctrine Arienne' (Letter VII), in each example (and there are many others) the English is more colourful than the French of the Basle edition; Harcourt Brown concludes that these letters must have been written originally in English. On the other hand, there exist in other letters gross howlers which are only explicable as the work of an anonymous hand working

[1] See Rousseau, *L'Angleterre et Voltaire*, iii. 1010–11.
[2] See Harcourt Brown, 'The Composition of the *Letters concerning the English Nation*'.

from French into English. For example, in Letter IX, discussing an order that officers might not seize horses except upon payment, we read the odd sentence: 'The People consider'd this Ordinance as a real Liberty, tho' it was a greater Tyranny'; the French of the Basle edition makes better sense: 'Ce reglement parût au peuple une vraie liberté parce qu'il ôtoit une plus grande tyrannie': the translator has misread *ôtoit* ('removed') as *étoit* ('was'). In Letter XIII, we read that Malebranche 'did not doubt of our living wholly in God', a nonsensical statement for which Voltaire could not be responsible; the French version is straightforward: 'il ne doutoit pas que nous ne vissions tout en Dieu'; the muddle of the English stems from a confusion between the past subjunctive of *voir* ('to see') and that of *vivre* ('to live'). In both cases, the French version must necessarily pre-date the English (mis-)translations. On the basis of internal evidence of this sort, Harcourt Brown was able to conclude that at least fourteen of the original twenty-four letters had been composed by Voltaire first in English; that three others might be 'of mixed origin'; and that the remaining part of the text, written by Voltaire in French at a later date, had been translated by an unknown hand from French into English. The composition of individual letters is therefore approximately as follows:

Composed in English: 1–8, 10, 12, 18, 19, 21, 22.
Composed (at least partly) in English: 20, 23, 24.
Composed in French: 9, 11, 13–17 (and 25).

The traditionally held view that the *Letters* are entirely a translation from the French by John Lockman (who translated others of Voltaire's works into English) goes back to a review of 1733 by the abbé Prévost (and is perpetuated to this day in the catalogue of the British Library). But even Prévost acknowledged that the earliest English readers did not regard the *Letters* as a translation: 'People were at first astonished to see the *Letters* in English only; and as there is nothing either on the title-page or in the preface to suggest that it is a translation, those who were well aware of Voltaire's ability to write correct English, believed that it was the original.'[3] These first English readers were right; the *Letters concerning the English Nation* are in large part the original work of Voltaire.

The text reproduced here follows the first edition in its most typical state, that is with two cancels (A4, G3). The probable text of the original version is found in the first Irish edition of the *Letters* (Dublin: Faulkner, 1733) which appears to have been composed from an uncancelled copy of the first London edition. The changes effected are as follows:

(i) p. 6 (A4): a whole sentence is removed; the first version of the text read: 'Even the most serious Letters, such as those which relate to Sir *Isaac Newton*'s Philosophy, will be found entertaining. Mr. *de Voltaire* remember'd, that he was writing to Mankind in general, and all are not Philosophers. He has infus'd into his Subject . . .' In a letter to Thiriot in July, 1733 (D631), Voltaire insisted on the removal of this sentence, presumably because it undermines completely the always tenuous fiction of a collection of intimate and spontaneous letters addressed to a close friend.

(ii) p. 50 (G3): the phrase 'in the opposite Party' has been inserted; the first version read: '*Bolingbroke* . . . (who having been his profess'd Enemy, might perhaps . . .).' The earlier version was simply inaccurate and would have caused offence to Voltaire's friend Bolingbroke, who had been a long-standing admirer of the great commander, even after Marlborough's drift to the Whigs.

Some states of the first edition contain one or two further cancels (F6 and/or S1), but neither affects the establishment of the text. F6 makes only a typographical correction; and S1 was introduced to change the Index in line with the alteration effected by G3. The first edition appears with a list of errata on the final page; these have all been incorporated in the text, except in two cases where Thiriot is too intrusive.[4] A small number of other obvious misprints

---

[3] Prévost, *Le Pour et Contre*, No. 11 (1733).

[4] The phrases, 'at a Time of Life' and 'this handsome and convincing reason' are corrected unnecessarily by Thiriot; see A.-M. Rousseau, 'Naissance d'un livre et d'un texte', 39.

(e.g. 'heen' for 'been') have been silently corrected. Origina
spelling, punctuation, and italics have otherwise been re
tained, and inconsistencies left unstandardized; for example
'it's' is sometimes used in place of 'its'; and 'Descartes
is usually, but not always, spelled 'Des Cartes'). Th
original footnotes remain as footnotes. The first editio:
also included a 'Letter concerning the Burning of Altena
(in connection with Voltaire's *History of Charles XII*) an(
an Index: these are omitted here. Voltaire had no contrc
over subsequent British and Irish editions of the *Letter*
and it is not therefore necessary to record their variants
which are insignificant. The most important later editio:
is 'The Second Edition, with large Additions' (Londor
Davis, 1741), which includes for the first time an Englis
version of the twenty-fifth letter on Pascal; this is given i
Appendix A.

SELECT BIBLIOGRAPHY

SVEC = Studies on Voltaire and the Eighteenth Century

(i) Editions

There is no previous critical edition of the *Letters concerning the English Nation*; the definitive edition of the final French version of the text, the *Lettres philosophiques*, is that of Gustave Lanson, revised by André-Michel Rousseau (2 vols., Paris, 1964), and contains invaluable information on sources; the edition of F. A. Taylor (revised edn., Oxford, 1946; republished Bristol Classical Press, 1992) has an excellent introduction and notes in English.

(ii) Letters concerning the English Nation

The article which decisively established Voltaire as the original author of almost two thirds of the English text is Harcourt Brown's 'The Composition of the *Letters concerning the English Nation*', in *The Age of the Enlightenment: Studies Presented to Theodore Besterman*, ed. W. H. Barber and others (Edinburgh, 1967), 15–34; his arguments are confirmed and elaborated by André-Michel Rousseau, 'Naissance d'un livre et d'un texte: les *Letters concerning the English Nation*', *SVEC* 179 (1979), 25–46, and by Hans Mattauch, 'A Translator's Hand in Voltaire's Fifth "Letter concerning the English Nation"', *SVEC* 106 (1973), 81–4. Details of the production of the first edition are discussed by Giles Barber in 'From Press to Purchase: The Making of the Book After its Printing', in *Trasmissione dei testi a stampa nel periodo moderno*, ed. G. Crapulli, vol. ii (Rome, 1987), 17–32.

(iii) Criticism

Literary critics have focused exclusively on the final French version of the text, and there is no critical study which takes proper account of the *Letters concerning the English Nation*. The following studies of the *Lettres philosophiques* are particularly recommended: André-Michel Rousseau, 'Introduction à une lecture des *Lettres philosophiques*', *L'Information littéraire*, 19 (1967), 10–16; T. J. Barling, 'The Literary Art of the *Lettres philosophiques*', *SVEC* 41 (1966), 7–69; Dennis Fletcher, *Voltaire: Lettres philosophiques* (London, 1986); Christiane Mervaud, 'Voltaire négociant en idées ou "merchant of a nobler kind" dans les *Lettres philosophiques*', *L'Information littéraire*, 40 (Oct.–Nov. 1988), 29–35; Jean Sareil, 'Les quatre premières *lettres philo-sophiques* ou les complications du jeu satirique', *Romanic Review*, 76 (1985), 277–86; Marsha Reisler, 'Rhetoric and Dialectic in Voltaire's *Lettres philosophiques*', *L'Esprit créateur*, 17 (1977), 311–24; and Julia L. Epstein, 'Voltaire's Ventriloquism: Voices in the First *Lettre philosophique*', *SVEC* 182 (1979), 219–35.

On genre and the relationship of the work to travel writing, see René Pomeau, 'Les *Lettres philosophiques*, œuvre épistolaire?', in *Beiträge zur französischen Aufklärung: Festgabe für Werner Krauss* ed. W. Bahner (Berlin, 1971), 271–9, and 'Les *Lettres philosophiques*: le projet de Voltaire', *SVEC* 179 (1979), 11–24; Shirley E. Jones, 'Voltaire's Use of Contemporary French Writing on England in His *Lettres philosophiques*', *Revue de littérature comparée*, 56 (1982), 139–56; Julia L. Epstein, 'Eighteenth-Century Travel Letters: The Case of Voltaire's *Lettres philoso-phiques*', *Genre*, 16 (1983), 115–35; and Christiane Mervaud, 'Des relations de voyage au mythe anglais des *Lettres philosophiques*', *SVEC* 296 (1992), 1–15.

On the twenty-fifth letter and its relationship to the work as a whole, see Roland Desné, 'The Role of England in Voltaire's Polemic Against Pascal: Apropos the Twenty-Fifth *Philosophical Letter*', in *Eighteenth-Century Studies: Presented to Arthur M. Wilson*, ed. P. Gay (New York, 1972), 41–57; and Alain Tichoux, 'Sur les origines de l'Anti-Pascal de Voltaire', *SVEC* 256 (1988), 21–47.

(iv) Voltaire's Thought

Haydn Mason's *Voltaire* (London, 1975) is a sound introduction to Voltaire's writing. Classic studies of Voltaire's thought include René Pomeau's *La Religion de Voltaire* (new edn., Paris, 1969), Peter Gay's *Voltaire's Politics: The Poet as Realist* (second edn., New Haven, Conn., 1988), and J. H. Brumfitt, *Voltaire Historian* (Oxford, 1958). The best general study of the impact of England upon Voltaire's thought is André-Michel Rousseau's *L'Angleterre et Voltaire*, 3 vols. (*SVEC* 145–7, 1976). See also Fernand Baldensperger, 'Voltaire anglophile avant son séjour d'Angleterre', *Revue de littérature comparée*, 9 (1929), 25–61, and articles by W. H. Barber: 'Voltaire and Quakerism: Enlightenment and the Inner Light', *SVEC* 24 (1963), 81–109; 'Voltaire and Samuel Clarke',

SVEC 179 (1979), 47–61; and 'Voltaire et Newton', *SVEC* 179 (1979), 193–202.

For evidence of Voltaire's engagement with British politics after his return to France, see Laurence L. Bongie, 'Voltaire's English, High Treason and a Manifesto for Bonnie Prince Charles', *SVEC* 171 (1977), 7–29; F. J. McLynn, 'Voltaire and the Jacobite Rising of 1745', *SVEC* 185 (1980), 7–20; and Graham Gargett, 'Voltaire, the Irish and the Battle of the Boyne', *French Studies Bulletin*, 35 (1990), 5–9.

(v) *Voltaire's Life*

The best biography in English is Haydn Mason's *Voltaire: A Biography* (London, 1981). The fullest description of Voltaire's early life, including the period spent in England, is René Pomeau's *D'Arouet à Voltaire: 1694–1734* (Oxford, 1985). This should be supplemented by the articles of Norma Perry (who is, however, unnecessarily sceptical about Voltaire's proficiency in English), including 'Voltaire's View of England', *Journal of European Studies*, 7 (1977), 77–94, 'Voltaire in London' (*The Times*, 22 Apr. 1978, p. 9), and 'Voltaire's First Months in England: Another Look at the Facts', *SVEC* 284 (1991), 115–38. *Voltaire's British Visitors*, ed. Sir Gavin de Beer and André-Michel Rousseau, *SVEC* 49 (1967), collects the accounts of English and Scots travellers who visited Voltaire in France. On eighteenth-century visitors to England, see Rosamond Bayne-Powell, *Travellers in Eighteenth-Century England* (London, 1951).

(vi) *Other Works by Voltaire*

Works by Voltaire available in translation include *Candide and Other Stories*, translated by Roger Pearson (The World's Classics, 1990), the *Philosophical Dictionary*, translated by Theodore Besterman (Penguin, 1972), and *The Selected Letters of Voltaire*, translated by Richard A. Brooks (New York, 1973). The *Historical Memoirs of the Author of the Henriade*, the English translation (1777) of Voltaire's autobiographical *Commentaire historique sur les œuvres de l'auteur de la Henriade*, is reprinted in Theodore Besterman's *Voltaire* (London, 1969), 543–601. There are other works apart from the *Letters concerning the English Nation* which Voltaire wrote first in English and later reworked in French: see *Voltaire's Essay on Epic Poetry: A Study and an Edition*, by Florence D. White (1915; repr. New York, 1970); and the volume containing both the *Essay on Epic Poetry* (ed. D. Williams) and the *Essay on the Civil Wars of France* (ed. R. Waller) in *The Complete Works of Voltaire* (The Voltaire Foundation, Taylor Institution, Oxford, 1996), vol. 3B. Voltaire's English notebooks have been edited by Theodore Besterman: *Notebooks*, second edn., vol. 1 (*The Complete Works of Voltaire*, vol. 81, Geneva, 1968). The standard edition of Voltaire's vast correspondence is the 'definitive edition' by Theodore Besterman, 51 vols. (Geneva and Oxford, 1968–77).

SUPPLEMENTARY BIBLIOGRAPHY (2005)

Since the first publication of this edition in 1994, it has been shown that Voltaire wrote all the text of the *Letters* in French, and that the *Letters concerning the English Nation* are a translation by John Lockman: J. Patrick Lee, 'The unexamined premise: Voltaire, John Lockman and the myth of the *English letters*', *SVEC*, 2001:10, 240–70; Nicholas Cronk, 'The *Letters concerning the English Nation* as an English work: reconsidering the Harcourt Brown thesis', *SVEC*, 2001:10, 226–39, and 'Lord Hervey and Voltaire's *Letters concerning the English Nation*', *Notes and Queries*, December 2001, 409–11. The *Letters concerning the English Nation* are none the less a text which Voltaire conceived with his English readership specifically in mind: Nicholas Cronk, 'Translation and imitation in the *Lettres anglaises*', in *Voltaire et ses combats*, ed. U. Kölving and C. Mervaud, 2 vols (Oxford, 1997), i.99–124, and 'Voltaire rencontre Monsieur le Spectateur: Addison et la genèse des *Lettres anglaises*', *Voltaire en Europe: hommage à Christiane Mervaud*, ed. M. Delon and C. Seth (Oxford, 2000), 13–21. On the reception of the work in the English-speaking world: Graham Gargett, 'Voltaire's *Lettres philosophiques* in eighteenth-century Ireland', *Eighteenth-Century Ireland*, 14 (1999), 77–98. On Voltaire and Oliver Goldsmith (see Appendix C): Graham Gargett, 'Oliver Goldsmith and Voltaire's *Lettres philosophiques*', *Modern Language Review*, 96 (2001), 952–63, and 'Plagiarism, translation and the problem of identity: Oliver Goldsmith and Voltaire', *Eighteenth-Century Ireland*, 16 (2001), 83–103.

A CHRONOLOGY OF VOLTAIRE

1694   Born François-Marie Arouet, in Paris.

1710   Writes his first poetry while at school, the Jesuit college
        Louis-le-Grand.

1713   First journey abroad, to The Hague.

1716   Exiled from Paris on account of a satire against the
        Regent.

1717   Another satire lands him in the Bastille.

1718   Adopts the name Voltaire: an anagram of Arouet l[e]
        j[eune], it evokes *volter*, 'to vault'. His first major work,
        the tragedy *Œdipe*, is staged with great success.

1722   His poem *Epître à Uranie* (not published until 1738)
        expresses views critical of Christianity.

1723   French government refuses to allow publication of *La
        Ligue*, an epic poem about Henry IV on the theme of
        religious intolerance.

1726   Quarrel with the chevalier de Rohan leads to a period of
        incarceration in the Bastille which delays his departure
        for England. May: arrives on the *Betty* at Gravesend, and
        travels to London. Renews his friendship with the silk-
        merchant Everard Fawkener, and lives for a time at his
        house in Wandsworth. Begins to learn English, and by
        the autumn is attending performances of Shakespeare
        (*Hamlet, Othello, Julius Caesar*) at Drury Lane and
        Lincoln's Inn Fields. Renews his friendship with
        Bolingbroke, and during the winter months uses his
        address in Pall Mall. Meets Alexander Pope several
        times, but has closer links with John Gay (who shows
        him *The Beggar's Opera* before its first performance)
        and with Jonathan Swift. Reads *Gulliver's Travels* on
        publication and urges his friend Thiriot to translate the
        work into French. Discusses metaphysics with Samuel
        Clarke, then Rector of St James's, Piccadilly.

1727   English newspapers report that the 'famous French
        poet' has been presented to George I, and later in the
        year he receives from Walpole a 'free gift and Royal
        Bounty' of £200. Meets the prominent Quaker Andrew
        Pitt at his house in Hampstead; is in London on the day

of Newton's state funeral in Westminster Abbey; and visits Mrs Conduitt, Newton's niece, who tells him the story of the apple. With Walpole's support, he opens a public subscription for the publication of his epic poem, now called *La Henriade*. Visits the ageing Duchess of Marlborough at Blenheim Palace (and presumably passes through Oxford, which he fails to mention); and meets the poets James Thomson and Edward Young, perhaps at Bubb Dodington's house in Dorset. Spends the winter months taken up with his various publishing projects, living in Maiden Lane (just north of the Strand), close to the London community of French Huguenot printers and booksellers. 6 December: publication of *An Essay upon the civil wars of France, extracted from curious manuscripts, and also upon the epick poetry of the European nations from Homer down to Milton*, price 1s. 6d.

1728   March: publication of *La Henriade*, dedicated to Queen Caroline, a magnificent quarto volume with engravings, price 3 guineas; followed by two octavo editions at 4s. June–August: returns to live in Wandsworth, and starts work on his next literary projects, the *Histoire de Charles XII*, the *Letters* on England, and a tragedy *Brutus*. These last two works are written in English: Voltaire has become an English author. Then, in October or November, he leaves England precipitately, in suspicious circumstances. He spends the winter lying low in Dieppe.

1729   Return to Paris and literary activity.

1733   *Letters concerning the English Nation* published in London.

1734   *Lettres écrites de Londres sur les Anglois et autres sujets* published in London. *Lettres philosophiques* (including the twenty-fifth letter on Pascal) published in Rouen; the work is condemned and burned by the Parlement of Paris, and sells well.

1734–43   Settles at Cirey (in Champagne) with his mistress Mme Du Châtelet, with whom he shares a period of intense literary and scientific activity.

1741   First performance of *Mahomet*, a play about religious fanaticism; he dedicated it first to Frederick the Great, then to Pope Benedict XIV; he would later say that

Ravaillac would not have murdered Henri IV if he had seen this play.

1743   Elected a Fellow of the Royal Society and of the Royal Society of Edinburgh. Supported by Mme de Pompadour, he enters a period of favour at Court: it was to be short-lived.

1745   Appointed Royal Historiographer by Louis XV.

1746   Elected to the Académie française (on the second attempt).

1747   *Zadig* (under title of *Memnon*) is first *conte* to be published. Indiscretions end his period of favour at Court.

1750–3   At the court of Frederick the Great in Berlin and Potsdam.

1752   The *Lettres philosophiques* are placed on the Index.

1755–9   Lives at *Les Délices* (now the Institut et Musée Voltaire) in Geneva.

1756   The first official edition of the *Essai sur les mœurs*, a history of the world.

1759   Publishes *Candide*.

1759–78   Moves into the château of Ferney, and becomes, in his own word, its 'patriarch'. He is hedging his bets: the village, now renamed Ferney-Voltaire, is in France but close to Geneva and the Swiss border.

1760   First use by Voltaire of the catch-phrase which epitomizes his crusade for religious toleration: *écrasez l'infâme* ('crush the unspeakable').

1761   Builds a church at Ferney, and devises for it an inscription which eliminates the middlemen: 'Deo erexit Voltaire' ('Voltaire erected this to God').

1762   Large collection of Voltaire appears in English translation (by Smollett and Francklin). Beginning of the long campaign to rehabilitate Jean Calas, Protestant victim of Catholic intolerance.

1764   Publishes *Dictionnaire philosophique*.

1778   Returns to Paris for the production of his tragedy *Irène*; in his presence, his bust is placed on stage at the Comédie française and crowned with a laurel wreath; he dies soon after, and his embalmed body has to be smuggled out of the capital to frustrate the attempts of the Catholic Church to deny him a proper burial. Buried secretly in the abbey of Seillières (Champagne), apart from his heart which is sent to Ferney (and is given in

1864 to the Bibliothèque nationale, where it is now in the 'Salon d'honneur').

1784–9 The first genuinely complete edition of Voltaire's writings is published in seventy volumes (the so-called Kehl edition), under the direction of the playwright Beaumarchais; the project ruins him financially but he writes that 'Europe will be satisfied'.

1791 In an act of Revolutionary piety, Voltaire's mortal (and heartless) remains are transferred to the recently completed Panthéon in Paris.

LETTERS

CONCERNING THE

ENGLISH NATION

BY

Mr. DE VOLTAIRE.

LONDON,
Printed for C. Davis in *Pater-Noster-Row,*
and A. Lyon in *Russel-Street, Covent-Garden.*
MDCCXXXIII.

THE CONTENTS.

(E) Written first in English.
(F) Written first in French.
(E/F) Written partly in English and partly in French.

THE PREFACE.

THE present Work* appears with Confidence in the Kingdom that gave Birth to it: and will be well satisfied with its Fortune, if it meets with as favourable a Reception as has been indulg'd to all the other Compositions of its Author.* The high Esteem which Mr. *de Voltaire* has always discover'd for the *English*, is a Proof how ambitious he is of their Approbation. 'Tis now grown familiar to him, but then he is not tir'd with it; and indeed one wou'd be apt to think that this Circumstance is pleasing to the Nation, from the strong Desire they have to peruse whatever is publish'd under his Name.

Without pretending therefore to any great Penetration, we may venture to assure him that his Letters will meet with all the Success that cou'd be wish'd. Mr. *de Voltaire* is the Author of them, they were written in *London*, and relate particularly to the *English* Nation; three Circumstances which must necessarily recommend them. The great Freedom with which Mr. *de Voltaire* delivers himself in his various Observations, cannot give him any Apprehensions of their being less favourably receiv'd upon that Account, by a judicious People who abhor Flattery. The *English* are pleas'd to have their Faults pointed out to them, because this shews at the same Time, that the Writer is able to distinguish their Merit.

We must however confess, that these Letters were not design'd for the Public. They are the Result of the Author's Complacency and Friendship for Mr. *Thiriot*, who had desir'd him, during his Stay in *England*, to favour him with such Remarks as he might make on the Manners and Customs of the *British* Nation. 'Tis well known that in a Correspondence of this kind, the most just and regular Writer does not propose to observe any Method. Mr. *de Voltaire* in all Probability follow'd no other Rule in the Choice of his Subjects than his particular Taste, or perhaps the Queries of his Friend. Be this as it will, 'twas thought that the most natural Order in which they cou'd be plac'd, would be that of their respective Dates. Several Particulars which are mention'd in them make it necessary for us to observe, that they were written between the latter End of 1728, and about 1731.* The only Thing that can be regretted on this Occasion is, that so agreeable a Correspondence should have continued no longer.

The Reader will no doubt observe, that the Circumstances in every Letter which had not an immediate relation to the Title of it, have been omitted. This was done on purpose; for Letters written with the Confidence and Simplicity of personal Friendship, generally include certain Things which are not proper for the Press. The Public indeed thereby often lose a great many agreeable Particulars; but why should they complain, if the want of them is compensated by a thousand Beauties of another kind? The Variety of the Subjects, the Graces of the Diction, the Solidity of the Reflexions, the delicate Turn of the Criticism; in fine, the noble Fire, which enlivens all the Compositions of Mr. *de Voltaire*, delight the Reader perpetually. Even the most serious Letters, such as those which relate to Sir *Isaac Newton*'s Philosophy, will be found entertaining.* The Author has infus'd into his Subject all the delicate Touches it was susceptible of; deep and abstruse enough to shew that he was Master of it, and always perspicuous enough to be understood.

Some of his *English* Readers may perhaps be dissatisfied at his not expatiating farther on their Constitution and their Laws, which most of them revere almost to Idolatry; but this Reservedness is an Effect of Mr. *de Voltaire*'s Judgment. He contented himself with giving his Opinion of them in general Reflexions, the Cast of which is entirely new, and which prove that he had made this Part of the *British* Polity his particular Study. Besides, how was it possible for a Foreigner to pierce thro' their Politicks, that gloomy Labyrinth, in which such of the *English* themselves as are best acquainted with it, confess daily that they are bewilder'd and lost?

While this Work was in the Press, there came to *London* a Manuscript Letter of Mr. *de Voltaire*, in answer to the Complaints made by the Citizens of *Hamburgh* against a Passage in the History of *Charles* the Twelfth, relating to the Burning of *Altena*. We thought proper to insert that Letter here,* for the Use of those who have the History of *Charles* the Twelfth in *English* only.

LETTER I.

On the Quakers.

I WAS of opinion, that the doctrine and history of so
extraordinary a people, were worthy the attention of the
curious. To acquaint myself with them, I made a visit* to
one of the most eminent Quakers in *England*, who after
having traded thirty years, had the wisdom to prescribe
limits to his fortune and to his desires, and was settled in a
little solitude not far from *London*. Being come into it, I
perceiv'd a small, but regularly built house, vastly neat, but
without the least pomp of furniture. The Quaker who
own'd it, was a hale ruddy complexion'd old man, who had
never been afflicted with sickness, because he had always
been insensible to passions, and a perfect stranger to intemperance. I never in my life saw a more noble or a more
engaging aspect than his. He was dress'd like those of his
persuasion, in a plain coat, without pleats in the sides, or
buttons on the pockets and sleeves; and had on a beaver,*
the brims of which were horizontal, like those of our clergy.
He did not uncover himself when I appear'd, and advanc'd
towards me without once stooping his body; but there
appear'd more politeness in the open, humane air of his
countenance, than in the custom of drawing one leg behind
the other, and taking that from the head, which is made to
cover it. Friend, says he to me, I perceive thou art a
stranger,* but if I can do any thing for thee, only tell me. Sir,
says I to him, bending forwards, and advancing as is usual
with us, one leg towards him; I flatter myself that my just
curiosity will not give you the least offence, and that you'll
do me the honour to inform me of the particulars of your
religion. The people of thy country, replied the Quaker, are
too full of their bows and compliments, but I never yet met
with one of them who had so much curiosity as thy self.
Come in, and let us first dine together. I still continued to
make some very unseasonable ceremonies, it not being easy

to disengage one's self at once from habits we have been long us'd to; and after taking part of a frugal meal, which began and ended with a prayer to God, I began to question my courteous host. I open'd with that which good Catholicks have more than once made to Huguenots. My dear sir, says I, were you ever baptiz'd? I never was, replied the Quaker, nor any of my brethren. Zouns, says I to him, you are not Christians then. Friend, replies the old man in a soft tone of voice, swear not; we are Christians, and endeavour to be good Christians, but we are not of opinion, that the sprinkling water on a child's head makes him a Christian. Heavens! says I, shock'd at his impiety, you have then forgot that *Christ* was baptiz'd by St. *John*. Friend, replies the mild Quaker once again, swear not. *Christ* indeed was baptiz'd by *John*, but he himself never baptiz'd any one. We are the disciples of *Christ*, not of *John*. I pitied very much the sincerity of my worthy Quaker, and was absolutely for forcing him to get himself christned. Were that all, replied he very gravely, we would submit chearfully to baptism, purely in compliance with thy weakness, for we don't condemn any person who uses it; but then we think, that those who profess a religion of so holy, so spiritual a nature as that of *Christ*, ought to abstain to the utmost of their power from the *Jewish* ceremonies. O unaccountable! says I, what! baptism a *Jewish* ceremony? Yes, my friend says he, so truly *Jewish*, that a great many *Jews* use the baptism of *John* to this day. Look into ancient authors, and thou wilt find that *John* only reviv'd this practice; and that it had been us'd by the *Hebrews*, long before his time, in like manner as the Mahometans imitated the *Ishmaelites* in their pilgrimages to *Mecca. Jesus* indeed submitted to the baptism of *John*, as he had suffer'd himself to be circumcis'd; but circumcision and the washing with water ought to be abolish'd by the baptism of *Christ*, that baptism of the spirit, that ablution of the soul, which is the salvation of mankind. Thus the forerunner said, *I indeed baptize you with water unto repentance; but he that cometh after me, is mightier than I, whose shoes I am not worthy to bear: he shall baptize you with the Holy Ghost and with* *fire.*[1] Likewise *Paul* the great apostle of the Gentiles, writes as follows to the *Corinthians; Christ sent me not to baptize, but to preach the Gospel;*[2] and indeed *Paul* never baptiz'd but two persons with water, and that very much against his inclinations. He circumcis'd his disciple *Timothy,* and the other disciples likewise circumcis'd all who were willing to submit to that carnal ordinance. But art thou circumcis'd, added he? I have not the honour to be so, says I. Well, friend, continues the Quaker, thou art a Christian without being circumcis'd, and I am one without being baptiz'd. Thus did this pious man make a wrong, but very specious* application, of four or five texts of scripture which seem'd to favour the tenets of his sect; but at the same time forgot very sincerely an hundred texts which made directly against them. I had more sense than to contest with him, since there is no possibility of convincing an enthusiast. A man shou'd never pretend to inform a lover of his mistress's faults, no more than one who is at law, of the badness of his cause; nor attempt to win over a fanatic by strength of reasoning. Accordingly I wav'd the subject.

Well, says I to him, what sort of a communion have you? We have none like that thou hintest at among us, replied he. How! no communion, says I? Only that spiritual one, replied he, of hearts. He then began again to throw out his texts of scripture; and preach'd a most eloquent sermon against that ordinance. He harangued in a tone as tho' he had been inspir'd, to prove that the sacraments were merely of human invention, and that the word *sacrament,* was not once mention'd in the gospel.* Excuse, says he, my ignorance, for I have not employ'd an hundredth part of the arguments which might be brought, to prove the truth of our religion, but these thou thy self mayest peruse in the Exposition of our Faith written by *Robert Barclay.** 'Tis one of the best pieces that ever was penn'd by man; and as our adversaries confess it to be of dangerous tendency, the arguments in it must necessarily be very convincing. I promis'd to peruse this piece, and my Quaker imagin'd he

---

[1] St. Matth. iii. 11.   [2] 1 Cor. i. 17.

had already made a convert of me. He afterwards gave me an account in few words, of some singularities which make this sect the contempt of others. Confess, says he, that 'twas very difficult for thee to refrain from laughter, when I answer'd all thy civilities without uncovering my head, and at the same time said *Thee* and *Thou* to thee. However, thou appearest to me too well read, not to know that in *Christ*'s time no nation was so ridiculous as to put the plural number for the singular. *Augustus Cæsar* himself was spoke to in such phrases as these, *I love thee, I beseech thee, I thank thee;* but he did not allow any person to call him *Domine*, Sir. 'Twas not till many ages after, that men wou'd have the word *You*, as tho' they were double, instead of *Thou* employ'd in speaking to them; and usurp'd the flattering titles of lordship, of eminence, and of holiness, which mere worms bestow on other worms, by assuring them that they are with a most profound respect, and an infamous falshood, their most obedient, humble servants. 'Tis to secure our selves more strongly from such a shameless traffick of lies and flattery, that we *thee* and *thou* a king with the same freedom as we do a beggar, and salute no person; we owing nothing to mankind but charity, and to the laws respect and obedience.

Our apparel is also somewhat different from that of others, and this purely, that it may be a perpetual warning to us not to imitate them. Others wear the badges and marks of their several dignities, and we those of christian humility. We fly from all assemblies of pleasure, from diversions of every kind, and from places where gaming is practis'd; and indeed our case wou'd be very deplorable, should we fill with such levities as those I have mention'd, the heart which ought to be the habitation of God. We never swear, not even in a court of justice, being of opinion that the most holy name of God ought not to be prostituted in the miserable contests betwixt man and man. When we are oblig'd to appear before a magistrate upon other people's account, (for law-suits are unknown among the friends) we give evidence to the truth by sealing it with our *yea* or *nay*; and the judges believe us on our bare affirmation, whilst so many other

Christians forswear themselves on the holy Gospels. We never war or fight in any case; but 'tis not that we are afraid, for so far from shuddering at the thoughts of death, we on the contrary bless the moment which unites us with the Being of Beings; but the reason of our not using the outward sword is, that we are neither wolves, tygers, nor mastiffs, but men and Christians. Our God, who has commanded us to love our enemies, and to suffer without repining, would certainly not permit us to cross the seas, merely because murtherers cloath'd in scarlet, and wearing caps two foot high enlist citizens by a noise made with two little sticks on an ass's skin extended. And when, after a victory is gain'd, the whole city of *London* is illuminated; when the sky is in a blaze with fireworks, and a noise is heard in the air of thanksgivings, of bells, of organs, and of the cannon, we groan in silence, and are deeply affected with sadness of spirit and brokenness of heart, for the sad havock which is the occasion of those public rejoycings.

LETTER II.

On the Quakers.

SUCH was the substance of the conversation I had with this very singular person; but I was greatly surpriz'd to see him come the *Sunday* following, and take me with him to the Quaker's meeting. There are several of these in *London*, but that which he carried me to stands near the famous pillar call'd the monument.* The brethren were already assembled at my entring it with my guide. There might be about four hundred men and three hundred women in the meeting. The women hid their faces behind their fans, and the men were cover'd with their broad-brimm'd hats; all were seated, and the silence was universal. I past through them, but did not perceive so much as one lift up his eyes to look at me. This silence lasted a quarter of an hour, when at last one of them rose up, took off his hat, and after making a variety of wry faces, and groaning in a most lamentable manner, he partly from his nose, and partly from his mouth, threw out a strange, confus'd jumble of words, (borrow'd as he imagin'd from the Gospel) which neither himself nor any of his hearers understood. When this dis-torter had ended his beautiful soliloquy, and that the stupid, but greatly edified, congregation were separated, I ask'd my friend how it was possible for the judicious part of their assembly to suffer such a babbling.* We are oblig'd, says he, to suffer it, because no one knows when a man rises up to hold forth, whether he will be mov'd by the spirit or by folly. In this doubt and uncertainty we listen patiently to every one, we even allow our women to hold forth; two or three of these are often inspir'd at one and the same time, and 'tis then that a most charming noise is heard in the Lord's house. You have then no priests, says I to him. No, no, friend, replies the Quaker, to our great happiness. Then opening one of the friend's books, as he call'd it, he read the following words in an emphatic tone: God forbid we should presume to ordain any one to receive the holy spirit on the Lord's day, to the prejudice of the rest of the brethren. Thanks to the almighty, we are the only people upon earth that have no priests. Wouldest thou deprive us of so happy a distinction? Why shou'd we abandon our babe to mercenary nurses, when we our selves have milk enough for it? These mercenary creatures wou'd soon domineer in our houses, and destroy both the mother and the babe. God has said, freely you have receiv'd, freely give. Shall we after these words cheapen, as it were, the Gospel; sell the Holy Ghost, and make of an assembly of Christians a mere shop of traders. We don't pay a sett of men cloath'd in black, to assist our poor, to bury our dead, or to preach to the brethren; these offices are all of too tender a nature, for us ever to entrust them to others. But how is it possible for you, says I, with some warmth, to know whether your discourse is really inspir'd by the Almighty? Whosoever, says he, shall implore *Christ* to enlighten him, and shall publish the Gospel truths, he may feel inwardly, such an one may be assur'd that he is inspir'd by the Lord.* He then pour'd forth a numberless multitude of Scripture-texts, which prov'd, as he imagin'd, that there is no such thing as Christianity without an immediate revelation, and added these remarkable words: When thou movest one of thy limbs, is it mov'd by thy own power? Certainly not, for this limb is often sensible to involuntary motions; consequently he who created thy body, gives motion to this earthly tabernacle. And are the several ideas of which thy soul receives the impression form'd by thy self? Much less are they, since these pour in upon thy mind whether thou wilt or no; consequently thou receivest thy ideas from him who created thy soul: But as he leaves thy affections at full liberty, he gives thy mind such ideas as thy affections may deserve; if thou livest in God, thou actest, thou thinkest in God. After this thou needest only but open thine eyes to that light which enlightens all mankind, and 'tis then thou wilt perceive the truth, and make others perceive it. Why this, says I, is *Malbranche*'s doctrine* to a tittle. I am acquainted with thy *Malbranche*, says he; he had something of the *friend* in him, but was not enough so. These are the most considerable particulars I learnt concerning the doctrine of the Quakers; in my next letter I shall acquaint you with their history, which you will find more singular than their opinions.

LETTER III.

On the Quakers.

YOU have already heard that the Quakers date from *Christ*, who according to them was the first Quaker. Religion, say these, was corrupted, a little after his death, and remain'd in that state of corruption about 1600 Years. But there were always a few Quakers conceal'd in the world, who carefully preserv'd the sacred fire, which was extinguish'd in all but themselves, 'till at last this light spread it self in *England* in 1642.

'Twas at the time when *Great-Britain* was torn to pieces by the intestine wars which three or four sects had rais'd in the name of God, that one *George Fox*, born in *Leicester-shire*, and son to a silk-weaver, took it into his head to preach; and, as he pretended, with all the requisites of a true apostle, that is, without being able either to read or write. He was about twenty five[1] years of age, irreproachable in his life and conduct, and a holy mad-man. He was equip'd in leather from head to foot, and travell'd from one village to another, exclaiming against war and the clergy. Had his invectives been levell'd against the soldiery only, he wou'd have been safe enough, but he inveigh'd against ecclesiasticks. *Fox* was seiz'd at *Derby*, and being carried before a justice of peace; he did not once offer to pull off his leathern hat; upon which an officer gave him a great box o'th' ear, and cried to him, Don't you know you are to appear uncover'd before his worship? *Fox* presented his other cheek to the officer, and begg'd him to give him another box for God's sake.* The justice wou'd have had him sworn before he ask'd him any questions: Know, friend, says *Fox* to him, that I never swear. The justice observing he *Thee'd* and *Thou'd* him, sent him to the house of correction in *Derby*, with orders that he should be whipp'd there. *Fox*

---

[1] *Fox* could read at that age.

prais'd the Lord all the way he went to the house of correction, where the justice's order was executed with the utmost severity. The men who whipp'd this enthusiast, were greatly surpriz'd to hear him beseech them to give him a few more lashes for the good of his soul. There was no need of intreating these people; the lashes were repeated, for which *Fox* thank'd them very cordially, and began to preach. At first, the spectators fell a laughing, but they afterwards listned to him; and as enthusiasm is an epidemical distemper, many were persuaded, and those who scourg'd him became his first disciples. Being set at liberty, he ran up and down the country with a dozen proselytes at his heels, still declaiming against the clergy, and was whipp'd from time to time. Being one day set in the pillory, he harangued the crowd in so strong and moving a manner, that fifty of the auditors became his converts; and he won the rest so much in his favour, that his head being freed tumultuously from the hole where it was fastned, the populace went and search'd for the church of *England* clergyman, who had been chiefly instrumental in bringing him to this punishment, and set him on the same pillory where *Fox* had stood.

 Fox was bold enough to convert some of *Oliver Cromwell*'s Soldiers, who thereupon quitted the service and refus'd to take the oaths. *Oliver* having as great a contempt for a sect which would not allow its members to fight, as *Sixtus Quintus* had for another sect, *Dove non si chiavava,* * began to persecute these new converts. The prisons were crouded with them, but persecution seldom has any other effect than to increase the number of proselytes. These came therefore from their confinement, more strongly confirmed in the principles they had imbib'd, and follow'd by their goalers whom they had brought over to their belief. But the circumstances which contributed chiefly to the spreading of this sect were as follows. *Fox* thought himself inspir'd, and consequently was of opinion, that he must speak in a manner different from the rest of mankind. He thereupon began to writhe his body, to screw up his face, to hold in his breath, and to exhale it in a forcible manner, insomuch that the priestess of the *Pythian* God at *Delphos* could not have acted her part to better advantage. Inspiration soon became so habitual to him, that he cou'd scarce deliver himself in any other manner. This was the first gift he communicated to his disciples. These ap'd very sincerely their master's several grimaces, and shook in every limb the instant the fit of inspiration came upon them, whence they were call'd Quakers.* The vulgar attempted to mimick them, they trembled, they spake thro' the nose; they quak'd and fancied themselves inspir'd by the Holy Ghost. The only thing now wanting was a few miracles, and accordingly they wrought some.

Fox, this modern patriarch, spoke thus to a justice of peace, before a large assembly of people. Friend, take care what thou dost: God will soon punish thee for persecuting his saints. This magistrate being one who besotted himself every day with bad beer and brandy, died of an apoplexy two days after, the moment he had sign'd a *mittimus* for imprisoning some Quakers. The sudden death with which this justice was seiz'd, was not ascrib'd to his intemperance, but was universally look'd upon as the effect of the holy man's predictions; so that this accident made more converts to Quakerism, than a thousand sermons and as many shaking fits cou'd have done. *Oliver** finding them increase daily was desirous of bringing them over to his party, and for that purpose attempted to bribe them by money. However, they were incorruptible, which made him one day declare, that this religion was the only one he had ever met with that had resisted the charms of gold.

The Quakers were several times persecuted under *Charles* the second, not upon a religious account, but for refusing to pay the tythes, for *Thee-ing* and *Thou-ing* the magistrates, and for refusing to take the oaths enacted by the laws.

At last *Robert Barclay*, a native of *Scotland*, presented to the king in 1675, his apology for the Quakers, a work as well drawn up as the subject cou'd possibly admit. The dedication to *Charles* the second is not fill'd with mean, flattering encomiums; but abounds with bold touches in favour of truth, and with the wisest counsels. 'Thou hast

tasted,'* says he to the king at the close of his epistle de-
dicatory, 'of prosperity and adversity; thou knowest what it
is to be banished thy native country; to be over-rul'd as well
as to rule, and sit upon the throne; and being oppressed,
thou hast reason to know how hateful the oppressor is both
to God and man: If after all these warnings and advertise-
ments, thou dost not turn unto the Lord with all thy heart;
but forget him who remembred thee in thy distress, and give
up thy self to follow lust and vanity, surely great will be thy
condemnation.

Against which snare, as well as the temptation of those,
that may or do feed thee, and prompt thee to evil, the most
excellent and prevalent remedy will be, to apply thy self to
that light of *Christ*, which shineth in thy conscience, which
neither can nor will flatter thee, nor suffer thee to be at ease
in thy sins; but doth and will deal plainly and faithfully with
thee, as those, that are followers thereof have plainly done—
Thy faithful friend and subject, ROBERT BARCLAY.'

A more surprizing circumstance is, that this epistle, written by a private man of no figure, was so happy in its effects
as to put a stop to the persecution.

LETTER IV.

On the Quakers.

ABOUT this[1] time arose the illustrious *William Pen*,
who establish'd the power of the Quakers in *America*,
and would have made them appear venerable in the eyes of
the *Europeans*, were it possible for mankind to respect virtue, when reveal'd in a ridiculous light. He was the only son
of vice-admiral *Pen*, favourite to the duke of *York*, afterwards king *James* the second.

William Pen at twenty years of age happening to meet
with a Quaker[2] in *Cork*, whom he had known at *Oxford*,
this man made a proselyte of him; and *William* being a
sprightly youth, and naturally eloquent, having a winning
aspect, and a very engaging carriage, he soon gain'd over
some of his Intimates. He carried matters so far that he
form'd by insensible degrees a society of young Quakers
who met at his house; so that he was at the head of a sect
when a little above twenty.

Being return'd, after his leaving *Cork*, to the vice-admiral
his father, instead of falling upon his knees to ask him
blessing, he went up to him with his hat on, and said,
Friend, I'm very glad to see thee in good health.* The vice-
admiral imagin'd his son to be crazy; but soon finding he
was turn'd Quaker, he employ'd all the methods that pru-
dence could suggest, to engage him to behave and act like
other people. The youth made no other answer to his father,
than by exhorting him to turn Quaker also. At last his father
confin'd himself to this single request, *viz*. that he shou'd
wait upon the king and the duke of *York* with his hat under
his arm, and shou'd not *Thee* and *Thou* them. *William*
answer'd, that he could not do these things for conscience
sake, which exasperated his father to such a degree, that he
turn'd him out of doors. Young *Pen* gave God thanks, for

---

[1] 1666.   [2] *Thomas Loe.*

permitting him to suffer so early in his cause, after which he went into the city, where he held forth,[1] and made a great number of converts.

The church of *England* clergy found their congregations dwindle away daily; and *Pen* being young, handsome, and of a graceful stature, the court as well as the city ladies flock'd very devoutly to his meeting. The patriarch *George Fox* hearing of his great reputation, came to *London*, (tho' the journey was very long) purely to see and converse with him. Both resolv'd to go upon missions into foreign countries, and accordingly they embark'd for *Holland*, after having left labourers sufficient to take care of the *London* vineyard.

Their labours were crown'd with success in *Amsterdam*; but a circumstance which reflected the greatest honour on them, and at the same time put their humility to the greatest trial, was the reception they met with from *Elizabeth* the princess *Palatine*, aunt to *George* the first of *Great-Britain*, a lady conspicuous for her genius and knowledge, and to whom *Des Cartes* had dedicated his *Philosophical Romance*.*

She was then retir'd to the *Hague*, where she receiv'd these *friends*, for so the Quakers were at that time call'd in *Holland*. This princess had several conferences with them in her palace, and she at last entertain'd so favourable an opinion of Quakerism, that they confess'd she was not far from the kingdom of heaven. The friends sow'd likewise the good seed in *Germany*, but reap'd very little fruit; for the mode of *Thee-ing* and *Thou-ing* was not approv'd of in a country, where a man is perpetually oblig'd to employ the titles of highness and excellency. *William Pen* return'd soon to *England* upon hearing of his father's sickness, in order to see him before he died. The vice-admiral was reconcil'd to his son, and tho' of a different persuasion, embrac'd him tenderly. *William* made a fruitless exhortation to his father not to receive the sacrament, but to die a Quaker; and the good old man intreated his son *William* to wear buttons on

---

[1] About 1668, and the 24th year of his age.

his sleeves, and a crape hatband in his beaver, but all to no purpose.

William Pen inherited very large possessions, part of which consisted in crown-debts due to the vice-admiral for sums he had advanc'd for the sea-service. No monies were at that time more secure than those owing from the king. *Pen* was oblig'd to go more than once, and *Thee* and *Thou* king *Charles* and his ministers, in order to recover the debt; and at last instead of specie, the government invested him with the right and sovereignty of a province of *America*, to the south of *Maryland*. Thus was a Quaker rais'd to sovereign power. *Pen* set sail for his new dominions with two ships freighted with Quakers, who follow'd his fortune. The country was then call'd *Pensilvania* from *William Pen*, who there founded *Philadelphia*, now the most flourishing city in that country. The first step he took was to enter into an alliance with his *American* neighbours; and this is the only treaty between those people and the Christians that was not ratified by an oath, and was never infring'd. The new sovereign was at the same time the legislator of *Pensilvania*, and enacted very wise and prudent laws, none of which have ever been chang'd since his time. The first is, to injure no person upon a religious account, and to consider as brethren all those who believe in one God.

He had no sooner settled his government, but several *American* merchants came and peopled this colony. The natives of the country instead of flying into the woods, cultivated by insensible degrees a friendship with the peaceable Quakers. They lov'd these foreigners as much as they detested the other Christians who had conquer'd and laid waste *America*. In a little time, a great number of these savages (falsely so call'd) charm'd with the mild and gentle disposition of their neighbours, came in crowds to *William Pen*, and besought him to admit them into the number of his vassals. 'Twas very rare and uncommon for a sovereign to be *Thee'd* and *Thou'd* by the meanest of his subjects, who never took their hats off when they came into his presence; and as singular for a government to be without one priest in it, and for a people to be without arms, either offensive or defensive; for a body of citizens to be absolutely undistinguish'd but by the publick employments, and for neighbours not to entertain the least jealousy one against the other.

William Pen might glory in having brought down upon earth the so much boasted golden age, which in all probability never existed but in *Pensilvania*. He return'd to *England* to settle some affairs relating to his new dominions. After the death of king *Charles* the second, king *James*, who had lov'd the father, indulg'd the same affection to the son, and no longer consider'd him as an obscure Sectary, but as a very great man. The king's politicks on this occasion agreed with his inclinations. He was desirous of pleasing the Quakers, by annulling the laws made against Nonconformists,* in order to have an opportunity, by this universal toleration, of establishing the *Romish* religion. All the sectarists in *England* saw the snare that was laid for them, but did not give into it; they never failing to unite when the *Romish* religion, their common enemy, is to be oppos'd. But *Pen* did not think himself bound in any manner to renounce his principles, merely to favour Protestants to whom he was odious, in opposition to a king who lov'd him. He had establish'd an universal toleration with regard to conscience in *America*, and wou'd not have it thought that he intended to destroy it in *Europe*; for which reason he adhered so inviolably to king *James*, that a report prevail'd universally of his being a Jesuit. This calumny affected him very strongly, and he was oblig'd to justify himself in print. However, the unfortunate king *James* the second, in whom, as in most princes of the *Stuart* family, grandeur and weakness were equally blended; and who, like them, as much overdid some things as he was short in others, lost his kingdom in a manner that is hardly to be accounted for.

All the *English* sectarists accepted from *William* the third and his parliament, the toleration and indulgence which they had refus'd when offer'd by king *James*. 'Twas then the Quakers began to enjoy, by virtue of the laws, the several privileges they possess at this time. *Pen* having at last seen

Quakerism firmly establish'd in his native country, went back to *Pensilvania.* His own people and the *Americans* receiv'd him with tears of joy, as tho' he had been a father who was return'd to visit his children. All the laws had been religiously observ'd in his absence, a circumstance in which no legislator had ever been happy but himself. After having resided some years in *Pensilvania*, he left it, but with great reluctance, in order to return to *England*, there to solicit some matters in favour of the commerce of *Pensilvania.* But he never saw it again, he dying in *Ruscomb* in *Berkshire*, *anno* 1718.

I am not able to guess what fate Quakerism may have in *America*, but I perceive it dwindles away daily in *England*. In all countries where liberty of conscience is allow'd, the establish'd religion will at last swallow up all the rest. Quakers are disqualified from being members of parliament; nor can they enjoy any post or preferment, because an oath must always be taken on these occasions, and they never swear. They are therefore reduc'd to the necessity of subsisting upon traffick. Their children, whom the industry of their parents has enrich'd, are desirous of enjoying honours, of wearing buttons and ruffles; and quite asham'd of being call'd Quakers, they become converts to the Church of *England*, merely to be in the fashion.

LETTER V.

On the Church of England.

ENGLAND is properly the country of sectarists. *Multæ sunt mansiones in domo patris mei* (in my father's house are many mansions.)* An *Englishman,* as one to whom liberty is natural, may go to heaven his own way.

Nevertheless, tho' every one is permitted to serve God in whatever mode or fashion he thinks proper, yet their true religion, that in which a man makes his fortune, is the sect of Episcoparians or Churchmen, call'd the Church of *England,* or simply the Church, by way of eminence. No person can possess an employment either in *England* or *Ireland,* unless he be rank'd among the faithful, that is, professes himself a member of the Church of *England.* This reason (which carries mathematical evidence with it) has converted such numbers of dissenters of all persuasions, that not a twentieth part of the nation is out of the pale of the establish'd church.* The *English* clergy have retain'd a great number of the Romish ceremonies, and especially that of receiving, with a most scrupulous attention, their tithes. They also have the pious ambition to aim at superiority.

Moreover, they inspire very religiously their flock with a holy zeal against Dissenters of all denominations. This zeal was pretty violent under the Tories, in the four last years of queen *Anne*; but was productive of no greater mischief than the breaking the windows of some meeting-houses, and the demolishing of a few of them. For religious rage ceas'd in *England* with the civil wars; and was no more under queen *Anne,* than the hollow noise of a sea whose billows still heav'd, tho' so long after the storm, when the Whigs and Tories laid waste their native country, in the same manner as the Guelphs and Gibelins* formerly did theirs. 'Twas absolutely necessary for both parties to call in religion on this occasion; the Tories declar'd for episcopacy, and the Whigs, as some imagin'd, were for abolishing it; however, after these had got the upper hand, they contented themselves with only abridging its power.

At the time when the earl of *Oxford* and the lord *Bolingbroke** us'd to drink healths to the Tories, the Church of *England* consider'd those noblemen as the defenders of it's holy privileges. The lower house of Convocation (a kind of house of Commons) compos'd wholly of the clergy, was in some credit at that time; at least the members of it had the liberty to meet, to dispute on ecclesiastical matters, to sentence impious books from time to time to the flames, that is, books written against themselves. The ministry, which is now compos'd of Whigs, does not so much as allow those gentlemen to assemble, so that they are at this time reduc'd (in the obscurity of their respective parishes) to the melancholy occupation of praying for the prosperity of the government, whose tranquillity they would willingly disturb. With regard to the bishops, who are twenty six in all, they still have seats in the house of lords in spite of the Whigs, because the ancient abuse of considering them as Barons subsists to this day. There is a clause however in the oath which the government requires from these gentlemen, that puts their christian patience to a very great trial, *viz.* that they shall be of the Church of *England* as by law establish'd. There are few bishops, deans, or other dignitaries, but imagine they are so *jure divino;** 'tis consequently a great mortification to them to be oblig'd to confess, that they owe their dignity to a pitiful law enacted by a sett of profane laymen. A learned monk (father *Courayer*) writ a book* lately to prove the validity and succession of *English* ordinations. This book was forbid in *France*; but do you believe that the *English* ministry were pleas'd with it? Far from it. Those damn'd Whigs don't value a straw, whether the episcopal succession among them hath been interrupted or not, or whether bishop *Parker* was consecrated (as 'tis pretended) in a tavern, or a church; for these Whigs are much better pleas'd that the bishops should derive their authority from the parliament, than from the apostles. The lord *B——** observ'd, that this notion of divine right would only make so many tyrants in lawn-sleeves, but that the laws made so many citizens.

With regard to the morals of the *English* clergy, they are more regular than those of *France*, and for this reason. All the clergy (a very few excepted) are educated in the universities of *Oxford* or *Cambridge*, far from the depravity and corruption which reign in the capital. They are not call'd to dignities till very late, at a time of life when men are sensible of no other passion but avarice, that is, when their ambition craves a supply. Employments are here bestow'd both in the church and the army, as a reward for long services; and we never see youngsters made bishops or colonels immediately upon their laying aside the academical gown; and besides, most of the clergy are married. The stiff and awkward air contracted by them at the university, and the little familiarity the men of this country have with the ladies, commonly oblige a bishop to confine himself to, and rest contented with his own. Clergymen sometimes take a glass at the tavern, custom giving them a sanction on this occasion; and if they fuddle themselves 'tis in a very serious manner, and without giving the least scandal.

That mixed Being (not to be defin'd) who is neither of the clergy nor of the laity; in a word, the thing call'd *Abbé* in *France*, is a species quite unknown in *England*. All the clergy here are very much upon the reserve, and most of them pedants. When these are told, that in *France*, young fellows famous for their dissoluteness and rais'd to the highest dignities of the church by female intrigues, address the fair publickly in an amorous way, amuse themselves in writing tender love-songs, entertain their friends very splendidly every night at their own houses, and after the banquet is ended, withdraw to invoke the assistance of the Holy Ghost, and call themselves boldly the successors of the apostles, they bless God for their being Protestants. But, these are shameless Hereticks, who deserve to be blown hence thro' the flames to old Nick, as *Rabelais* says,* and for this reason I don't trouble my self about them.

LETTER VI.

On the Presbyterians.

THE Church of *England* is confin'd almost to the kingdom whence it receiv'd its name, and to *Ireland*, for
Presbyterianism is the establish'd religion in *Scotland*. This
Presbyterianism is directly the same with Calvinism, as it
was establish'd in *France*, and is now profess'd at *Geneva*.
As the priests of this sect receive but very inconsiderable
stipends from their churches, and consequently cannot
emulate the splendid luxury of bishops, they exclaim very
naturally against honours which they can never attain to.
Figure to your self the haughty *Diogenes*, trampling under
foot the pride of *Plato*. The *Scotch* Presbyterians are not
very unlike that proud, tho' tatter'd reasoner. *Diogenes* did
not use *Alexander** half so impertinently as these treated
king *Charles* the second; for when they took up arms in his
cause, in opposition to *Oliver*, who had deceiv'd them, they
forc'd that poor monarch to undergo the hearing of three or
four sermons every day; wou'd not suffer him to play,
reduc'd him to a state of penitence and mortification; so that
Charles soon grew sick of these pedants, and accordingly
elop'd from them with as much joy as a youth does from
school.

A Church of *England* minister appears as another *Cato**
in presence of a juvenile, sprightly *French* graduate, who
bawls for a whole morning together in the divinity schools,
and hums a song in chorus with ladies in the evening: But
this *Cato* is a very spark, when before a *Scotch* Presbyterian.
The latter affects a serious gate, puts on a sour look, wears
a vastly broad-brimm'd hat, and a long cloak over a very
short coat; preaches thro' the nose, and gives the name of
the whore of *Babylon* to all churches, where the ministers
are so fortunate as to enjoy an annual revenue of five or six
thousand pounds; and where the people are weak enough to

suffer this, and to give them the titles of my lord, your lordship, or your eminence.

These gentlemen, who have also some churches in *England*, introduc'd there the mode of grave and severe exhortations. To them is owing the sanctification of *Sunday* in the three kingdoms. People are there forbid to work or take any recreation on that day, in which the severity is twice as great as that of the *Romish* church. No opera's, plays or concerts are allow'd in *London* on *Sundays*; and even cards are so expressly forbid, that none but persons of quality and those we call the genteel, play on that day; the rest of the nation go either to church, to the tavern, or to see their mistresses.

Tho' the Episcopal and Presbyterian sects are the two prevailing ones in *Great-Britain*, yet all others are very welcome to come and settle in it, and live very sociably together, tho' most of their preachers hate one another almost as cordially as a Jansenist damns a Jesuit.

Take a view of the *Royal-Exchange** in *London*, a place more venerable than many courts of justice, where the representatives of all nations meet for the benefit of mankind. There the Jew, the Mahometan, and the Christian transact together as tho' they all profess'd the same religion, and give the name of Infidel to none but bankrupts. There the Presbyterian confides in the Anabaptist, and the Churchman depends on the Quaker's word. At the breaking up of this pacific and free assembly, some withdraw to the synagogue, and others to take a glass. This man goes and is baptiz'd in a great tub, in the name of the Father, Son, and Holy Ghost: That man has his son's foreskin cut off, whilst a sett of *Hebrew* words (quite unintelligible to him) are mumbled over his child. Others retire to their churches, and there wait for the inspiration of heaven with their hats on, and all are satisfied.

If one religion only were allowed in *England*, the government would very possibly become arbitrary; if there were but two, the people wou'd cut one another's throats; but as there are such a multitude, they all live happy and in peace.

LETTER VII.

On the Socinians, or Arians, or Antitrinitarians.

THERE is a little sect here compos'd of clergymen, and of a few very learned persons among the laity, who, tho' they don't call themselves *Arians* or *Socinians*,* do yet dissent entirely from St. *Athanasius*, with regard to their notions of the Trinity, and declare very frankly, that the Father is greater than the Son.

Do you remember what is related of a certain orthodox bishop, who in order to convince an emperor of the reality of consubstantiation, put his hand under the chin of the monarch's son, and took him by the nose in presence of his sacred majesty? The emperor was going to order his attendants to throw the bishop out of the window, when the good old man gave him this handsome and convincing reason: Since your majesty, says he, is angry when your son has not due respect shown him, what punishment do you think will God the father inflict on those who refuse his son *Jesus* the titles due to him? The persons I just now mention'd, declare that the holy bishop took a very wrong step; that his argument was inconclusive, and that the emperor should have answer'd him thus: Know that there are two ways by which men may be wanting in respect to me; first, in not doing honour sufficient to my son; and secondly, in paying him the same honour as to me.

Be this as it will, the principles of *Arius* begin to revive, not only in *England* but in *Holland* and *Poland*. The celebrated sir *Isaac Newton* honour'd this opinion so far as to countenance it. This philosopher thought that the Unitarians argued more mathematically than we do. But the most sanguine stickler for Arianism is the illustrious Dr. *Clark*.* This man is rigidly virtuous, and of a mild disposition; is more fond of his tenets than desirous of propagating them; and absorb'd so entirely in problems and calculations, that he is a mere reasoning machine.

'Tis he who wrote a book which is much esteem'd and little understood, on the existence of God; and another more intelligible, but pretty much contemned, on the truth of the Christian religion.*

He never engag'd in scholastic disputes, which our friend calls venerable trifles. He only publish'd a work* containing all the testimonies of the primitive ages, for and against the Unitarians, and leaves to the reader the counting of the voices, and the liberty of forming a judgment. This book won the doctor a great number of partizans, and lost him the See of *Canterbury:* But in my humble opinion, he was out in his calculation, and had better have been Primate of all *England*, than meerly an *Arian* parson.

You see that opinions are subject to revolutions as well as Empires. *Arianism* after having triumph'd during three centuries, and been forgot twelve, rises at last out of its own ashes; but it has chose a very improper season to make its appearance in, the present age being quite cloy'd with disputes and Sects. The members of this Sect are, besides, too few to be indulg'd the liberty of holding public assemblies, which however they will doubtless be permitted to do, in case* they spread considerably. But people are now so very cold with respect to all things of this kind, that there is little probability any new religion, or old one that may be reviv'd, will meet with favour. Is it not whimsical enough that *Luther, Calvin* and *Zvinglius*, all of 'em wretched authors, should have founded Sects which are now spread over a great part of *Europe*; that *Mahomet*, tho' so ignorant, should have given a religion to *Asia* and *Africa*; and that Sir *Isaac Newton*, Dr. *Clark*, Mr. *Locke*, Mr. *Le Clerc &c.** the greatest philosophers, as well as the ablest writers of their ages, should scarce have been able to raise a little flock, which even decreases daily.

This it is to be born at a proper period of time. Were Cardinal *de Retz** to return again into the world, neither his eloquence nor his intrigues would draw together ten women in *Paris*.

Were *Oliver Cromwell*, he who beheaded his Sovereign and seiz'd upon the kingly dignity, to rise from the dead, he wou'd be a wealthy city trader, and no more.

LETTER VIII.

On the Parliament.

THE Members of the *English* Parliament are fond of comparing themselves to the old *Romans*.*

Not long since, Mr. *Shippen** open'd a speech in the house of Commons with these words, *The Majesty of the People of* England *would be wounded*. The singularity of the expression occasion'd a loud laugh; but this Gentleman, so far from being disconcerted, repeated the same words with a resolute tone of voice, and the laugh ceas'd. In my opinion, the Majesty of the people of *England* has nothing in common with that of the people of *Rome*, much less is there any affinity between their governments. There is in *London* a Senate, some of the members whereof are accus'd, (doubtless very unjustly)* of selling their voices on certain occasions, as was done in *Rome*; this is the only resemblance. Besides, the two nations appear to me quite opposite in character, with regard both to good and evil. The *Romans* never knew the dreadful folly of religious Wars, an abomination reserv'd for devout Preachers of patience and humility. *Marius* and *Sylla*, *Cæsar* and *Pompey*, *Anthony* and *Augustus*, did not draw their swords and set the world in a blaze, merely to determine whether the *Flamen** should wear his shirt over his robe, or his robe over his shirt; or whether the sacred Chickens should eat and drink, or eat only, in order to take the augury. The *English* have hang'd one another by law, and cut one another to pieces in pitch battles, for quarrels of as trifling a nature. The Sects of the Episcoparians and Presbyterians quite distracted these very serious Heads for a time. But I fancy they'll hardly ever be so silly again, they seeming to be grown wiser at their own expence; and I don't perceive the least inclination in them to murther one another merely about syllogisms, as some Zealots among them once did.

But here follows a more essential difference between *Rome* and *England*, which gives the advantage entirely to the latter, *viz.* that the civil wars of *Rome* ended in slavery, and those of the *English* in liberty. The *English* are the only people upon earth who have been able to prescribe limits to the power of Kings by resisting them; and who, by a series of struggles, have at last establish'd that wise Government, where the Prince is all powerful to do good, and at the same time is restrain'd from committing evil; where the Nobles are great without insolence, tho' there are no Vassals; and where the People share in the government without confusion.

The house of Lords and that of the Commons divide the legislative power under the King, but the *Romans* had no such balance. The Patricians and Plebeians in *Rome* were perpetually at variance, and there was no intermediate Power to reconcile them. The *Roman* Senate who were so unjustly, so criminally proud, as not to suffer the Plebeians to share with them in any thing, cou'd find no other artifice to keep the latter out of the Administration than by employing them in foreign wars. They consider'd the Plebeians as a wild beast, whom it behov'd them to let loose upon their neighbours, for fear they should devour their masters. Thus the greatest defect in the Government of the *Romans* rais'd 'em to be Conquerors. By being unhappy at home, they triumph'd over, and possess'd themselves of the world, till at last their divisions sunk them to Slavery.

The government of *England* will never rise to so exalted a pitch of glory, nor will its end be so fatal. The *English* are not fir'd with the splendid folly of making conquests, but would only prevent their neighbours from conquering. They are not only jealous of their own Liberty, but even of that of other nations. The *English* were exasperated against *Lewis* the Fourteenth, for no other reason but because he was ambitious; and declar'd war against him merely out of levity, not from any interested motives.*

The *English* have doubtless purchas'd their Liberties at a very high price, and waded thro' seas of blood to drown the Idol of arbitrary Power. Other nations have been involv'd in as great calamities, and have shed as much blood; but then the blood they spilt in defence of their Liberties, only enslaved them the more.

That which rises to a Revolution in *England* is no more than a Sedition in other countries. A city in *Spain*, in *Barbary*, or in *Turkey*, takes up arms in defence of its Privileges, when immediately 'tis storm'd by mercenary Troops, 'tis punish'd by Executioners, and the rest of the Nation kiss the chains they are loaded with. The *French* are of opinion, that the government of this Island is more tempestuous than the sea which surrounds it, which indeed is true; but then 'tis never so but when the King raises the storm; when he attempts to seize the Ship of which he is only the chief Pilot. The civil wars of *France* lasted longer; were more cruel, and productive of greater evils than those of *England:* But none of these civil Wars had a wise and prudent Liberty for their object.

In the detestable Reigns of *Charles* the ninth, and *Henry* the third, the whole affair was only whether the people should be slaves to the *Guises*.* With regard to the last war of *Paris*, it deserves only to be hooted at. Methinks I see a croud of School-boys rising up in arms against their Master, and afterwards whipp'd for it. Cardinal *de Retz*, who was witty and brave, but to no purpose; rebellious without a cause; factious without design, and head of a defenceless Party, caball'd for caballing sake, and seem'd to foment the civil War merely out of diversion. The Parliament did not know what he intended, nor what he did not intend. He levied troops by act of Parliament, and the next moment cashier'd them. He threatned, he begg'd pardon; he set a price upon Cardinal *Mazarine*'s head, and afterwards congratulated him in a public manner. Our civil wars under *Charles* the sixth were bloody and cruel, those of the *League* execrable, and that of the *Frondeurs*[1] ridiculous.

That for which the *French* chiefly reproach the *English*

---

[1] *Frondeurs*, in its proper sense *Slingers*, and figuratively *Cavillers*, or lovers of contradiction; was a name given to a league or party that oppos'd the *French* ministry, i.e. Cardinal *Mazarine* in 1648. See *Rochefoucault*'s Memoirs.*

Nation, is, the murther of King *Charles* the First, whom his subjects treated exactly as he wou'd have treated them, had his Reign been prosperous. After all, consider on one side, *Charles* the first defeated in a pitch'd battle, imprison'd, try'd, sentenc'd to die in *Westminster-hall*, and then beheaded: And on the other, the Emperor *Henry* the seventh, poison'd by his chaplain at his receiving the sacrament; *Henry* the third stabb'd by a Monk; thirty assassinations projected against *Henry* the fourth;* several of them put in execution, and the last bereaving that great Monarch of his life. Weigh, I say, all these wicked attempts, and then judge.

LETTER IX.

On the Government.

THAT mixture in the *English* government, that harmony between King, Lords and Commons, did not always subsist. *England* was enslav'd for a long series of years by the *Romans*, the *Saxons*, the *Danes*, and the *French* successively. *William* the conqueror particularly rul'd them with a rod of iron. He dispos'd as absolutely of the lives and fortunes of his conquer'd subjects as an eastern Monarch; and forbid, upon pain of death, the *English* both fire or candle in their houses after eight a clock; whether he did this to prevent their nocturnal meetings, or only to try, by this odd and whimsical prohibition, how far it was possible for one Man to extend his power over his fellow Creatures. 'Tis true indeed that the *English* had Parliaments before and after *William* the Conqueror; and they boast of them, as tho' these assemblies then call'd Parliaments, compos'd of ecclesiastical Tyrants, and of plunderers entitled Barons, had been the guardians of the publick liberty and happiness.

The Barbarians who came from the shores of the *Baltick*, and settled in the rest of *Europe*, brought with them the form of government call'd States or Parliaments, about which so much noise is made, and which are so little understood. Kings indeed were not absolute in those days, but then the people were more wretched upon that very account, and more completely enslav'd. The Chiefs of these savages who had laid waste *France, Italy, Spain* and *England*, made themselves Monarchs. Their generals divided among themselves the several countries they had conquer'd, whence sprung those Margraves, those Peers, those Barons, those petty Tyrants, who often contested with their Sovereigns for the spoils of whole nations. These were birds of prey, fighting with an Eagle for Doves, whose blood the Victorious was to suck. Every nation, instead of being govern'd by one Master, was trampled upon by an hundred Tyrants. The priests soon play'd a part among them.* Before this, it had been the fate of the *Gauls*, the *Germans* and the *Britons*, to be always govern'd by their Druids, and the Chiefs of their villages, an ancient kind of Barons, not so tyrannical as their successors. These Druids pretended to be mediators between God and man. They enacted laws, they fulminated their excommunications, and sentenc'd to death. The Bishops succeeded, by insensible degrees, to their temporal authority in the *Goth* and *Vandal* government. The Popes set themselves at their head, and arm'd with their Briefs, their Bulls, and reinforc'd by Monks, they made even Kings tremble; depos'd and assassinated them at pleasure, and employ'd every artifice to draw into their own purses, monies from all parts of *Europe*. The weak *Ina*, one of the tyrants of the *Saxon* Heptarchy in *England*, was the first Monarch that submitted, in his pilgrimage to *Rome*, to pay St. *Peter*'s penny (equivalent very near to a *French* crown) for every house in his dominions. The whole Island soon follow'd his example; *England* became insensibly one of the Pope's provinces, and the holy Father us'd to send from time to time his Legates thither to levy exorbitant taxes. At last King *John* deliver'd up by a public instrument, the Kingdom of *England* to the Pope, who had excommunicated him; but the Barons not finding their account in this resignation, dethron'd the wretched King *John* and seated *Lewis*, father to St. *Lewis* King of *France* in his place. However they were soon weary of their new Monarch, and accordingly oblig'd him to return back to *France*.

Whilst that the Barons, the Bishops, and the Popes, all laid waste *England*, where all were for ruling; the most numerous, the most useful, even the most virtuous, and consequently the most venerable part of mankind, consisting of those who study the laws and the sciences; of traders, of artificers, in a word, of all who were not tyrants; that is, those who are call'd the people; these, I say, were by them look'd upon as so many animals beneath the dignity of the human species. The Commons in those ages were far from sharing in the government, they being *Villains* or Peasants whose labour, whose blood were the property of their Masters who entitled themselves the Nobility. The major part of men in *Europe* were at that time what they are to this day in several parts of the world, they were *Villains* or Bondsmen of Lords, that is, a kind of cattle bought and sold with the land. Many ages past away before justice cou'd be done to human nature; before mankind were conscious, that 'twas abominable numbers should sow, and but few reap: And was not *France* very happy, when the power and authority of those petty Robbers was abolish'd by the lawful authority of Kings and of the People?

Happily in the violent shocks which the divisions between Kings and the Nobles gave to empires, the chains of Nations were more or less heavy. Liberty, in *England*, sprung from the quarrels of Tyrants. The Barons forc'd King *John* and King *Henry* the third, to grant the famous *Magna Charta*, the chief design of which was indeed to make Kings dependant on the Lords, but then the rest of the nation were a little favour'd in it, in order that they might join, on proper occasions, with their pretended Masters. This great Charter which is consider'd as the sacred origin of the *English* Liberties, shews in it self how little Liberty was known.

The Title alone proves, that the King thought he had a just right to be absolute; and that the Barons, and even the Clergy forc'd him to give up that pretended right, for no other reason but because they were the most powerful.

Magna Charta begins in this stile, We grant, of our own free will, the following Privileges to the Archbishops, Bishops, Priors and Barons of our Kingdom, &c.

The House of Commons is not once mention'd in the Articles of this Charter, a Proof that it did not yet exist, or that it existed without Power. Mention is therein made, by name, of the Freemen of *England*, a melancholy Proof that some were not so. It appears by the thirty second Article, that these pretended Freemen ow'd Service to their Lords. Such a Liberty as this, was not many removes from Slavery.

By article XXI, the King ordains that his Officers shall not henceforward seize upon, unless they pay for them, the

Horses and Carts of Freemen. The People consider'd this
Ordinance as a real Liberty, tho' it was a greater Tyranny.*
Henry the seventh, that happy Usurper and great Politician,
who pretended to love the Barons, tho' he in reality hated
and fear'd them, got their Lands alienated. By this means
the *Villains*, afterwards acquiring Riches by their Industry,
purchas'd the Estates and Country-Seats of the illustrious
Peers who had ruin'd themselves by their Folly and Extravagance, and all the Lands got by insensible Degrees into
other Hands.

The Power of the House of Commons increas'd every
Day. The Families of the ancient Peers were at last extinct;
and as Peers only are properly noble in *England*, there
would be no such thing in strictness of Law, as Nobility in
that Island, had not the Kings created new Barons from
Time to Time, and preserv'd the Body of Peers, once a
Terror to them, to oppose them to the Commons since
become so formidable.*

All these new Peers who compose the higher House,
receive nothing but their Titles from the King, and very few
of them have Estates in those Places whence they take their
Titles. One shall be Duke of *D——* tho' he has not a Foot
of Land in *Dorsetshire*; and another is Earl of a Village, tho'
he scarce knows where it is situated. The Peers have Power,
but 'tis only in the Parliament House.

There is no such thing here, as *haute, moyenne, & basse
justice*,[1] that is, a Power to judge in all Matters civil and
criminal; nor a Right or Privilege of Hunting in the
Grounds of a Citizen, who at the same time is not permitted
to fire a Gun in his own Field.

No one is exempted in this Country from paying certain
Taxes, because he is a Nobleman or a Priest. All Duties and

---

[1] *La haute justice*, is that of a Lord, who has Power to sentence capitally,
and to judge of all Causes civil and criminal, those of the Crown excepted.
La moyenne justice, is empower'd to judge of Actions relating to
Guardianships, and Offences. *La basse justice* takes Cognizance of the Fees
due to the Lord, of the Havock of Beasts, and of Offences. The *moyenne
justice* is imaginary, and there is perhaps no Instance of its ever being put
in Execution.

Taxes are settled by the House of Commons, whose Power is greater than that of the Peers, tho' inferiour to it in dignity. The spiritual as well as temporal Lords have the Liberty to reject a Money Bill brought in by the Commons, but they are not allow'd to alter any thing in it, and must either pass or throw it out without Restriction. When the Bill has pass'd the Lords and is sign'd by the King, then the whole Nation pays, every Man in proportion to his Revenue or Estate, not according to his Title, which would be absurd. There is no such thing as an arbitrary Subsidy or Poll-Tax, but a real Tax on the Lands, of all which an Estimate was made in the Reign of the famous King *William* the Third.

The Land-Tax continues still upon the same foot, tho' the Revenue of the Lands is increas'd. Thus no one is tyranniz'd over, and every one is easy. The Feet of the Peasants are not bruis'd by wooden Shoes; they eat white Bread, are well cloath'd, and are not afraid of increasing their Stock of Cattle, nor of tiling their Houses, from any Apprehensions that their Taxes will be rais'd the Year following. The annual Income of the Estates of a great many Commoners in *England*, amounts to two hundred thousand Livres; and yet these don't think it beneath them to plough the Lands which enrich them, and on which they enjoy their Liberty.

LETTER X.

On Trade.

AS Trade enrich'd the Citizens in *England*, so it contri-
buted to their Freedom, and this Freedom on the other
Side extended their Commerce, whence arose the Grandeur
of the State. Trade rais'd by insensible Degrees the naval
Power, which gives the *English* a Superiority over the Seas,
and they now are Masters of very near two hundred Ships of
War. Posterity will very possibly be surpriz'd to hear that
an Island whose only Produce is a little Lead, Tin, Fuller's
Earth, and coarse Wool, should become so powerful by its
Commerce, as to be able to send in 1723,* three Fleets at the
same Time to three different and far distanc'd Parts of the
Globe. One before *Gibraltar*, conquer'd and still possess'd
by the *English*; a second to *Porto Bello*, to dispossess the
King of *Spain* of the Treasures of the *West-Indies*; and a
third into the *Baltick*, to prevent the *Northern* Powers from
coming to an Engagement.

At the Time when *Lewis* XIV made all *Italy* tremble, and
that his Armies, which had already possess'd themselves of
Savoy and *Piedmont*, were upon the Point of taking *Turin*;
Prince *Eugene* was oblig'd to march from the Middle of
Germany in order to succour *Savoy*. Having no Money,
without which Cities cannot be either taken or defended, he
address'd himself to some *English* Merchants. These, at an
Hour and half's Warning, lent him five Millions, whereby
he was enabled to deliver *Turin*, and to beat the *French*; after
which he wrote the following short Letter to the Persons
who had disburs'd him the abovemention'd Sums: 'Gentlemen, I have receiv'd your Money, and flatter my self that I
have laid it out to your Satisfaction.' Such a Circumstance as
this raises a just Pride in an *English* Merchant, and makes
him presume (not without some Reason) to compare himself to a *Roman* Citizen; and indeed a Peer's Brother does
not think Traffic beneath him. When the Lord *Townshend**

was Minister of State, a Brother of his was content to be a City Merchant; and at the Time that the Earl of *Oxford* govern'd *Great-Britain*, his younger Brother was no more than a Factor in *Aleppo*,* where he chose to live, and where he died. This Custom, which begins however to be laid aside, appears monstruous to *Germans*, vainly puff'd up with their Extraction. These think it morally impossible that the Son of an *English* Peer should be no more than a rich and powerful Citizen, for all are Princes in *Germany*. There have been thirty Highnesses of the same Name, all whose Patrimony consisted only in their Escutcheons and their Pride.

In *France* the Title of Marquis is given *gratis* to any one who will accept of it; and whosoever arrives at *Paris* from the midst of the most remote Provinces with Money in his Purse, and a Name terminating in *ac* or *ille*, may strut about, and cry, Such a Man as I! A Man of my Rank and Figure! And may look down upon a Trader with sovereign Contempt;* whilst the Trader on the other Side, by thus often hearing his Profession treated so disdainfully, is Fool enough to blush at it. However, I cannot say which is most useful to a Nation; a Lord, powder'd in the tip of the Mode, who knows exactly at what a Clock the King rises and goes to bed; and who gives himself Airs of Grandeur and State, at the same Time that he is acting the Slave in the Anti-chamber of a prime Minister; or a Merchant, who enriches his Country, dispatches Orders from his Compting-House to *Surat* and *Grand Cairo*, and contributes to the Felicity of the World.

LETTER XI.
On Inoculation.

IT is inadvertently affirm'd in the Christian Countries of *Europe*, that the *English* are Fools and Madmen. Fools, because they give their Children the Small-Pox to prevent their catching it; and Mad-men, because they wantonly communicate a certain and dreadful Distemper to their Children, merely to prevent an uncertain Evil. The *English*, on the other Side, call the rest of the *Europeans* cowardly and unnatural. Cowardly, because they are afraid of putting their Children to a little Pain; unnatural, because they expose them to die one Time or other of the Small-Pox. But that the Reader may be able to judge, whether the *English* or those who differ from them in opinion, are in the right, here follows the History of the fam'd Inoculation, which is mention'd with so much Dread in *France*.

The *Circassian* Women have, from Time immemorial, communicated the Small-Pox to their Children when not above six Months old, by making an Incision in the arm, and by putting into this Incision a Pustle, taken carefully from the Body of another Child. This Pustle produces the same Effect in the arm it is laid in, as Yest* in a Piece of Dough: It ferments, and diffuses through the whole Mass of Blood, the Qualities with which it is impregnated. The Pustles of the Child, in whom the artificial Small-Pox has been thus inoculated, are employ'd to communicate the same Distemper to others. There is an almost perpetual Circulation of it in *Circassia*; and when unhappily the Small-Pox has quite left the Country, the Inhabitants of it are in as great Trouble and Perplexity, as other Nations when their Harvest has fallen short.

The Circumstance that introduc'd a Custom in *Circassia*, which appears so singular to others, is nevertheless a Cause common to all Nations, I mean maternal Tenderness and Interest.

The *Circassians* are poor, and their Daughters are beautiful, and indeed 'tis in them they chiefly trade. They furnish with Beauties, the Seraglios of the *Turkish* Sultan, of the *Persian* Sophy, and of all those who are wealthy enough to purchase and maintain such precious Merchandize. These Maidens are very honourably and virtuously instructed to fondle and caress Men; are taught Dances of a very polite and effeminate kind; and how to heighten by the most voluptuous Artifices, the Pleasures of their disdainful Masters for whom they are design'd. These unhappy Creatures repeat their Lesson to their Mothers, in the same manner as little Girls among us repeat their Catechism, without understanding one Word they say.

Now it often happen'd, that after a Father and Mother had taken the utmost Care of the Education of their Children, they were frustrated of all their Hopes in an Instant. The Small-Pox getting into the Family, one Daughter died of it, another lost an Eye, a third had a great Nose at her Recovery, and the unhappy Parents were completely ruin'd. Even frequently, when the Small-Pox became epidemical, Trade was suspended for several Years, which thinn'd very considerably the Seraglios of *Persia* and *Turkey*.

A trading Nation is always watchful over its own Interests, and grasps at every Discovery that may be of Advantage to its Commerce. The *Circassians* observ'd, that scarce one Person in a Thousand was ever attack'd by a Small-Pox of a violent kind. That some indeed had this Distemper very favourably three or four Times, but never twice so as to prove fatal; in a Word, that no one ever had it in a violent Degree twice in his Life. They observ'd farther, that when the Small-Pox is of the milder Sort, and the Pustles have only a tender, delicate Skin to break thro', they never leave the least Scar in the Face. From these natural Observations they concluded, that in case an Infant of six Months or a Year old, should have a milder Sort of Small-Pox, he wou'd not die of it, would not be mark'd, nor be ever afflicted with it again.

In order therefore to preserve the Life and Beauty of their Children, the only Thing remaining was, to give them the

Small-Pox in their infant Years. This they did, by inoculating in the Body of a Child, a Pustle taken from the most regular, and at the same Time the most favourable Sort of Small-Pox that could be procur'd.

The Experiment cou'd not possibly fail. The *Turks*, who are People of good Sense, soon adopted this Custom, insomuch that at this Time there is not a Bassa* in *Constantinople*, but communicates the Small-Pox to his Children of both Sexes, immediately upon their being wean'd.

Some pretend, that the *Circassians* borrow'd this Custom anciently from the *Arabians*; but we shall leave the clearing up of this Point of History to some learned Benedictine, who will not fail to compile a great many Folio's on this Subject, with the several Proofs or Authorities. All I have to say upon it, is, that in the beginning of the Reign of King *George* the First, the Lady *Wortley Mountague*, a Woman of as fine a Genius, and endu'd with as great a Strength of Mind, as any of her Sex in the *British* Kingdoms, being with her Husband who was Ambassador at the Port, made no scruple to communicate the Small-Pox to an Infant of which she was deliver'd in *Constantinople*. The Chaplain represented to his Lady, but to no purpose, that this was an unchristian Operation, and therefore that it cou'd succeed with none but Infidels. However, it had the most happy Effect upon the Son of the Lady *Wortley Mountague*, who, at her Return to *England*, communicated the Experiment to the Princess of *Wales*, now Queen of *England*.* It must be confess'd that this Princess, abstracted from her Crown and Titles, was born to encourage the whole Circle of Arts, and to do good to Mankind. She appears as an amiable Philosopher on the Throne, having never let slip one Opportunity of improving the great Talents she receiv'd from Nature, nor of exerting her Beneficence. 'Tis she, who being inform'd that a Daughter of *Milton* was living, but in miserable Circumstances, immediately sent her a considerable Present. 'Tis she who protects the learned Father *Courayer*.* 'Tis she who condescended to attempt a Reconciliation between Dr. *Clark* and Mr. *Leibnitz*.* The Moment this Princess heard of Inoculation, she caus'd an

Experiment of it to be made on four Criminals sentenc'd to die, and by that means preserv'd their Lives doubly; for she not only sav'd them from the Gallows, but by means of this artificial Small-Pox, prevented their ever having that Distemper in a natural Way, with which they would very probably have been attack'd one Time or other, and might have died of in a more advanc'd Age.

The Princess being assur'd of the Usefulness of this Operation, caus'd her own Children to be inoculated. A great Part of the Kingdom follow'd her Example, and since that Time ten thousand Children, at least, of Persons of Condition owe in this Manner their Lives to her Majesty, and to the Lady *Wortley Mountague*; and as many of the Fair Sex are oblig'd to them for their Beauty.*

Upon a general Calculation, threescore Persons in every hundred have the Small-Pox. Of these threescore, twenty die of it in the most favourable Season of Life, and as many more wear the disagreeable Remains of it in their Faces so long as they live. Thus, a fifth Part of Mankind either die, or are disfigur'd by this Distemper. But it does not prove fatal to so much as one, among those who are inoculated in *Turkey* or in *England*, unless the Patient be infirm, or would have died had not the Experiment been made upon him. Besides, no one is disfigur'd, no one has the Small-Pox a second Time, if the Inoculation was perfect. 'Tis therefore certain, that had the Lady of some *French* Ambassador brought this Secret from *Constantinople* to *Paris*, the Nation would have been for ever oblig'd to her. Then the Duke *de Villequier*, Father to the Duke *d'Aumont*, who enjoys the most vigorous Constitution, and is the healthiest Man in *France*, would not have been cut off in the Flower of his Age.

The Prince of *Soubise*, happy in the finest Flush of Health, would not have been snatch'd away at five and twenty; nor the Dauphin, Grandfather to *Lewis* the Fifteenth, have been laid in his Grave in his fiftieth Year. Twenty thousand Persons whom the Small-Pox swept away at *Paris* in 1723, would have been alive at this Time. But are not the *French* fond of Life, and is Beauty so inconsiderable an Advantage as to be disregarded by the Ladies! It must be confess'd that we are an odd kind of People. Perhaps our Nation will imitate, ten Years hence, this Practice of the *English*, if the Clergy and the Physicians will but give them Leave to do it: Or possibly our Country Men may introduce Inoculation three Months hence in *France* out of mere whim, in case the *English* should discontinue it thro' Fickleness.

I am inform'd that the *Chinese* have practis'd Inoculation these hundred Years, a Circumstance that argues very much in its Favour, since they are thought to be the wisest and best govern'd People in the World. The *Chinese* indeed don't communicate this Distemper by Inoculation, but at the Nose, in the same Manner as we take Snuff. This is a more agreeable way, but then it produces the like Effects; and proves at the same Time, that had Inoculation been practis'd in *France*, 'twould have sav'd the Lives of Thousands.

LETTER XII.

On the Lord Bacon.

NOT long since, the trite and frivolous Question following was debated in a very polite and learned Company, *viz.* who was the greatest Man, *Cæsar, Alexander, Tamerlane, Cromwell,* &c.

Some Body answer'd, that Sir *Isaac Newton* excell'd them all. The Gentleman's Assertion was very just; for if true Greatness consists in having receiv'd from Heaven a mighty Genius, and in having employ'd it to enlighten our own Minds and that of others; a Man like Sir *Isaac Newton,* whose equal is hardly found in a thousand Years, is the truly great Man. And those Politicians and Conquerors, (and all ages produce some) were generally so many illustrious wicked Men. That Man claims our Respect, who commands over the Minds of the rest of the World by the Force of Truth, not those who enslave their Fellow Creatures; He who is acquainted with the Universe, not They who deface it.

Since therefore you desire me to give you an Account of the famous Personages which *England* has given birth to, I shall begin with Lord *Bacon,* Mr. *Locke,* Sir *Isaac Newton,* &c. Afterwards the Warriors and Ministers of State shall come in their order.*

I must begin with the celebrated Viscount *Verulam,* known in *Europe* by the Name of *Bacon,* which was that of his Family. His Father had been Lord Keeper, and himself was a great many Years Lord Chancellor under King *James* the First. Nevertheless, amidst the Intrigues of a Court, and the Affairs of his exalted Employment, which alone were enough to engross his whole Time, he yet found so much Leisure for Study, as to make himself a great Philosopher, a good Historian, and an elegant Writer; and a still more surprizing Circumstance is, that he liv'd in an Age in which the Art of writing justly and elegantly was little known,

much less true Philosophy. Lord *Bacon*, as is the Fate
of Man, was more esteem'd after his Death than in his
Life-time. His Enemies were in the *British* Court, and his
Admirers were Foreigners.

When the Marquis *d'Essiat* attended in *England* upon the
Princess *Henrietta Maria*, Daughter to *Henry* the Fourth,
whom King *Charles* the First had married, that Minister
went and visited the Lord *Bacon*, who being at that Time
sick in his Bed, receiv'd him with the Curtains shut close.
You resemble the Angels, says the Marquis to him; we hear
those Beings spoken of perpetually, and we believe them
superiour to Men, but are never allow'd the Consolation to
see them.

You know that this great Man was accus'd of a Crime
very unbecoming a Philosopher, I mean Bribery and Extor-
tion. You know that he was sentenc'd by the House of
Lords, to pay a Fine of about four hundred thousand *French*
Livres; to lose his Peerage and his Dignity of Chancellor.
But in the present Age, the *English* revere his Memory to
such a Degree, that they will scarce allow him to have been
guilty. In case you should ask what are my Thoughts on this
Head, I shall answer you in the Words which I heard the
Lord *Bolingbroke* use on another Occasion. Several Gentlemen were speaking, in his Company, of the Avarice with
which the late Duke of *Marlborough* had been charg'd,
some Examples whereof being given, the Lord *Bolingbroke*
was appeal'd to, (who having been in the opposite Party,*
might perhaps, without the Imputation of Indecency, have
been allow'd to clear up that Matter:) 'He was so great a
Man, replied his Lordship, that I have forgot his Vices.'

I shall therefore confine my self to those Things which so
justly gain'd Lord *Bacon* the Esteem of all *Europe*.

The most singular, and the best of all his Pieces, is that
which, at this Time, is the most useless and the least read, I
mean his *Novum Scientiarum Organum*. This is the Scaffold with which the new Philosophy was rais'd; and when
the Edifice was built, Part of it at least, the Scaffold was no
longer of Service.

The Lord *Bacon* was not yet acquainted with Nature, but
then he knew, and pointed out, the several Paths that lead

to it. He had despis'd in his younger Years the Thing
call'd Philosophy in the Universities; and did all that lay
in his Power to prevent those Societies of Men, instituted
to improve human Reason, from depraving it by their
Quiddities, their Horrors of the *Vacuum*, their substantial
Forms, and all those impertinent* Terms which not only
Ignorance had rendred venerable, but which had been
made sacred, by their being ridiculously blended with
Religion.

He is the Father of experimental Philosophy. It must
indeed be confess'd, that very surprizing Secrets had been
found out before his Time. The Sea-Compass, Printing,
engraving on Copper Plates, Oil-Painting, Looking-
Glasses; the Art of restoring, in some Measure, old Men to
their Sight by Spectacles; Gun-Powder, &c. had been
discover'd. A new World had been sought for, found, and
conquer'd. Would not one suppose that these sublime Discoveries had been made by the greatest Philosophers, and in
Ages much more enlightened than the present? But 'twas far
otherwise; all these great Changes happen'd in the most
stupid and barbarous Times. Chance only gave Birth to
most of those Inventions; and 'tis very probable that what
is call'd Chance, contributed very much to the Discovery
of *America*; at least it has been always thought, that
Christopher Columbus undertook his Voyage, merely on
the Relation of a Captain of a Ship, which a Storm had drove
as far Westward as the *Caribee* Islands. Be this as it will,
Men had sail'd round the World, and cou'd destroy Cities
by an artificial Thunder more dreadful than the real one:
But, then they were not acquainted with the Circulation of
the Blood, the Weight of the Air, the Laws of Motion,
Light, the Number of our Planets, &c. And a Man who
maintain'd a Thesis on *Aristotle*'s Categories; on the
universals *a parte rei*,* or such like Nonsense, was look'd
upon as a Prodigy.

The most astonishing, the most useful Inventions, are not
those which reflect the greatest Honour on the human
Mind. 'Tis to a mechanical Instinct, which is found in many
Men, and not to true Philosophy, that most Arts owe their
Origin.

The Discovery of Fire, the Art of making Bread, of melting and preparing Metals, of building Houses, and the Invention of the Shuttle, are infinitely more beneficial to Mankind than Printing or the Sea-Compass: And yet these Arts were invented by uncultivated, savage Men.

What a prodigious use the *Greeks* and *Romans* made afterwards of Mechanicks! Nevertheless, they believ'd that there were crystal Heavens; that the Stars were small Lamps which sometimes fell into the Sea; and one of their greatest Philosophers,* after long Researches, found that the Stars were so many Flints which had been detach'd from the Earth.

In a Word, no one, before the Lord *Bacon*, was acquainted with experimental Philosophy, nor with the several physical Experiments which have been made since his Time. Scarce one of them but is hinted at in his Work, and he himself had made several. He made a kind of pneumatic Engine, by which he guess'd the elasticity of the Air. He approach'd, on all Sides as it were, to the Discovery of its Weight, and had very near attain'd it, but some Time after *Toricelli* seiz'd upon this Truth. In a little Time experimental Philosophy began to be cultivated on a sudden in most Parts of *Europe*. 'Twas a hidden Treasure which the Lord *Bacon* had some Notion of, and which all the Philosophers, encourag'd by his Promises, endeavour'd to dig up.

But that which surpriz'd me most was to read in his Work, in express Terms, the new Attraction, the Invention of which is ascrib'd to Sir *Isaac Newton*.

We must search, says Lord *Bacon*, whether there may not be a kind of magnetic Power, which operates between the Earth and heavy Bodies, between the Moon and the Ocean, between the Planets, &c. In another Place he says, either heavy Bodies must be carried towards the Center of the Earth, or must be reciprocally attracted by it; and in the latter Case 'tis evident, that the nearer Bodies, in their falling, draw towards the Earth, the stronger they will attract one another. We must, says he, make an Experiment to see whether the same Clock will go faster on the Top of a Mountain or at the Bottom of a Mine. Whether the Strength of the Weights decreases on the Mountain, and increases in the Mine. 'Tis probable that the Earth has a true attractive Power.

This Fore-runner in Philosophy was also an elegant Writer, an Historian and a Wit.

His moral Essays are greatly esteem'd, but they were drawn up in the View of instructing rather than of pleasing: And as they are not a Satyr upon Mankind, like *Rochefoucaults*'s Maxims, nor written upon a sceptical Plan, like *Montagne*'s Essays, they are not so much read as those two ingenious Authors.

His History of *Henry* the Seventh was look'd upon as a Master-Piece, but how is it possible that some Persons can presume to compare so little a Work with the History of our illustrious *Thuanus?**

Speaking about the famous Impostor *Perkin*, Son to a converted *Jew*,[1] who assum'd boldly the Name and Title of *Richard* the Fourth, King of *England*, at the Instigation of the Duchess of *Burgundy*; and who disputed the Crown with *Henry* the Seventh, the Lord *Bacon* writes as follows:

'At this Time the King began again to be haunted with Sprites, by the Magick and curious Arts of the Lady *Margaret*; who raised up the Ghost of *Richard* Duke of *York*, second Son to King *Edward* the Fourth, to walk and vex the King.'[2]

'After such Time as she (*Margaret* of *Burgundy*) thought he (*Perkin Warbeck*) was perfect in his Lesson, she began to cast with her self from what Coast this *Blazing-Starre* should first appear, and at what Time it must be upon the Horizon of *Ireland*; for there had the like Meteor strong Influence before.'[3]

Methinks our sagacious *Thuanus* does not give into such Fustian,* which formerly was look'd upon as Sublime, but in this Age is justly call'd Nonsense.

---

[1] *John Osbeck.*

[2] The History of the Reign of King *Henry* the Seventh, *page* 112. *London*, printed in 1641. Folio.

[3] Idem. *p.* 116.

LETTER XIII.

On Mr. Locke.

PERHAPS no Man ever had a more judicious or more methodical Genius, or was a more acute Logician than Mr. *Locke*, and yet he was not deeply skill'd in the Mathematicks. This great Man could never subject himself to the tedious Fatigue of Calculations, nor to the dry Pursuit of Mathematical Truths, which do not at first present any sensible Objects to the Mind; and no one has given better Proofs than he, that 'tis possible for a Man to have a geometrical Head without the Assistance of Geometry. Before his Time, several great Philosophers had declar'd, in the most positive Terms, what the Soul of Man is; but as these absolutely knew nothing about it, they might very well be allow'd to differ entirely in opinion from one another.

In *Greece*, the infant Seat of Arts and of Errors, and where the Grandeur as well as Folly of the human Mind went such prodigious Lengths, the People us'd to reason about the Soul in the very same Manner as we do.

The divine *Anaxagoras*, in whose Honour an Altar was erected, for his having taught Mankind that the Sun was greater than *Peloponnesus*, that Snow was black, and that the Heavens were of Stone; affirm'd that the Soul was an aerial Spirit, but at the same Time immortal. *Diogenes*, (not he who was a cynical Philosopher after having coyn'd base Money) declar'd that the Soul was a Portion of the Substance of God; an Idea which we must confess was very sublime. *Epicurus* maintain'd that it was compos'd of Parts in the same Manner as the Body.

Aristotle who has been explain'd a thousand Ways, because he is unintelligible, was of Opinion, according to some of his Disciples, that the Understanding in all Men is one and the same Substance.

The divine *Plato*, Master of the divine *Aristotle*, and the divine *Socrates* Master of the divine *Plato*, us'd to say that

the Soul was corporeal and eternal. No doubt but the De-
mon of *Socrates* had instructed him in the Nature of it.
Some People, indeed, pretend, that a Man who boasted his
being attended by a familiar Genius, must infallibly be either a Knave or a Madman, but this kind of People are
seldom satisfied with any Thing but Reason.

With regard to the Fathers of the Church, several in the
primitive Ages believ'd that the Soul was human, and the
Angels and God corporeal. Men naturally improve upon
every System. St. *Bernard*, as Father *Mabillon* confesses,
taught that the Soul after Death does not see God in the
celestial Regions, but converses with *Christ's* human Nature
only. However, he was not believ'd this Time on his bare
Word; the Adventure of the Crusade having a little sunk the
Credit of his Oracles. Afterwards a thousand Schoolmen
arose, such as the irrefragable Doctor,[1] the subtil Doctor,[2]
the angelic Doctor,[3] the seraphic Doctor,[4] and the cherubic
Doctor,* who were all sure that they had a very clear and
distinct Idea of the Soul, and yet wrote in such a Manner,
that one would conclude they were resolv'd no one should
understand a Word in their Writings. Our *Des Cartes*, born
not to discover the Errors of Antiquity, but to substitute his
own in the Room of them; and hurried away by that sys-
tematic Spirit which throws a Cloud over the Minds of the
greatest Men, thought he had demonstrated that the Soul is
the same Thing as Thought, in the same Manner as Matter,
in his Opinion, is the same as Extension. He asserted, that
Man thinks eternally, and that the Soul, at its coming into
the Body, is inform'd with the whole Series of metaphysical
Notions; knowing God, infinite Space, possessing all ab-
stract Ideas; in a Word, completely endued with the most
sublime Lights, which it unhappily forgets at its issuing
from the Womb.

Father *Malbranche*, in his sublime Illusions, not only
admitted innate Ideas, but did not doubt of our living
wholly in God,* and that God is, as it were, our Soul.

[1] *Alexander de Hales.*   [2] *Duns Scotus.*   [3] St. *Thomas.*
[4] St. *Bonaventure.*

Such a Multitude of Reasoners having written the Romance of the Soul, a Sage at last arose, who gave, with an Air of the greatest Modesty, the History of it. Mr. *Locke* has display'd the human Soul, in the same Manner as an excellent Anatomist explains the Springs of the human Body. He every where takes the Light of Physicks for his Guide. He sometimes presumes to speak affirmatively, but then he presumes also to doubt. Instead of concluding at once what we know not, he examines gradually what we wou'd know. He takes an Infant at the Instant of his Birth; he traces, Step by Step, the Progress of his Understanding; examines what Things he has in common with Beasts, and what he possesses above them. Above all he consults himself; the being conscious that he himself thinks.

I shall leave, says he, to those who know more of this Matter than my self, the examining whether the Soul exists before or after the Organization of our Bodies. But I confess that 'tis my Lot to be animated with one of those heavy Souls which do not think always; and I am even so unhappy as not to conceive, that 'tis more necessary the Soul should think perpetually, than that Bodies shou'd be for ever in Motion.

With regard to my self, I shall boast that I have the Honour to be as stupid in this Particular as Mr. *Locke*. No one shall ever make me believe, that I think always; and I am as little inclin'd as he cou'd be, to fancy that some Weeks after I was conceiv'd, I was a very learned Soul; knowing at that Time a thousand Things which I forgot at my Birth; and possessing when in the Womb, (tho' to no Manner of Purpose,) Knowledge which I lost the Instant I had occasion for it; and which I have never since been able to recover perfectly.

Mr. *Locke* after having destroy'd innate Ideas; after having fully renounc'd the Vanity of believing that we think always; after having laid down, from the most solid Principles, that Ideas enter the Mind through the Senses; having examin'd our simple and complex Ideas; having trac'd the human Mind through its several Operations; having shew'd that all the Languages in the World are imperfect, and the great Abuse that is made of Words every Moment; he at last comes to consider the Extent or rather the narrow Limits of human Knowledge. 'Twas in this Chapter he presum'd to advance, but very modestly, the following Words, 'We shall, perhaps, never be capable of knowing, whether a Being, purely material, thinks or not.'* This sage Assertion was, by more Divines than one, look'd upon as a scandalous Declaration that the Soul is material and mortal. Some *Englishmen*, devout after their Way, sounded an Alarm. The Superstitious are the same in Society as Cowards in an Army; they themselves are seiz'd with a panic Fear, and communicate it to others. 'Twas loudly exclaim'd, that Mr. *Locke* intended to destroy Religion; nevertheless, Religion had nothing to do in the Affair, it being a Question purely Philosophical, altogether independent on Faith and Revelation.* Mr. *Locke*'s Opponents needed but to examine, calmly and impartially, whether the declaring that Matter can think, implies a Contradiction; and whether God is able to communicate Thought to Matter. But Divines are too apt to begin their Declarations with saying, that God is offended when People differ from them in Opinion; in which they too much resemble the bad Poets, who us'd to declare publickly that *Boileau* spake irreverently of *Lewis* the Fourteenth, because he ridicul'd their stupid Productions. Bishop *Stillingfleet* got the Reputation of a calm and unprejudic'd Divine, because he did not expressly make use of injurious Terms in his Dispute with Mr. *Locke*.* That Divine entred the Lists against him, but was defeated; for he argued as a Schoolman, and *Locke* as a Philosopher, who was perfectly acquainted with the strong as well as the weak Side of the human Mind, and who fought with Weapons whose Temper he knew. If I might presume to give my Opinion on so delicate a Subject after Mr. *Locke*, I would say, that Men have long disputed on the Nature and the Immortality of the Soul. With regard to its Immortality, 'tis impossible to give a Demonstration of it, since its Nature is still the Subject of Controversy; which however must be thoroughly understood, before a Person can be able to determine whether it be immortal or not. Human Reason is so little able, merely by its own Strength, to demonstrate the Immortality of the Soul, that 'twas absolutely necessary Religion should reveal it to us. 'Tis of Advantage to Society in general, that Mankind should believe the Soul to be immortal; Faith commands us to do this; nothing more is requir'd, and the Matter is clear'd up at once. But 'tis otherwise with respect to its Nature; 'tis of little Importance to Religion, which only requires the Soul to be virtuous, what Substance it may be made of. 'Tis a Clock which is given us to regulate, but the Artist has not told us of what Materials the Spring of this Clock is compos'd.

I am a Body and, I think, that's all I know of the Matter. Shall I ascribe to an unknown Cause, what I can so easily impute to the only second Cause I am acquainted with? Here all the School Philosophers interrupt me with their Arguments, and declare that there is only Extension and Solidity in Bodies, and that there they can have nothing but Motion and Figure. Now Motion, Figure, Extension and Solidity cannot form a Thought, and consequently the Soul cannot be Matter. All this, so often repeated, mighty Series of Reasoning, amounts to no more than this; I am absolutely ignorant what Matter is; I guess, but imperfectly, some Properties of it; now, I absolutely cannot tell whether these Properties may be joyn'd to Thought. As I therefore know nothing, I maintain positively that Matter cannot think. In this Manner do the Schools reason.

Mr. *Locke* address'd these Gentlemen in the candid, sincere Manner following. At least confess your selves to be as ignorant as I. Neither your Imaginations nor mine are able to comprehend in what manner a Body is susceptible of Ideas; and do you conceive better in what manner a Substance, of what kind soever, is susceptible of them? As you cannot comprehend either Matter or Spirit, why will you presume to assert any thing?

The superstitious Man comes afterwards, and declares, that all those must be burnt for the Good of their Souls, who so much as suspect that 'tis possible for the Body to think without any foreign Assistance. But what would these People say should they themselves be prov'd irreligious?

And indeed, what Man can presume to assert, without being guilty at the same time of the greatest Impiety, that 'tis impossible for the Creator to form Matter with Thought and Sensation? Consider only, I beg you, what a Dilemma you bring yourselves into; you who confine in this Manner the Power of the Creator. Beasts have the same Organs, the same Sensations, the same Perceptions as we; they have Memory, and combine certain Ideas. In case it was not in the Power of God to animate Matter, and inform it with Sensation, the Consequence would be, either that Beasts are mere Machines, or that they have a spiritual Soul.

Methinks 'tis clearly evident that Beasts cannot be mere Machines, which I prove thus. God has given them the very same Organs of Sensation as to us: If therefore they have no Sensation, God has created a useless Thing; now according to your own Confession God does nothing in vain; he therefore did not create so many Organs of Sensation, merely for them to be uninform'd with this Faculty; consequently Beasts are not mere Machines. Beasts, according to your Assertion, cannot be animated with a spiritual Soul; you will therefore, in spight of your self, be reduc'd to this only Assertion, *viz.* that God has endued the Organs of Beasts, who are mere Matter, with the Faculties of Sensation and Perception, which you call Instinct in them. But why may not God if he pleases, communicate to our more delicate Organs, that Faculty of feeling, perceiving, and thinking, which we call human Reason? To whatever Side you turn, you are forc'd to acknowledge your own Ignorance, and the boundless Power of the Creator. Exclaim therefore no more against the sage, the modest Philosophy of Mr. *Locke*, which so far from interfering with Religion, would be of use to demonstrate the Truth of it, in case Religion wanted any such Support. For what Philosophy can be of a more religious Nature than that, which affirming nothing but what it conceives clearly; and conscious of its own Weakness, declares that we must always have recourse to God in our examining of the first Principles.

Besides, we must not be apprehensive, that any philosophical Opinion will ever prejudice the Religion of a

Country. Tho' our Demonstrations clash directly with our Mysteries, that's nothing to the Purpose, for the latter are not less rever'd upon that Account by our Christian Philosophers, who know very well that the Objects of Reason and those of Faith are of a very different Nature. Philosophers will never form a religious Sect, the Reason of which is, their Writings are not calculated for the Vulgar, and they themselves are free from Enthusiasm. If we divide Mankind into twenty Parts, 'twill be found that nineteen of these consist of Persons employ'd in manual Labour, who will never know that such a Man as Mr. *Locke* existed. In the remaining twentieth Part how few are Readers? And among such as are so, twenty amuse themselves with Romances to one who studies Philosophy. The thinking Part of Mankind are confin'd to a very small Number, and these will never disturb the Peace and Tranquillity of the World.

Neither *Montagne*, *Locke*, *Bayle*, *Spinoza*, *Hobbes*, the Lord *Shaftsbury*, *Collins* nor *Toland* lighted up the Firebrand of Discord in their Countries;* this has generally been the Work of Divines, who being at first puff'd up with the Ambition of becoming Chiefs of a Sect, soon grew very desirous of being at the Head of a Party. But what do I say? All the Works of the modern Philosophers put together will never make so much Noise as even the Dispute which arose among the *Franciscans*, merely about the Fashion of their Sleeves and of their Cowls.

LETTER XIV.

On Des Cartes and Sir Isaac Newton.

A FRENCHMAN who arrives in *London*, will find Philosophy, like every Thing else, very much chang'd there. He had left the World a *plenum*, and he now finds it a *vacuum*. At *Paris* the Universe is seen, compos'd of Vortices of subtile Matter; but nothing like it is seen in *London*. In *France*, 'tis the Pressure of the Moon that causes the Tides; but in *England* 'tis the Sea that gravitates towards the Moon; so that when you think that the Moon should make it Flood with us, those Gentlemen fancy it should be Ebb, which, very unluckily, cannot be prov'd. For to be able to do this, 'tis necessary the Moon and the Tides should have been enquir'd into, at the very instant of the Creation.

You'll observe farther, that the Sun, which in *France* is said to have nothing to do in the Affair, comes in here for very near a quarter of its Assistance. According to your *Cartesians*, every Thing is perform'd by an Impulsion, of which we have very little Notion; and according to Sir *Isaac Newton*, 'tis by an Attraction, the Cause of which is as much unknown to us. At *Paris* you imagine that the Earth is shap'd like a Melon, or of an oblique Figure; at *London* it has an oblate one. A *Cartesian* declares that Light exists in the Air; but a *Newtonian* asserts that it comes from the Sun in six Minutes and a half. The several Operations of your Chymistry are perform'd by Acids, Alkalies and subtile Matter; but Attraction prevails even in Chymistry among the *English*.

The very Essence of Things is totally chang'd. You neither are agreed upon the Definition of the Soul, nor on that of Matter. *Descartes*, as I observ'd in my last, maintains that the Soul is the same Thing with Thought, and Mr. *Locke* has given a pretty good Proof of the contrary.

Descartes asserts farther, that Extension alone constitutes Matter, but Sir *Isaac* adds Solidity to it.

How furiously contradictory are these Opinions!

Non nostrum inter vos tantas componere lites.

VIRGIL, Eclog. III.

'Tis not for us to end such great Disputes.

This famous *Newton*, this Destroyer of the *Cartesian* System, died in *March Anno* 1727. His Countrymen honour'd him in his Life-Time, and interr'd him as tho' he had been a King who had made his People happy.

The *English* read with the highest Satisfaction, and translated into their Tongue, the Elogium of Sir *Isaac Newton*, which Mr. *de Fontenelle*, spoke in the Academy of Sciences. Mr. *de Fontenelle* presides as Judge over Philosophers; and the *English* expected his Decision, as a solemn Declaration of the Superiority of the *English* Philosophy over that of the *French*. But when 'twas found that this Gentleman had compar'd *Des Cartes* to Sir *Isaac*, the whole Royal Society in *London* rose up in Arms. So far from acquiescing with Mr. *Fontenelle*'s Judgment, they criticis'd his Discourse. And even several (who however were not the ablest Philosophers in that Body) were offended at the Comparison; and for no other Reason but because *Des Cartes* was a *Frenchman*.

It must be confess'd that these two great Men differ'd very much in Conduct, in Fortune, and in Philosophy.

Nature had indulg'd *Des Cartes* a shining and strong Imagination, whence he became a very singular Person both in private Life, and in his Manner of Reasoning. This Imagination could not conceal it self even in his philosophical Works, which are every where adorn'd with very shining, ingenious Metaphors and Figures. Nature had almost made him a Poet; and indeed he wrote a Piece of Poetry for the Entertainment of *Christina* Queen of *Sweden*, which however was suppress'd in Honour to his Memory.

He embrac'd a Military Life for some Time, and afterwards becoming a complete Philosopher, he did not think the Passion of Love derogatory to his Character. He had by his Mistress a Daughter call'd *Froncine*, who died young, and was very much regretted by him. Thus he experienc'd every Passion incident to Mankind.

He was a long Time of Opinion, that it would be necessary for him to fly from the Society of his Fellow Creatures, and especially from his native Country, in order to enjoy the Happiness of cultivating his philosophical Studies in full Liberty.

Des Cartes was very right, for his Cotemporaries were not knowing enough to improve and enlighten his Understanding, and were capable of little else than of giving him Uneasiness.

He left *France* purely to go in search of Truth, which was then persecuted by the wretched Philosophy of the Schools. However, he found that Reason was as much disguis'd and deprav'd in the Universities of *Holland*, into which he withdrew, as in his own Country. For at the Time that the *French* condemn'd the only Propositions of his Philosophy which were true, he was persecuted by the pretended Philosophers of *Holland*, who understood him no better; and who, having a nearer View of his Glory, hated his Person the more, so that he was oblig'd to leave *Utrecht*. *Des Cartes* was injuriously accus'd of being an Atheist, the last Refuge of religious Scandal: And he who had employ'd all the Sagacity and Penetration of his Genius, in searching for new Proofs of the Existence of a God, was suspected to believe there was no such Being.

Such a Persecution from all Sides, must necessarily suppose a most exalted Merit as well as a very distinguish'd Reputation, and indeed he possess'd both. Reason at that Time darted a Ray upon the World thro' the Gloom of the Schools, and the Prejudices of popular Superstition. At last his Name spread so universally, that the *French* were desirous of bringing him back into his native Country by Rewards, and accordingly offer'd him an annual Pension of a thousand Crowns. Upon these Hopes *Des Cartes* return'd to *France*; paid the Fees of his Patent, which was sold at that Time, but no Pension was settled upon him. Thus disappointed, he return'd to his Solitude in *North-Holland*, where he again pursued the Study of Philosophy, whilst the great *Galileo*, at fourscore Years of Age, was groaning in the Prisons of the Inquisition, only for having demonstrated the Earth's Motion.

At last *Des Cartes* was snatch'd from the World in the Flower of his Age at *Stockholm*. His Death was owing to a bad Regimen, and he expir'd in the Midst of some *Literati* who were his Enemies, and under the Hands of a Physician to whom he was odious.

The Progress of Sir *Isaac Newton*'s Life was quite different. He liv'd happy, and very much honour'd in his native Country, to the Age of fourscore and five Years.

'Twas his peculiar Felicity, not only to be born in a Country of Liberty, but in an Age when all scholastic Impertinencies were banish'd from the World. Reason alone was cultivated, and Mankind cou'd only be his Pupil, not his Enemy.

One very singular Difference in the Lives of these two great Men is, that Sir *Isaac*, during the long Course of Years he enjoy'd was never sensible to any Passion, was not subject to the common Frailties of Mankind, nor ever had any Commerce with Women; a Circumstance which was assur'd me by the Physician and Surgeon who attended him in his last Moments.

We may admire Sir *Isaac Newton* on this Occasion, but then we must not censure *Des Cartes*.

The Opinion that generally prevails in *England* with regard to these two Philosophers is, that the latter was a Dreamer, and the former a Sage.

Very few People in *England* read *Descartes*, whose Works indeed are now useless. On the other Side, but a small Number peruse those of Sir *Isaac*, because to do this the Student must be deeply skill'd in the Mathematicks, otherwise those Works will be unintelligible to him. But notwithstanding this, these great Men are the Subject of every One's Discourse. Sir *Isaac Newton* is allow'd every Advantage, whilst *Des Cartes* is not indulg'd a single one. According to some, 'tis to the former that we owe the Discovery of a *Vacuum*, that the Air is a heavy Body, and the Invention of Telescopes. In a Word, Sir *Isaac Newton* is here as the *Hercules* of fabulous Story, to whom the Ignorant ascrib'd all the Feats of ancient Heroes.

In a Critique that was made in *London* on Mr. *de*

Fontenelle's Discourse, the Writer presum'd to assert that *Des Cartes* was not a great Geometrician. Those who make such a Declaration may justly be reproach'd with flying in their Master's Face. *Des Cartes* extended the Limits of Geometry as far beyond the Place where he found them, as Sir *Isaac* did after him. The former first taught the Method of expressing Curves by Equations. This Geometry which, Thanks to him for it, is now grown common, was so abstruse in his Time, that not so much as one Professor would undertake to explain it; and *Schotten* in *Holland*, and *Format** in *France*, were the only Men who understood it.

He applied this geometrical and inventive Genius to Dioptricks, which, when treated of by him, became a new Art. And if he was mistaken in some Things, the Reason of that is, a Man who discovers a new Tract of Land cannot at once know all the Properties of the Soil. Those who come after him, and make these Lands fruitful, are at least oblig'd to him for the Discovery. I will not deny but that there are innumerable Errors in the rest of *Des Cartes*'s Works.

Geometry was a Guide he himself had in some Measure fashion'd, which would have conducted him safely thro' the several Paths of natural Philosophy. Nevertheless he at last abandon'd this Guide, and gave entirely into the Humour of forming Hypotheses; and then Philosophy was no more than an ingenious Romance, fit only to amuse the Ignorant. He was mistaken in the Nature of the Soul, in the Proofs of the Existence of a God, in Matter, in the Laws of Motion, and in the Nature of Light. He admitted innate Ideas, he invented new Elements, he created a World; he made Man according to his own Fancy; and 'tis justly said, that the Man of *Des Cartes* is in Fact that of *Des Cartes* only, very different from the real one.

He push'd his metaphysical Errors so far, as to declare that two and two make four, for no other Reason but because God would have it so. However, 'twill not be making him too great a Compliment if we affirm that he was valuable even in his Mistakes. He deceiv'd himself, but then it was at least in a methodical Way. He destroy'd all the absurd Chimæra's with which Youth had been infatuated for two thousand Years. He taught his Cotemporaries how to reason, and enabled them to employ his own Weapons against himself. If *Des Cartes* did not pay in good Money, he however did great Service in crying down that of a base Alloy.

I indeed believe, that very few will presume to compare his Philosophy in any respect with that of Sir *Isaac Newton*. The former is an Essay, the latter a Master-Piece: But then the Man who first brought us to the Path of Truth, was perhaps as great a Genius as he who afterwards conducted us through it.

Des Cartes gave Sight to the Blind. These saw the Errors of Antiquity and of the Sciences. The Path he struck out is since become boundless. *Rohault*'s little Work* was during some Years a complete System of Physicks; but now all the Transactions of the several Academies in *Europe* put together do not form so much as the Beginning of a System. In fathoming this Abyss no Bottom has been found. We are now to examine what Discoveries Sir *Isaac Newton* has made in it.

LETTER XV.

On Attraction.

THE Discoveries which gain'd Sir *Isaac Newton* so universal a Reputation, relate to the System of the World, to Light, to Geometrical Infinites; and lastly to Chronology, with which he us'd to amuse himself after the Fatigue of his severer Studies.

I will now acquaint you (without Prolixity if possible) with the few Things I have been able to comprehend of all these sublime Ideas. With Regard to the System of our World, Disputes were a long Time maintain'd, on the Cause that turns the Planets, and keeps them in their Orbits; and on those Causes which make all Bodies here below descend towards the Surface of the Earth.

The System of *Des Cartes* explain'd and improv'd since his Time seem'd to give a plausible Reason for all those Phænomena; and this Reason seem'd more just, as 'tis simple, and intelligible to all Capacities. But in Philosophy, a Student ought to doubt of the Things he fancies he understands too easily, as much as of those he does not understand.

Gravity, the falling of accelerated Bodies on the Earth, the Revolution of the Planets in their Orbits, their Rotations round their Axis, all this is mere Motion. Now Motion can't perhaps be conceiv'd any otherwise than by Impulsion; therefore all those Bodies must be impelled. But by what are they impelled? All Space is full, it therefore is fill'd with a very subtile Matter, since this is imperceptible to us; this Matter goes from West to East, since all the Planets are carried from West to East. Thus from Hypothesis to Hypothesis, from one Appearance to another, Philosophers have imagin'd a vast Whirlpool of subtile Matter, in which the Planets are carried round the Sun: They also have created another particular Vortex which floats in the great one, and which turns daily round the Planets. When all this is done, 'tis pretended that Gravity depends on this diurnal Motion; for, say these, the Velocity of the subtile Matter that turns round our little Vortex, must be seventeen Times more rapid than that of the Earth; or, in case its Velocity is seventeen Times greater than that of the Earth, its centrifugal Force must be vastly greater, and consequently impell all Bodies towards the Earth. This is the Cause of Gravity, according to the *Cartesian* System. But the Theorist, before he calculated the centrifugal Force and Velocity of the subtile Matter, should first have been certain that it existed.

Sir *Isaac Newton* seems to have destroy'd all these great and little Vortices, both that which carries the Planets round the Sun, as well as the other which supposes every Planet to turn on its own Axis.

First, with regard to the pretended little Vortex of the Earth, 'tis demonstrated that it must lose its Motion by insensible Degrees; 'tis demonstrated, that if the Earth swims in a Fluid, its Density must be equal to that of the Earth; and in case its Density be the same, all the Bodies we endeavour to move must meet with an insuperable Resistance.

With regard to the great Vortices, they are still more chimerical, and 'tis impossible to make them agree with *Kepler*'s Law, the Truth of which has been demonstrated. Sir *Isaac* shows, that the Revolution of the Fluid in which *Jupiter* is suppos'd to be carried, is not the same with regard to the Revolution of the Fluid of the Earth, as the Revolution of *Jupiter* with respect to that of the Earth. He proves, that as the Planets make their Revolutions in Elipsis's, and consequently being at a much greater Distance one from the other in their *Aphelia*, and a little nearer in their *Perihelia*; the Earth's Velocity, for Instance, ought to be greater, when 'tis nearer *Venus* and *Mars*, because the Fluid that carries it along, being then more press'd, ought to have a greater Motion; and yet 'tis even then that the Earth's Motion is slower.

He proves that there is no such Thing as a celestial Matter which goes from West to East, since the Comets traverse those Spaces, sometimes from East to West, and at other Times from North to South.

In fine, the better to resolve, if possible, every Difficulty, he proves, and even by Experiments, that 'tis impossible there should be a *Plenum*; and brings back the *Vacuum*, which *Aristotle* and *Des Cartes* had banish'd from the World.

Having by these and several other Arguments destroy'd the *Cartesian* Vortices, he despair'd of ever being able to discover, whether there is a secret Principle in Nature which, at the same Time, is the Cause of the Motion of all celestial Bodies, and that of Gravity on the Earth. But being retir'd in 1666, upon Account of the Plague, to a Solitude near *Cambridge*; as he was walking one Day in his Garden, and saw some Fruits fall from a Tree,* he fell into a profound Meditation on that Gravity, the Cause of which had so long been sought, but in vain, by all the Philosophers, whilst the Vulgar think there is nothing mysterious in it. He said to himself, that from what height soever, in our Hemisphere, those Bodies might descend, their Fall wou'd certainly be in the Progression discover'd by *Galileo*; and the Spaces they run thro' would be as the Square of the Times. Why may not this Power which causes heavy Bodies to descend, and is the same without any sensible Diminution at the remotest Distance from the Center of the Earth, or on the Summits of the highest Mountains; Why, said Sir *Isaac*, may not this Power extend as high as the Moon? And in Case its Influence reaches so far, is it not very probable that this Power retains it in its Orbit, and determines its Motion? But in case the Moon obeys this Principle (whatever it be) may we not conclude very naturally, that the rest of the Planets are equally subject to it? In case this Power exists (which besides is prov'd) it must increase in an inverse *Ratio* of the Squares of the Distances. All therefore that remains is, to examine how far a heavy Body, which should fall upon the Earth from a moderate height, would go; and how far in the same Time, a Body which should fall from the Orbit of the Moon, would descend. To find this, nothing is wanted but the Measure of the Earth, and the Distance of the Moon from it.

Thus Sir *Isaac Newton* reason'd. But at that Time the *English* had but a very imperfect Measure of our Globe, and depended on the uncertain Supposition of Mariners, who computed a Degree to contain but sixty *English* Miles, whereas it consists in reality of near seventy. As this false Computation did not agree with the Conclusions which Sir *Isaac* intended to draw from them, he laid aside this Pursuit. A half-learn'd Philosopher, remarkable only for his Vanity, would have made the Measure of the Earth agree, any how, with his System: Sir *Isaac*, however, chose rather to quit the Researches he was then engag'd in. But after Mr. *Picart** had measur'd the Earth exactly, by tracing that Meridian, which redounds so much to the Honour of the *French*, Sir *Isaac Newton* resum'd his former Reflexions, and found his Account in Mr. *Picart*'s Calculation.

A Circumstance which has always appear'd wonderful to me, is, that such sublime Discoveries should have been made by the sole Assistance of a Quadrant and a little Arithmetic.

The Circumference of the Earth is one hundred twenty three Millions, two hundred forty nine thousand six hundred Feet. This, among other Things, is necessary to prove the System of Attraction.

The instant we know the Earth's Circumference, and the Distance of the Moon, we know that of the Moon's Orbit, and the Diameter of this Orbit. The Moon performs its Revolution in that Orbit in twenty seven Days, seven Hours, forty three Minutes. 'Tis demonstrated, that the Moon in its mean Motion makes an hundred and fourscore and seven thousand, nine hundred and sixty Feet (of *Paris*)* in a Minute. 'Tis likewise demonstrated, by a known Theorem, that the central Force which should make a Body fall from the height of the Moon, would make its Velocity no more than fifteen *Paris* Feet in a Minute of Time. Now, if the Law by which Bodies gravitate, and attract one another in an inverse Ratio of the Squares of the Distances be true; if the same Power acts, according to that Law, throughout all Nature; 'tis evident that as the Earth is sixty Semi-diameters distant from the Moon, a heavy Body must necessarily fall (on the Earth) fifteen Feet in the first Second, and fifty four thousand Feet in the first Minute.

Now a heavy Body falls, in reality, fifteen Feet in the first Second, and goes in the first Minute fifty four thousand Foot, which Number is the Square of sixty multiplied by fifteen. Bodies therefore gravitate in an inverse Ratio of the Squares of the Distances; consequently, what causes Gravity on Earth, and keeps the Moon in its Orbit, is one and the same Power; it being demonstrated that the Moon gravitates on the Earth, which is the Center of its particular Motion, 'tis demonstrated that the Earth and the Moon gravitate on the Sun which is the Center of their annual Motion.

The rest of the Planets must be subject to this general Law; and if this Law exists, these Planets must follow the Laws which *Kepler* discover'd. All these Laws, all these Relations are indeed observ'd by the Planets with the utmost Exactness; therefore the Power of Attraction causes all the Planets to gravitate towards the Sun, in like Manner as the Moon gravitates towards our Globe.

Finally, as in all Bodies, Re-action is equal to Action, 'tis certain that the Earth gravitates also towards the Moon; and that the Sun gravitates towards both: That every one of the Satellites of *Saturn* gravitates towards the other four, and the other four towards it: All five towards S*aturn*, and *Saturn* towards all. That 'tis the same with regard to *Jupiter*; and that all these Globes are attracted by the Sun, which is reciprocally attracted by them.

This Power of Gravitation acts proportionably to the Quantity of Matter in Bodies, a Truth which Sir *Isaac* has demonstrated by Experiments. This new Discovery has been of use to show, that the Sun (the Center of the planetary System) attracts them all in a direct Ratio of their Quantity of Matter combin'd with their Nearness. From hence Sir *Isaac*, rising by Degrees to Discoveries which seem'd not to be form'd for the human Mind, is bold enough to compute the Quantity of Matter contain'd in the Sun and in every Planet; and in this Manner shows, from the simple Laws of Mechanicks, that every celestial Globe ought necessarily to be where it is plac'd.

His bare Principle of the Laws of Gravitation, accounts for all the apparent Inequalities in the Coarse of the celestial

Globes. The Variations of the Moon are a necessary Consequence of those Laws. Moreover, the Reason is evidently seen why the Nodes of the Moon perform their Revolutions in nineteen Years, and those of the Earth in about twenty six Thousand. The several Appearances observ'd in the Tides, are also a very simple Effect of this Attraction. The Proximity of the Moon when at the full, and when it is new, and its Distance in the Quadratures or Quarters combin'd with the Action of the Sun, exhibit a sensible Reason why the Ocean swells and sinks.

After having shown, by his sublime Theory, the Course and Inequalities of the Planets, he subjects Comets to the same Law. The Orbit of these Fires (unknown for so great a Series of Years,) which was the Terror of Mankind, and the Rock against which Philosophy split; plac'd by *Aristotle* below the Moon, and sent back by *Des Cartes* above the Sphere of *Saturn*, is at last plac'd in its proper Seat by Sir *Isaac Newton*.

He proves that Comets are solid Bodies which move in the Sphere of the Sun's Activity; and that they describe an Ellipsis so very eccentric, and so near to Parabola's, that certain Comets must take up above five hundred Years in their Revolution.

The learned Dr. *Halley* is of opinion, that the Comet seen in 1680, is the same which appear'd in *Julius Cæsar*'s Time. This shows more than any other, that Comets are hard, opake Bodies; for it descended so near to the Sun, as to come within a sixth Part of the Diameter of this Planet from it; and consequently might have contracted a Degree of Heat two thousand Times stronger than that of red hot Iron; and would have been soon dispers'd in Vapour, had it not been a firm, dense Body. The guessing the Course of Comets began then to be very much in vogue: The celebrated *Bernoulli* concluded by his System, that the famous Comet of 1680, would appear again the 17th of *May* 1719. Not a single Astronomer in *Europe* went to Bed that Night; however they needed not to have broke their Rest, for the famous Comet never appear'd. There is at least more Cunning, if not more Certainty, in fixing its Return to so remote a Distance as five hundred and seventy five Years. As to Mr. *Whiston*,* he affirm'd very seriously, that in the Time of the Deluge a Comet overflow'd the terrestrial Globe; and he was so unreasonable as to wonder that People laugh'd at him for making such an Assertion. The Ancients were almost in the same way of Thinking with Mr. *Whiston*, and fancied that Comets were always the Fore-runners of some great Calamity which was to befall Mankind. Sir *Isaac Newton*, on the contrary, suspected that they are very beneficent; and that Vapours exhale from them merely to nourish and vivify the Planets, which imbibe in their Course the several Particles the Sun has detach'd from the Comets; an Opinion which at least is more probable than the former. But this is not all. If this Power of Gravitation or Attraction acts on all the celestial Globes, it acts undoubtedly on the several Parts of these Globes. For in case Bodies attract one another in Proportion to the Quantity of Matter contain'd in them, it can only be in Proportion to the Quantity of their Parts; and if this Power is found in the whole, 'tis undoubtedly in the half, in the quarter, in the eighth Part, and so on in *infinitum*.

This is Attraction, the great Spring by which all Nature is mov'd. Sir *Isaac Newton* after having demonstrated the Existence of this Principle, plainly foresaw that its very Name wou'd offend; and therefore this Philosopher in more Places than one of his Books, gives the Reader some Caution about it. He bids him beware of confounding this Name with what the Ancients call'd occult Qualities; but to be satisfied with knowing that there is in all Bodies a central Force which acts to the utmost Limits of the Universe, according to the invariable Laws of Mechanicks.

'Tis surprising, after the solemn Protestations Sir *Isaac* made, that such eminent Men as Mr. *Sorin* and Mr. *de Fontenelle*, should have imputed to this great Philosopher the verbal and chimerical Way of Reasoning of the *Aristoteleans*; Mr. *Sorin* in the Memoirs of the Academy of 1709, and Mr. *de Fontenelle* in the very Elogium of Sir *Isaac Newton*.*

Most of the *French*, the Learned and others, have repeated this Reproach. These are for ever crying out, why did he not imploy the Word *Impulsion*, which is so well understood, rather than that of *Attraction*, which is unintelligible.

Sir *Isaac* might have answer'd these Criticks thus: First, you have as imperfect an Idea of the Word Impulsion, as of that of Attraction; and in case you cannot conceive how one Body tends towards the Center of another Body, neither can you conceive by what Power one Body can impell another.

Secondly, I cou'd not admit of Impulsion, for to do this, I must have known that a celestial Matter was the Agent; but so far from knowing that there is any such Matter, I have prov'd it to be merely imaginary.

Thirdly, I use the Word Attraction for no other Reason, but to express an Effect which I discover'd in Nature; a certain and indisputable Effect of an unknown Principle; a Quality inherent in Matter, the Cause of which Persons of greater Abilities than I can pretend to, may, if they can, find out.

What have you then taught us? Will these People say further: And to what Purpose are so many Calculations to tell us what you yourself don't comprehend?

I have taught you, may Sir *Isaac* rejoin, that all Bodies gravitate towards one another in proportion to their Quantity of Matter; that these central Forces alone, keep the Planets and Comets in their Orbits, and cause them to move in the Proportion before set down. I demonstrate to you, that 'tis impossible there should be any other Cause which keeps the Planets in their Orbits, than that general Phenomenon of Gravity. For heavy Bodies fall on the Earth according to the Proportion demonstrated of central Forces; and the Planets finishing their Course according to these same Proportions, in case there were another Power that acted upon all those Bodies, it would either increase their Velocity, or change their Direction. Now not one of those Bodies ever has a single Degree of Motion or Velocity, or has any Direction but what is demonstrated to be the Effect of the central Forces; consequently 'tis impossible there should be any other Principle.

Give me Leave once more to introduce Sir *Isaac* speaking: Shall he not be allow'd to say, My Case and that of the Ancients is very different. These saw, for Instance, Water ascend in Pumps, and said, the Water rises because it abhors a *Vacuum*. But with regard to my self, I am in the Case of a Man who should have first observ'd that Water ascends in Pumps, but should leave others to explain the Cause of this Effect. The Anatomist who first declar'd, that the Motion of the Arm is owing to the Contraction of the Muscles, taught Mankind an indisputable Truth; but are they less oblig'd to him because he did not know the Reason why the Muscles contract? The Cause of the Elasticity of the Air is unknown, but he who first discover'd this Spring perform'd a very signal Service to natural Philosophy. The Spring that I discover'd was more hidden and more universal, and for that very Reason Mankind ought to thank me the more. I have discover'd a new Property of Matter, one of the Secrets of the Creator; and have calculated and discover'd the Effects of it. After this shall People quarrel with me about the Name I give it.

Vortices may be call'd an occult Quality because their Existence was never prov'd: Attraction on the contrary is a real Thing, because its Effects are demonstrated, and the Proportions of it are calculated. The Cause of this Cause is among the *Arcana* of the Almighty.

*Procedes huc, & non amplius.**

Hither thou shalt go, and no farther.

LETTER XVI.

On *Sir* Isaac Newton's *Opticks.*

THE Philosophers of the last Age found out a new Universe; and a Circumstance which made its Discovery more difficult, was, that no one had so much as suspected its Existence. The most Sage and Judicious were of Opinion, that 'twas a frantic Rashness to dare so much as to imagine that it was possible to guess the Laws by which the celestial Bodies move, and the manner how Light acts. *Galileo* by his astronomical Discoveries, *Kepler* by his Calculation, *Des Cartes* (at least in his Dioptricks) and Sir *Isaac Newton* in all his Works, severally saw the Mechanism of the Springs of the World. The Geometricians have subjected Infinity to the Laws of Calculation. The Circulation of the Blood in Animals, and of the Sap in Vegetables, have chang'd the Face of Nature with regard to us. A new kind of Existence has been given to Bodies in the Air-Pump. By the Assistance of Telescopes Bodies have been brought nearer to one another. Finally, the several Discoveries which Sir *Isaac Newton* has made on Light, are equal to the boldest Things which the Curiosity of Man could expect, after so many philosophical Novelties.

Till *Antonio de Dominis*,* the Rainbow was consider'd as an inexplicable Miracle. This Philosopher guess'd that it was a necessary Effect of the Sun and Rain. *Des Cartes* gain'd immortal Fame, by his mathematical Explication of this so natural a Phænomenon. He calculated the Reflexions and Refractions of Light in Drops of Rain; and his Sagacity on this Occasion was at that Time look'd upon as next to divine.

But what would he have said had it been prov'd to him that he was mistaken in the Nature of Light; that he had not the least Reason to maintain that 'tis a globular Body: That 'tis false to assert, that this Matter spreading it self through the whole, waits only to be projected forward by the Sun, in order to be put in Action, in like Manner as a long Staff acts at one end when push'd forward by the other. That Light is certainly darted by the Sun; in fine, that Light is transmitted from the Sun to the Earth in about seven Minutes, tho' a Cannon Ball, which were not to lose any of its Velocity, cou'd not go that Distance in less than twenty five Years. How great wou'd have been his Astonishment, had he been told, that Light does not reflect directly by impinging against the solid Parts of Bodies; that Bodies are not transparent when they have large Pores; and that a Man should arise, who would demonstrate all these Paradoxes, and anatomize a single Ray of Light with more Dexterity than the ablest Artist dissects a human Body. This Man is come. Sir *Isaac Newton* has demonstrated to the Eye, by the bare Assistance of the Prism, that Light is a Composition of colour'd Rays, which, being united, form the white Colour. A single Ray is by him divided into seven, which all fall upon a Piece of Linen, or a Sheet of white Paper, in their Order one above the other, and at unequal Distances. The first is Red, the second Orange, the third Yellow, the fourth Green, the fifth Blue, the sixth Indigo, the seventh a Violet Purple. Each of these Rays transmitted afterwards by an hundred other Prisms, will never change the Colour it bears; in like Manner as Gold, when completely purg'd from its Dross, will never change afterwards in the Crucible. As a superabundant Proof that each of these elementary Rays has inherently in it self that which forms its Colour to the Eye, take a small Piece of yellow Wood for Instance, and set it in the Ray of a red Colour, this Wood will instantly be ting'd red; but set it in the Ray of a green Colour, it assumes a green Colour, and so of all the rest.

From what Cause therefore do Colours arise in Nature? 'Tis nothing but the Disposition of Bodies to reflect the Rays of a certain Order, and to absorb all the rest.

What then is this secret Disposition? Sir *Isaac Newton* demonstrates, that 'tis nothing more than the Density of the small constituent Particles of which a Body is compos'd. And how is this Reflexion perform'd? 'Twas suppos'd to arise from the Rebounding of the Rays, in the same Manner as a Ball on the Surface of a solid Body; but this is a Mistake, for Sir *Isaac* taught the astonish'd Philosophers, that Bodies are opake for no other Reason, but because their Pores are large; that Light reflects on our Eyes from the very Bosom of those Pores; that the smaller the Pores of a Body are, the more such a Body is transparent. Thus Paper which reflects the Light when dry, transmits it when oil'd, because the Oil, by filling its Pores, makes them much smaller.

'Tis there that examining the vast Porosity of Bodies, every Particle having its Pores, and every Particle of those Particles having its own; he shows we are not certain that there is a cubic Inch of solid Matter in the Universe, so far are we from conceiving what Matter is. Having thus divided, as it were, Light into its Elements, and carried the Sagacity of his Discoveries so far, as to prove the Method of distinguishing compound Colours from such as are primitive; he shews, that these elementary Rays separated by the Prism, are rang'd in their Order for no other Reason but because they are refracted in that very Order; and 'tis this Property (unknown till he discover'd it) of breaking or splitting in this Proportion; 'tis this unequal Refraction of Rays, this Power of refracting the red less than the orange Colour, &c. which he calls the different Refrangibility. The most reflexible Rays are the most refrangible, and from hence he evinces that the same Power is the Cause both of the Reflection and Refraction of Light.

But all these Wonders are merely but the Opening of his Discoveries. He found out the Secret to see the Vibrations or Fits of Light, which come and go incessantly, and which either transmit Light or reflect it according to the Density of the Parts they meet with. He has presum'd to calculate the Density of the Particles of Air necessary between two Glasses, the one flat, the other convex on one side, set one upon the other; in order to operate such a Transmission or Reflexion, or to form such and such a Colour.

From all these Combinations he discovers the Proportion in which Light acts on Bodies, and Bodies act on Light.

He saw Light so perfectly, that he has determin'd to what

Degree of Perfection the Art of increasing it, and of assisting our Eyes by Telescopes can be carried.

Des Cartes, from a noble Confidence, that was very excusable considering how strongly he was fir'd at the first Discoveries he made in an Art which he almost first found out; *Des Cartes*, I say, hop'd to discover in the Stars, by the Assistance of Telescopes, Objects as small as those we discern upon the Earth.

But Sir *Isaac* has shown, that Dioptric Telescopes cannot be brought to a greater Perfection; because of that Refraction, and of that very Refrangibility, which at the same Time that they bring Objects nearer to us, scatter too much the elementary Rays; he has calculated in these Glasses the Proportion of the scattering of the red and of the blue Rays; and proceeding so far as to demonstrate Things which were not suppos'd even to exist, he examines the Inequalities which arise from the Shape or Figure of the Glass, and that which arises from the Refrangibility. He finds, that the object Glass of the Telescope being convex on one side and flat on the other, in case the flat Side be turn'd towards the Object, the Error which arises from the Construction and Position of the Glass, is above five thousand Times less than the Error which arises from the Refrangibility: And therefore, that the Shape or Figure of the Glasses is not the Cause why Telescopes cannot be carried to a greater Perfection, but arises wholly from the Nature of Light.

For this Reason he invented a Telescope, which discovers Objects by Reflection and not by Refraction. Telescopes of this new kind are very hard to make, and their Use is not easy. But according to the *English*, a reflective Telescope of but five Feet, has the same Effect as another of an hundred Feet in Length.

LETTER XVII.

On Infinites in Geometry, and Sir Isaac Newton's Chronology.

THE Labyrinth and Abyss of Infinity, is also a new Course Sir *Isaac Newton* has gone through, and we are oblig'd to him for the Clue by whose Assistance we are enabled to trace its various Windings.

Des Cartes got the Start of him also in this astonishing Invention. He advanc'd with mighty Steps in his Geometry, and was arriv'd at the very Borders of Infinity, but went no farther. Dr. *Wallis** about the Middle of the last Century, was the first who reduc'd a Fraction by a perpetual Division to an infinite Series.

The Lord *Brounker** employ'd this Series to square the Hyperbola.

Mercator publish'd a Demonstration of this Quadrature, much about which Time, Sir *Isaac Newton* being then twenty three Years of Age, had invented a general Method to perform, on all geometrical Curves, what had just before been try'd on the Hyperbola.

'Tis to this Method of subjecting every where Infinity to algebraical Calculations, that the Name is given of differential Calculations or of Fluxions, and integral Calculation. 'Tis the Art of numbring and measuring exactly a Thing whose Existence cannot be conceiv'd.

And, indeed, would you not imagine that a Man laugh'd at you, who should declare that there are Lines infinitely great which form an Angle infinitely little?

That a right Line, which is a right Line so long as it is finite, by changing infinitely little its Direction, becomes an infinite Curve; and that a Curve may become infinitely less than another Curve?

That there are infinite Squares, infinite Cubes; and Infinites of Infinites all greater than one another, and the last but one of which, is nothing in Comparison of the last?

All these Things which at first appear to be the utmost Excess of Frenzy, are in reality an Effort of the Subtilty and Extent of the human Mind, and the Art of finding Truths which till then had been unknown.

This so bold Edifice is even founded on simple Ideas. The Business is to measure the Diagonal of a Square, to give the Area of a Curve, to find the square Root of a Number, which has none in common Arithmetic. After all, the Imagination ought not to be startled any more at so many Orders of Infinites, than at the so well known Proposition, *viz.* that Curve Lines may always be made to pass between a Circle and a Tangent; or at that other, namely that Matter is divisible in *infinitum.* These two Truths have been demonstrated many Years, and are no less incomprehensible than the Things we have been speaking of.

For many Years the Invention of this famous Calculation was denied Sir *Isaac Newton.* In *Germany* Mr. *Leibnitz* was consider'd as the Inventor of the Differences or Moments, call'd[1] *Fluxions,* and Mr. *Bernouilli* claim'd the integral Calculation. However, Sir *Isaac* is now thought to have first made the Discovery, and the other two have the Glory of having once made the World doubt whether 'twas to be ascrib'd to him or them. Thus some contested with Dr. *Harvey* the Invention of the Circulation of the Blood, as others disputed with Mr. *Perrault** that of the Circulation of the Sap.

Hartsocher and *Lewenhoeck* disputed with each other the Honour of having first seen the *Vermiculi* of which Mankind are form'd. This *Hartsocher* also contested with *Huygens* the Invention of a new Method of calculating the Distance of a fix'd Star. 'Tis not yet known to what Philosopher we owe the Invention of the Cycloid.

Be this as it will, 'tis by the Help of this Geometry of Infinites that Sir *Isaac Newton* attain'd to the most sublime Discoveries. I am now to speak of another Work,* which tho' more adapted to the Capacity of the human Mind, does nevertheless display some Marks of that creative Genius

---

[1] By Sir *Isaac Newton.*

with which Sir *Isaac Newton* was inform'd in all his Researches. The Work I mean is a Chronology of a new kind,
for what Province soever he undertook, he was sure to
change the Ideas and Opinions receiv'd by the rest of Men.

Accustom'd to unravel and disintangle Chaos's, he was
resolv'd to convey at least some Light into that of the Fables
of Antiquity which are blended and confounded with History, and fix an uncertain Chronology. 'Tis true, that there
is no Family, City or Nation, but endeavours to remove its
Original as far backward as possible. Besides, the first Historians were the most negligent in setting down the Æra's;
Books were infinitely less common than they are at this
Time, and consequently Authors being not so obnoxious to
Censure, they therefore impos'd upon the World with
greater Impunity; and as 'tis evident that these have related
a great Number of fictitious Particulars, 'tis probable
enough that they also gave us several false Æra's.

It appear'd in general to Sir *Isaac*, that the World was five
hundred Years younger than Chronologers declare it to be.
He grounds his Opinion on the ordinary Course of Nature,
and on the Observations which Astronomers have made.

By the Course of Nature we here understand the Time
that every Generation of Men lives upon the Earth. The
Egyptians first employ'd this vague and uncertain Method
of calculating, when they began to write the Beginning of
their History. These computed three hundred and forty one
Generations from *Menes* to *Sethon*; and having no fix'd
Æra, they suppos'd three Generations to consist of an hundred Years. In this Manner they computed eleven thousand
three hundred and forty Years from *Menes*'s Reign to that
of *Sethon*.

The *Greeks* before they counted by Olympiads, follow'd
the Method of the *Egyptians*, and even gave a little more
Extent to Generations, making each to consist of forty
Years.

Now here both the *Egyptians* and the *Greeks* made an
erroneous Computation. 'Tis true indeed, that according to
the usual Course of Nature three Generations last about an
hundred and twenty Years: But three Reigns are far from

taking up so many. 'Tis very evident, that Mankind in general live longer than Kings are found to reign: So that an Author who should write a History, in which there were no Dates fix'd, and should know that nine Kings had reign'd over a Nation; such an Historian, would commit a great Error should he allow three hundred Years to these nine Monarchs. Every Generation takes about thirty six Years; every Reign is, one with the other, about twenty. Thirty Kings of *England* have sway'd the Scepter from *William* the Conqueror to *George* the First, the Years of whose Reigns added together, amount to six hundred and forty eight Years; which being divided equally among the thirty Kings, give to every one a Reign of twenty one Years and a half very near. Sixty three Kings of *France* have set upon the Throne; these have, one with another, reign'd about twenty Years each. This is the usual Course of Nature: The Ancients therefore were mistaken, when they suppos'd the Durations in general, of Reigns, to equal that of Generations. They therefore allow'd too great a Number of Years, and consequently some Years must be substracted from their Computation.

Astronomical Observations seem to have lent a still greater Assistance to our Philosopher. He appears to us stronger when he fights upon his own Ground.

You know that the Earth, besides its annual Motion which carries it round the Sun from West to East in the Space of a Year, has also a singular Revolution which was quite unknown till within these late Years. Its Poles have a very slow retrograde Motion from East to West, whence it happens that their Position every Day does not correspond exactly with the same Point of the Heavens. This difference which is so insensible in a Year, becomes pretty considerable in Time; and in threescore and twelve Years the Difference is found to be of one Degree, that is to say, the three hundred and sixtieth Part of the Circumference of the whole Heaven. Thus after seventy two Years the *Colure* of the vernal Equinox which pass'd thro' a fix'd Star, corresponds with another fix'd Star. Hence it is, that the Sun, instead of being in that Part of the Heavens in which the

Ram was situated in the Time of *Hipparchus*, is found to correspond with that Part of the Heavens in which the *Bull* was situated; and the *Twins* are plac'd where the *Bull* then stood. All the Signs have chang'd their Situation, and yet we still retain the same Manner of speaking as the Ancients did. In this Age we say that the Sun is in the *Ram* in the Spring, from the same Principle of Condescension that we say that the Sun turns round.

Hipparchus was the first among the *Greeks* who observ'd some Change in the Constellations with regard to the Equinoxes, or rather who learnt it from the *Egyptians*. Philosophers ascrib'd this Motion to the Stars; for in those Ages People were far from imagining such a Revolution in the Earth, which was suppos'd to be immoveable in every respect. They therefore created a Heaven in which they fix'd the several Stars, and gave this Heaven a particular Motion by which it was carried towards the East, whilst that all the Stars seem'd to perform their diurnal Revolution from East to West. To this Error they added a second of much greater Consequence, by imagining that the pretended Heaven of the fix'd Stars advanc'd one Degree eastward every hundred Years. In this Manner they were no less mistaken in their astronomical Calculation than in their System of Natural Philosophy. As for Instance, an Astronomer in that Age would have said, that the Vernal Equinox was in the Time of such and such an Observation, in such a Sign, and in such a Star. It has advanc'd two Degrees of each since the Time that Observation was made to the present. Now two Degrees are equivalent to two hundred Years; consequently the Astronomer who made that Observation liv'd just so many Years before me. 'Tis certain that an Astronomer who had argued in this Manner would have mistook just fifty four Years; hence it is that the Ancients, who were doubly deceiv'd, made their great Year of the World, that is, the Revolution of the whole Heavens, to consist of thirty six thousand Years. But the Moderns are sensible that this imaginary Revolution of the Heaven of the Stars, is nothing else than the Revolution of the Poles of the Earth, which is perform'd in twenty five thousand nine hundred Years. It may be proper to observe transiently in this Place, that Sir *Isaac*, by determining the Figure of the Earth, has very happily explain'd the Cause of this Revolution.

All this being laid down, the only Thing remaining to settle Chronology, is, to see thro' what Star, the *Colure* of the Equinoxes passes, and where it intersects at this Time the Ecliptick in the Spring; and to discover whether some ancient Writer does not tell us in what Point the Ecliptic was intersected in his Time, by the same *Colure* of the Equinoxes.

Clemens Alexandrinus informs us, that *Chiron*, who went with the *Argonauts*, observ'd the Constellations at the Time of that famous Expedition, and fix'd the vernal Equinox to the Middle of the *Ram*; the autumnal Equinox to the Middle of *Libra*; our Summer Solstice to the Middle of *Cancer*, and our Winter Solstice to the Middle of *Capricorn*.

A long Time after the Expedition of the *Argonauts*, and a Year before the *Peloponnesian* War, *Methon* observ'd that the Point of the Summer Solstice pass'd thro' the eighth Degree of *Cancer*.

Now every Sign of the Zodiack contains thirty Degrees. In *Chiron*'s Time, the Solstice was arriv'd at the Middle of the Sign, that is to say to the fifteenth Degree. A Year before the *Peloponnesian* War it was at the eighth, and therefore it had retarded seven Degrees. A Degree is equivalent to seventy two Years; consequently, from the Beginning of the *Peloponnesian* War to the Expedition of the *Argonauts*, there is no more than an Interval of seven times seventy two Years, which make five hundred and four Years, and not seven hundred Years, as the *Greeks* computed. Thus in comparing the Position of the Heavens at this Time, with their Position in that Age, we find that the Expedition of the *Argonauts* ought to be plac'd about nine hundred Years before *Christ*, and not about fourteen hundred; and consequently that the World is not so old by five hundred Years as it was generally suppos'd to be. By this Calculation all the Æra's are drawn nearer, and the several Events are found to have happen'd later than is computed. I don't know whether this ingenious System will be favourably receiv'd;

and whether these Notions will prevail so far with the Learned, as to prompt them to reform the Chronology of the World. Perhaps these Gentlemen would think it too great a Condescension, to allow one and the same Man the Glory of having improv'd natural Philosophy, Geometry and History. This would be a kind of universal Monarchy, which the Principle of Self-Love that is in Man, will scarce suffer him to indulge his Fellow-Creature; and, indeed, at the same Time that some very great Philosophers attack'd Sir *Isaac Newton*'s attractive Principle, others fell upon his chronological System. Time that shou'd discover to which of these the Victory is due, may perhaps only leave the Dispute still more undetermin'd.

LETTER XVIII.
On Tragedy.

THE *English* as well as the *Spaniards* were possess'd of Theatres, at a Time when the *French* had no more than moving, itinerant Stages. *Shakespear*, who was consider'd as the *Corneille* of the first mention'd Nation, was pretty near Cotemporary with *Lopez de Vega*, and he created, as it were, the *English* Theatre. *Shakespear* boasted a strong, fruitful Genius: He was natural and sublime, but had not so much as a single Spark of good Taste, or knew one Rule of the Drama. I will now hazard a random, but, at the same Time, true Reflection, which is, that the great Merit of this Dramatic Poet has been the Ruin of the *English* Stage. There are such beautiful, such noble, such dreadful Scenes in this Writer's monstrous Farces, to which the Name of Tragedy is given, that they have always been exhibited with great Success. Time, which only gives Reputation to Writers, at last makes their very Faults venerable. Most of the whimsical, gigantic Images of this Poet, have, thro' Length of Time (it being an hundred and fifty Years since they were first drawn) acquir'd a Right of passing for sublime. Most of the modern dramatic Writers have copied him; but the Touches and Descriptions which are applauded in *Shakespear*, are hiss'd at in these Writers; and you'll easily believe that the Veneration in which this Author is held, increases in Proportion to the Contempt which is shown to the Moderns. Dramatic Writers don't consider that they should not imitate him; and the ill Success of *Shakespear*'s Imitators, produces no other Effect, than to make him be consider'd as inimitable. You remember that in the Tragedy of OTHELLO* *Moor of Venice*, (a most tender Piece) a Man strangles his Wife on the Stage; and that the poor Woman, whilst she is strangling, cries aloud, that she dies very unjustly. You know that in HAMLET *Prince of Denmark*, two Grave-Diggers make a Grave, and are all the Time drinking, singing Ballads, and making humourous Reflexions, (natural indeed enough to Persons of their Profession) on the several Skulls they throw up with their Spades; but a Circumstance which will surprize you is, that this ridiculous Incident has been imitated. In the Reign of King *Charles* the Second, which was that of Politeness, and the Golden Age of the Liberal Arts; *Otway*, in his VENICE PRESERV'D, introduces *Antonio* the Senator, and *Naki* his Curtezan, in the Midst of the Horrors of the Marquis of *Bedemar*'s Conspiracy. *Antonio*, the superannuated Senator plays, in his Mistress's Presence, all the apish Tricks of a lewd, impotent Debauchee who is quite frantic and out of his Senses. He mimicks a Bull and a Dog; and bites his Mistress's Legs, who kicks and whips him. However, the Players have struck these Buffooneries (which indeed were calculated merely for the Dregs of the People) out of *Otway*'s Tragedy; but they have still left in *Shakespear*'s JULIUS CÆSAR, the Jokes of the *Roman* Shoemakers and Coblers, who are introduc'd in the same Scene with *Brutus* and *Cassius*. You will undoubtedly complain, that those who have hitherto discours'd with you on the *English* Stage, and especially on the celebrated *Shakespear*, have taken Notice only of his Errors; and that no one has translated any of those strong, those forcible Passages which atone for all his Faults. But to this I will answer, that nothing is easier than to exhibit in Prose all the silly Impertinencies which a Poet may have thrown out; but that 'tis a very difficult Task to translate his fine Verses. All your junior academical *Sophs*,* who set up for Censors of the eminent Writers, compile whole Volumes; but methinks two Pages which display some of the Beauties of great Genius's, are of infinitely more Value than all the idle Rhapsodies of those Commentators; and I will join in Opinion with all Persons of good Taste in declaring, that greater Advantage may be reap'd from a Dozen Verses of *Homer* or *Virgil*, than from all the Critiques put together which have been made on those two great Poets.

I have ventur'd to translate some Passages of the most celebrated *English* Poets, and shall now give you one from *Shakespear*. Pardon the Blemishes of the Translation for the

Sake of the Original; and remember always that when you see a Version, you see merely a faint Print of a beautiful Picture. I have made Choice of Part of the celebrated Soliloquy in *Hamlet*, which you may remember is as follows.

To be, or not to be! that is the Question!
Whether 'tis nobler in the Mind to suffer
The Stings and Arrows of outrageous Fortune,
Or to take Arms against a Sea of Troubles,
And by opposing, end them? To dye! to sleep!
No more! and by a Sleep to say we end
The Heart-ach, and the thousand natural Shocks
That Flesh is Heir to! 'Tis a Consummation
Devoutly to be wish'd. To die! to sleep!
To sleep, perchance to dream! Oy, there's the Rub;
For in that Sleep of Death, what Dreams may come
When we have shuffled off this mortal Coyle,
Must give us Pause. There's the respect
That makes Calamity of so long Life:
For who wou'd bear the Whips and Scorns of Time,
Th' Oppressor's Wrong, the poor Man's contumely,
The Pangs of despis'd Love, the Laws Delay,
The Insolence of Office, and the Spurns
That patient Merit of th' unworthy takes,
When he himself might his Quietus make
With a bare Bodkin? Who would these Fardles bear
To groan and sweat under a weary Life,
But that the Dread of something after Death,
Th' undiscover'd Country, from whose Bourn
No Traveller returns, puzzles the Will,
And makes us rather bear those Ills we have,
Than fly to others that we know not of?
Thus Conscience does make Cowards of us all;
And thus the native Hue of Resolution
Is sicklied o'er with the pale Cast of Thought:
And Enterprizes of great Weight and Moment
With this Regard their Currents turn away,
And lose the Name of Action——

My Version of it runs thus:

> *Demeure, il faut choisir & passer à l'instant*
> *De la vie, à la mort, ou de l'Etre au neant.*
> *Dieux cruels, s'il en est, éclairez mon courage.*
> *Faut-il vieillir courbé sous la main qui m'outrage,*
> *Supporter, ou finir mon malheur & mon sort?*
> *Qui suis je? Qui m'arrete! & qu'est-ce que la Mort?*
> *C'est la fin de nos maux, c'est mon unique Azile*
> *Après de longs transports, c'est un sommeil tranquile.*
> *On s'endort, & tout meurt, mais un affreux reveil*
> *Doit succeder peut etre aux douceurs du sommeil!*
> *On nous menace, on dit que cette courte Vie,*
> *De tourmens éternels est aussi-tôt suivie.*
> *O Mort! moment fatal! affreuse Eternité!*
> *Tout cœur à ton seul nom se glace épouvanté.*
> *Eh! qui pourroit sans Toi supporter cette vie,*
> *De nos Prêtres menteurs benir l'hypocrisie;*
> *D'une indigne Maitresse encenser les erreurs,*
> *Ramper sous un Ministre, adorer ses hauteurs;*
> *Et montrer les langueurs de son ame abattüe,*
> *A des Amis ingrats qui detournent la vüe?*
> *La Mort seroit trop douce en ces extrémitez,*
> *Mais le scrupule parle, & nous crie, Arrêtez;*
> *Il defend à nos mains cet heureux homicide*
> *Et d'un Heros guerrier, fait un Chrétien timide, &c.*

Don't imagine that I have translated *Shakespear* in a servile Manner.* Woe to the Writer who gives a literal Version; who by rendring every Word of his Original, by that very means enervates the Sense, and extinguishes all the Fire of it. 'Tis on such an Occasion one may justly affirm, that the Letter kills, but the Spirit quickens.

Here follows another Passage copied from a celebrated Tragic Writer among the *English*. 'Tis *Dryden*, a Poet in the Reign of *Charles* the Second; a Writer whose Genius was too exuberant, and not accompanied with Judgment enough. Had he writ only a tenth Part of the Works he left behind him, his Character wou'd have been conspicuous in every Part; but his great Fault is his having endeavour'd to be universal.

The Passage in Question is as follows:*

> When I consider Life, 'tis all a Cheat,
> Yet fool'd by Hope, Men favour the Deceit;
> Trust on and think, to Morrow will repay;
> To Morrow's falser than the former Day;
> Lies more; and whilst it says we shall be blest
> With some new Joy cuts off what we possess;
> Strange Cozenage! none wou'd live past Years again,
> Yet all hope Pleasure in what yet remain,
> And from the Dregs of Life think to receive
> What the first sprightly Running could not give.
> I'm tir'd with waiting for this chymic Gold,
> Which fools us young, and beggars us when old.

I shall now give you my Translation.

> De desseins en regrets & d'erreurs en desirs
> Les Mortels insensés promenent leur Folie.
> Dans des malheurs presents, dans l'espoir des plaisirs
> Nous ne vivons jamais, nous attendons la vie.
> Demain, demain, dit-on, va combler tous nos vœux.
> Demain vient, & nous laisse encore plus malheureux.
> Qu'elle est l'erreur, helas! du soin qui nous dévore,
> Nul de nous ne voudroit recommencer son cours.
> De nos premiers momens nous maudissons l'aurore,
> Et de la nuit qui vient, nous attendons encore
> Ce qu'ont en vain promis les plus beaux de nos jours, &c.

'Tis in these detach'd Passages that the *English* have hitherto excell'd. Their dramatic Pieces, most of which are barbarous and without Decorum, Order or Verisimilitude, dart such resplendent Flashes, thro' this Gloom, as amaze and astonish. The Style is too much inflated, too unnatural, too closely copied from the *Hebrew* Writers, who abound so much with the *Asiatic* Fustian.* But then it must be also confess'd, that the *Stilts* of the figurative Style on which the

English Tongue is lifted up, raises the Genius at the same Time very far aloft, tho' with an irregular Pace. The first *English* Writer who compos'd a regular Tragedy and infus'd a Spirit of Elegance thro' every Part of it, was the illustrious Mr. *Addison*. His CATO is a Master-piece both with regard to the Diction, and to the Beauty and Harmony of the Numbers. The Character of *Cato* is, in my Opinion, vastly superiour to that of *Cornelia* in the POMPEY of *Corneille*: For *Cato* is great without any Thing like Fustian, and *Cornelia*, who besides is not a necessary Character, tends sometimes to bombast. Mr. *Addison*'s *Cato* appears to me the greatest Character that was ever brought upon any Stage, but then the rest of them don't correspond to the Dignity of it: And this dramatic Piece so excellently well writ, is disfigur'd by a dull Love-Plot, which spreads a certain Languor over the whole, that quite murders it.

The Custom of introducing Love at random and at any rate in the Drama, pass'd from *Paris* to *London* about 1660, with our Ribbons and our Peruques. The Ladies who adorn the Theatrical Circle, there, in like Manner as in this City, will suffer Love only to be the Theme of every Conversation. The judicious Mr. *Addison* had the effeminate Complaisance to soften the Severity of his dramatic Character so, as to adapt it to the Manners of the Age; and from an Endeavour to please, quite ruin'd a Master-Piece in its kind. Since his Time, the Drama is become more regular, the Audience more difficult to be pleas'd, and Writers more correct and less bold. I have seen some new Pieces that were written with great Regularity, but which at the same Time were very flat and insipid. One would think that the *English* had been hitherto form'd to produce irregular Beauties only. The shining Monsters of *Shakespear*, give infinite more Delight than the judicious Images of the Moderns. Hitherto the poetical Genius of the *English* resembles a tufted Tree planted by the Hand of Nature, that throws out a thousand Branches at random, and spreads unequally, but with great Vigour. It dies if you attempt to force its Nature, and to lop and dress it in the same Manner as the Trees of the Garden of *Marli*.

LETTER XIX.
On Comedy.

I AM surpriz'd that the judicious and ingenious Mr. *de Muralt*, who has publish'd some Letters on the *English* and *French* Nations,* should have confin'd himself, in treating of Comedy, merely to censure *Shadwell* the comic Writer. This Author was had in pretty great Contempt in Mr. *de Muralt*'s Time, and was not the Poet of the polite Part of the Nation. His dramatic Pieces which pleas'd some Time in acting, were despis'd by all Persons of Taste and might be compar'd to many Plays which I have seen in *France*, that drew Crowds to the Play-house, at the same Time that they were intolerable to read; and of which it might be said, that the whole City of *Paris* exploded them, and yet all flock'd to see 'em represented on the Stage. Methinks Mr. *de Muralt* should have mention'd an excellent comic Writer (living when he was in *England*) I mean Mr. *Wycherley*, who was a long Time known publickly to be happy in the good Graces of the most celebrated Mistress of King *Charles* the Second. This Gentleman who pass'd his Life among Persons of the highest Distinction, was perfectly well acquainted with their Lives and their Follies, and painted them with the strongest Pencil, and in the truest Colours. He has drawn a *Misantrope** or Man-hater, in Imitation of that of *Moliere*. All *Wycherley*'s Strokes are stronger and bolder than those of our *Misantrope*, but then they are less delicate, and the Rules of Decorum are not so well observ'd in this Play. The *English* Writer has corrected the only Defect that is in *Moliere*'s Comedy, the Thinness of the Plot, which also is so dispos'd that the Characters in it do not enough raise our Concern. The *English* Comedy affects us, and the Contrivance of the Plot is very ingenious, but at the same Time 'tis too bold for the *French* Manners. The Fable is this.——A Captain of a Man of War, who is very brave, open-hearted, and enflam'd with a Spirit of

Contempt for all Mankind, has a prudent, sincere Friend whom he yet is suspicious of, and a Mistress that loves him with the utmost Excess of Passion. The Captain so far from returning her Love, will not even condescend to look upon her; but confides intirely in a false Friend, who is the most worthless Wretch living. At the same Time he has given his Heart to a Creature who is the greatest Coquet, and the most perfidious of her Sex, and is so credulous as to be confident she is a *Penelope*, and his false Friend a *Cato*. He embarks on board his Ship in order to go and fight the *Dutch*, having left all his Money, his Jewels and every Thing he had in the World to this virtuous Creature, whom at the same Time he recommends to the Care of his suppos'd faithful Friend. Nevertheless the real Man of Honour whom he suspects so unaccountably, goes on board the Ship with him; and the Mistress on whom he would not bestow so much as one Glance, disguises herself in the Habit of a Page, and is with him the whole Voyage, without his once knowing that she is of a Sex different from that she attempts to pass for, which, by the Way, is not over natural.

The Captain having blown up his own Ship in an Engagement, returns to *England* abandon'd and undone, accompanied by his Page and his Friend, without knowing the Friendship of the one, or the tender Passion of the other. Immediately he goes to the Jewel among Women, who he expected had preserv'd her Fidelity to him, and the Treasure he had left in her Hands. He meets with her indeed, but married to the honest Knave in whom he had repos'd so much Confidence; and finds she had acted as treacherously with regard to the Casket he had entrusted her with. The Captain can scarce think it possible, that a Woman of Virtue and Honour can act so vile a Part; but to convince him still more of the Reality of it, this very worthy Lady falls in Love with the little Page, and will force him to her Embraces. But as it is requisite Justice should be done, and that in a dramatick Piece Virtue ought to be rewarded and Vice punish'd; 'tis at last found that the Captain takes his Page's Place, and lyes with his faithless Mistress, cuckolds his treacherous Friend, thrusts his Sword through his Body, recovers his Casket and marries his Page. You'll observe that this Play is also larded with a petulant, litigious old Woman (a Relation of the Captain) who is the most comical Character that was ever brought upon the Stage.

Wycherley has also copied from *Moliere* another Play, of as singular and bold a Cast, which is a kind of *Ecole des Femmes*, or, *School for married Women.**

The principal Character in this Comedy is one *Horner*, a sly Fortune-Hunter, and the Terror of all the City Husbands. This Fellow in order to play a surer Game, causes a Report to be spread, that in his last Illness, the Surgeons had found it necessary to have him made an Eunuch. Upon his appearing in this noble Character, all the Husbands in Town flock to him with their Wives, and now poor *Horner* is only puzzled about his Choice. However, he gives the Preference particularly to a little female Peasant; a very harmless, innocent Creature, who enjoys a fine Flush of Health, and cuckolds her Husband with a Simplicity that has infinitely more Merit than the witty Malice of the most experienc'd Ladies. This Play cannot indeed be call'd the School of good Morals, but 'tis certainly the School of Wit and true Humour.

Sir *John Vanbrugh* has writ several Comedies which are more humourous than those of Mr. *Wycherley*, but not so ingenious. Sir *John* was a Man of Pleasure, and likewise a Poet and an Architect. The general Opinion is, that he is as sprightly in his Writings as he is heavy in his Buildings. 'Tis he who rais'd the famous Castle of *Blenheim*, a ponderous and lasting Monument of our unfortunate Battle of *Hockstet*. Were the Apartments but as spacious as the Walls are thick, this Castle wou'd be commodious enough. Some Wag, in an Epitaph he made on Sir *John Vanbrugh*, has these Lines:

> *Earth lye light on him, for he*
> *Laid many a heavy Load on thee.**

Sir *John* having taken a Tour into *France* before the glorious War that broke out in 1701, was thrown into the *Bastile*, and detain'd there for some Time, without being ever able to discover the Motive which had prompted our Ministry to indulge him this Mark of their Distinction. He writ a Comedy during his Confinement; and a Circumstance which appears to me very extraordinary is, that we don't meet with so much as a single satyrical Stroke against the Country in which he had been so injuriously treated.

The late Mr. *Congreve* rais'd the Glory of Comedy to a greater Height than any English Writer before or since his Time. He wrote only a few Plays, but they are all excellent in their kind. The Laws of the Drama are strictly observ'd in them; they abound with Characters all which are shadow'd with the utmost Delicacy, and we don't meet with so much as one low, or coarse Jest. The Language is every where that of Men of Honour, but their Actions are those of Knaves; a Proof that he was perfectly well acquainted with human Nature, and frequented what we call polite Company. He was infirm, and come to the Verge of Life when I knew him. Mr. *Congreve* had one Defect, which was, his entertaining too mean an Idea of his first Profession, (that of a Writer) tho' 'twas to this he ow'd his Fame and Fortune. He spoke of his Works as of Trifles that were beneath him; and hinted to me in our first Conversation, that I should visit him upon no other Foot than that of a Gentleman, who led a Life of Plainness and Simplicity. I answer'd, that had he been so unfortunate as to be a mere Gentleman I should never have come to see him; and I was very much disgusted at so unseasonable a Piece of Vanity.

Mr. *Congreve*'s Comedies are the most witty and regular, those of Sir *John Vanbrugh* most gay and humourous, and those of Mr. *Wycherley* have the greatest Force and Spirit. It may be proper to observe, that these fine Genius's never spoke disadvantageously of *Moliere*; and that none but the contemptible Writers among the *English* have endeavour'd to lessen the Character of that great comic Poet. Such *Italian* Musicians as despise *Lully* are themselves Persons of no Character or Ability; but a *Buononcini** esteems that great Artist, and does Justice to his Merit.

The *English* have some other good comic Writers living, such as Sir *Richard Steele*, and Mr. *Cibber*, who is an excellent Player, and also Poet Laureat, a Title which how ridiculous soever it may be thought, is yet worth a thousand Crowns a Year, (besides some considerable Privileges) to the Person who enjoys it. Our illustrious *Corneille* had not so much.

To conclude. Don't desire me to descend to Particulars with regard to these *English* Comedies, which I am so fond of applauding; nor to give you a single smart Saying, or humorous Stroke from *Wycherley* or *Congreve.* We don't laugh in reading a Translation. If you have a Mind to understand the *English* Comedy, the only way to do this will be for you to go to *England,* to spend three Years in *London,* to make your self Master of the *English* Tongue, and to frequent the Play-house every Night.* I receive but little Pleasure from the Perusal of *Aristophanes* and *Plautus,* and for this Reason, because I am neither a *Greek* nor a *Roman.* The Delicacy of the Humour, the Allusion, the *à propos,* all these are lost to a Foreigner.

But 'tis different with respect to Tragedy, this treating only of exalted Passions and heroical Follies, which the antiquated Errors of Fable or History have made sacred. *Oedipus, Electra* and such like Characters, may with as much Propriety, be treated of by the *Spaniards,* the *English,* or Us, as by the *Greeks.* But true Comedy is the speaking Picture of the Follies and ridiculous Foibles of a Nation; so that he only is able to judge of the Painting, who is perfectly acquainted with the People it represents.

LETTER XX.

On such of the Nobility as cultivate the
Belles Lettres.

THERE once was a Time in *France* when the polite Arts were cultivated by Persons of the highest Rank in the State. The Courtiers particularly, were conversant in them, altho' Indolence, a Taste for Trifles, and a Passion for Intrigue, were the Divinities of the Country. The Court methinks at this Time seems to have given into a Taste quite opposite to that of polite Literature, but perhaps the Mode of Thinking may be reviv'd in a little Time. The *French* are of so flexible a Disposition, may be moulded into such a Variety of Shapes, that the Monarch needs but command and he is immediately obey'd. The *English* generally think, and Learning is had in greater Honour among them than in our Country; an Advantage that results naturally from the Form of their Government. There are about eight hundred Persons in *England* who have a Right to speak in publick, and to support the Interest of the Kingdom; and near five or six Thousand may in their Turns, aspire to the same Honour. The whole Nation set themselves up as Judges over these, and every Man has the Liberty of publishing his Thoughts with regard to publick Affairs; which shews, that all the People in general are indispensably oblig'd to cultivate their Understandings. In *England* the Governments of *Greece* and *Rome* are the Subject of every Conversation, so that every Man is under a Necessity of perusing such Authors as treat of them, how disagreeable soever it may be to him; and this Study leads naturally to that of polite Literature. Mankind in general speak well in their respective Professions. What is the Reason why our Magistrates, our Lawyers, our Physicians, and a great Number of the Clergy are abler Scholars, have a finer Taste and more Wit than Persons of all other Professions? The Reason is, because their Condition of Life requires a cultivated and enlightned

Mind, in the same Manner as a Merchant is oblig'd to be acquainted with his Traffick. Not long since an *English* Nobleman,* who was very young, came to see me at *Paris* in his Return from *Italy*. He had writ a poetical Description of that Country, which, for Delicacy and Politeness may vie with any Thing we meet with in the Earl of *Rochester*, or in our *Chaulieu*, our *Sarrasin*, or *Chapelle*. The Translation I have given of it is so inexpressive of the Strength and delicate Humour of the Original, that I am oblig'd seriously to ask Pardon of the Author, and of all who understand *English*. However, as this is the only Method I have to make his Lordship's Verses known, I shall here present you with them in our Tongue.*

> *Qu'ay je donc vû dans l'Italie?*
> *Orgueil, Astuce, & Pauvreté,*
> *Grands Complimens, peu de Bonté*
> *Et beaucoup de Ceremonie.*
>
> *L'extravagante Comedie,*
> *Que souvent l'Inquisition*[1]
> *Veut qu'on nomme Religion;*
> *Mais qu'ici nous nommons Folie.*
>
> *La Nature en vain bienfaisante*
> *Veut enricher ses Lieux charmans,*
> *Des Prêtres la main desolante*
> *Etouffe ses plus beaux présens.*
>
> *Les Monsignors, soy disant Grands,*
> *Seuls dans leurs Palais magnifiques*
> *Y sont d'illustres faineants,*
> *Sans argent, & sans domestiques.*
>
> *Pour les Petits, sans liberté,*
> *Martyrs du joug qui les domine,*
> *Ils ont fait vœu de pauvreté,*
> *Priant Dieu par oisiveté*
> *Et toûjours jeunant par famine.*

---

[1] His Lordship undoubtedly hints at the Farces which certain Preachers act in the open Squares.

Ces beaux lieux du Pape benis
Semblent habitez par les Diables;
Et les Habitans miserables
Sont damnez dans le Paradis.

LETTER XXI.

On the Earl of Rochester and Mr. Waller.

THE Earl of *Rochester*'s Name is universally known. Mr. *de St. Evremont* has made very frequent mention of him,* but then he has represented this famous Nobleman in no other Light than as the Man of Pleasure, as one who was the Idol of the Fair; but with regard to my self, I would willingly describe in him the Man of Genius, the great Poet. Among other Pieces which display the shining Imagination his Lordship only cou'd boast, he wrote some Satyrs on the same Subjects as those our celebrated *Boileau* made choice of. I don't know any better Method of improving the Taste, than to compare the Productions of such great Genius's as have exercis'd their Talent on the same Subject. *Boileau* declaims as follows against human Reason in his Satyr on Man.*

> *Cependant à le voir plein de vapeurs légeres,*
> *Soi-même se bercer de ses propres chimeres,*
> *Lui seul de la nature est la baze & l'appui,*
> *Et le dixieme ciel ne tourne que pour lui.*
> *De tous les Animaux il est ici le Maître;*
> *Qui pourroit le nier, poursuis tu? Moi peut-être.*
> *Ce maître prétendu qui leur donne des loix,*
> *Ce Roi des Animaux, combien a-t'il de Rois?*

> Yet, pleas'd with idle Whimsies of his Brain,
> And puff'd with Pride, this haughty Thing wou'd fain
> Be thought himself the only Stay and Prop
> That holds the mighty Frame of Nature up.
> The Skies and Stars his Properties must seem,

> Of all the Creatures he's the Lord, he cries.

And who is there, *say you*, that dares deny

So own'd a Truth? That may be, Sir, do I.

—— —— ——

This boasted Monarch of the World who awes
The Creatures here, and with his Nod gives Laws;
This self-nam'd King, who thus pretends to be
The Lord of all, how many Lords has he?

OLDHAM a little alter'd.*

The Lord *Rochester* expresses himself, in his Satyr against Man,* in pretty near the following Manner: But I must first desire you always to remember, that the Versions I give you from the *English* Poets are written with Freedom and Latitude; and that the Restraint of our Versification, and the Delicacies of the *French* Tongue, will not allow a Translator to convey into it the licentious Impetuosity and Fire of the *English* Numbers.

Cet Esprit que je haïs, cet Esprit plein d'erreur,
Ce n'est pas ma raison, c'est la tienne Docteur.
C'est la raison frivôle, inquiete, orgeuilleuse
Des sages Animaux, rivale dédaigneuse,
Qui croit entr'eux & l'Ange, occuper le milieu,
Et pense être ici bas l'image de son Dieu.
Vil atôme imparfait, qui croit, doute, dispute
Rampe, s'eleve, tombe, & nie encore sa chûte.
Qui nous dit je suis libre, en nous montrant ses fers,
Et dont l'œil trouble & faux, croit percer l'univers.
Allez, reverends Fous, bienheureux Fanatiques,
Compilez bien l'Amas de vos Riens scholastiques,
Peres de Visions, & d'Enigmes sacrez,
Auteurs du Labirinthe, ou vous vous égarez.
Allez obscurement éclaircir vos misteres,
Et courez dans l'école adorer vos chimeres.
Il est d'autres erreurs, il est de ces dévots
Condamné par eux mêmes à l'ennui du repos.
Ce mystique encloîtré, fier de son Indolence
Tranquille, au sein de Dieu. Que peut il faire? Il pense.
Non, tu ne penses point, misérable, tu dors:
Inutile à la terre, & mis au rang des Morts.
Ton esprit énervé croupit dans la Molesse.

Reveille toi, sois homme, & sors de ton Yvresse.
L'homme est né pour agir, & tu pretens penser? &c.

The Original runs thus:

Hold, mighty Man, I cry all this we know,
And 'tis this very Reason I despise,
This supernatural Gift, that makes a Mite
Think he's the Image of the Infinite;
Comparing his short Life, void of all rest,
To the eternal and the ever blest.
This busy, puzzling Stirrer up of Doubt,
That frames deep Mysteries, then finds 'em out,
Filling, with frantic Crowds of thinking Fools,
Those reverend Bedlams, Colleges and Schools;
Borne on whose Wings, each heavy Sot can pierce
The Limits of the boundless Universe.
So charming Ointments make an old Witch fly,
And bear a crippled Carcass through the Sky.
'Tis this exalted Power, whose Business lies
In Nonsense and Impossibilities.
This made a whimsical Philosopher,
Before the spacious World his Tub prefer;
And we have modern cloyster'd Coxcombs, who
Retire to think, 'cause they have nought to do:
But Thoughts are giv'n for Action's Government,
Where Action ceases, Thought's impertinent.

Whether these Ideas are true or false, 'tis certain they are express'd with an Energy and Fire which form the Poet. I shall be very far from attempting to examine philosophically into these Verses; to lay down the Pencil and take up the Rule and Compass on this Occasion; my only Design in this Letter, being to display the Genius of the *English* Poets, and therefore I shall continue in the same View.

The celebrated Mr. *Waller* has been very much talk'd of in *France*, and Mr. *de la Fontaine*, St. *Evremont* and *Bayle* have written his Elogium, but still his Name only is known. He had much the same Reputation in *London* as *Voiture** had in *Paris*, and in my Opinion deserv'd it better. *Voiture* was born in an Age that was just emerging from Barbarity; an Age that was still rude and ignorant, the People of which aim'd at Wit, tho' they had not the least Pretensions to it, and sought for Points and Conceits instead of Sentiments. *Bristol* Stones* are more easily found than Diamonds. *Voiture*, born with an easy and frivolous Genius, was the first who shone in this Aurora of *French* Literature. Had he come into the World after those great Genius's who spread such a Glory over the Age of *Lewis* the Fourteenth, he would either have been unknown, wou'd have been despis'd, or wou'd have corrected his Style. *Boileau* applauded him, but 'twas in his first Satyr, at a Time when the Taste of that great Poet was not yet form'd. He was young, and in an Age when Persons form a Judgment of Men from their Reputation, and not from their Writings. Besides, *Boileau* was very partial both in his Encomiums and his Censures. He applauded *Segrais*, whose Works no Body reads; he abus'd *Quinault*, whose poetical Pieces every one has got by Heart, and is wholly silent upon *La Fontaine*. *Waller*, tho' a better Poet than *Voiture*, was not yet a finish'd Poet. The Graces breathe in such of *Waller*'s Works as are writ in a tender Strain, but then they are languid thro' Negligence, and often disfigur'd with false Thoughts. The *English* had not, in his Time, attain'd the Art of correct Writing. But his serious Compositions exhibit a Strength and Vigour which cou'd not have been expected from the Softness and Effeminacy of his other Pieces. He wrote an Elegy on *Oliver Cromwell*, which with all it's Faults is nevertheless look'd upon as a Master-Piece. To understand this Copy of Verses, you are to know that the Day *Oliver* died was remarkable for a great Storm. His Poem begins in this Manner:*

> *Il n'est plus, s'en est fait, soumettons nous au sort,*
> *Le ciel a signalé ce jour par des tempêtes,*
> *Et la voix des tonnerres éclatant sur nos têtes*
> *Vient d'annoncer sa mort.*
>
> *Par ses derniers soupirs il ébranle cet île;*
> *Cet île que son bras fit trembler tant de fois,*

Quand dans le cours de ses Exploits,
Il brisoit la tête des Rois,
Et soumettoit un peuple à son joug seul docile.

Mer tu t'en és troublé; O Mer tes flots émus
Semblent dire en grondant aux plus lointains rivages
Que l'effroi de la terre & ton Maître n'est plus.

Tel au ciel autrefois s'envola Romulus,
Tel il quita la Terre, au milieu des orages,
Tel d'un peuple guerrier il reçut les homages;
Obéï dans sa vie, à sa mort adoré,
Son palais fut un Temple, &c.

We must resign! Heav'n his great Soul does claim
In Storms as loud as his immortal Fame:
His dying Groans, his last Breath shakes our Isle,
And Trees uncut fall for his fun'ral Pile:
About his Palace their broad Roots are tost
Into the Air; so Romulus *was lost!*
New Rome *in such a Tempest miss'd her King,*
And from obeying fell to worshipping:
On Œta's *Top thus* Hercules *lay dead,*
With ruin'd Oaks and Pines about him spread.
Nature herself took Notice of his Death,
And, sighing, swell'd the Sea with such a Breath,
That to remotest Shores the Billows roul'd,
Th'approaching Fate of his great Ruler told.

WALLER.

'Twas this Elogium that gave Occasion to the Reply
(taken Notice of in *Bayle*'s Dictionary,)* which *Waller*
made to King *Charles* the Second. This King, to whom
Waller had a little before, (as is usual with Bards and Monarchs) presented a Copy of Verses embroider'd with
Praises; reproach'd the Poet for not writing with so much
Energy and Fire as when he had applauded the Usurper
(meaning *Oliver;*) *Sir*, reply'd *Waller* to the King, *we Poets*
succeed better in Fiction than in Truth. This Answer was not
so sincere as that which a *Dutch* Ambassador made, who,

when the same Monarch complain'd that his Masters paid less Regard to him than they had done to *Cromwell*; *Ah Sir!* says the Ambassador, Oliver *was quite another Man*——— 'Tis not my Intent to give a Commentary on *Waller*'s Character, nor on that of any other Person; for I consider Men after their Death in no other Light than as they were Writers, and wholly disregard every Thing else. I shall only observe, that *Waller*, tho' born in a Court, and to an Estate of five or six thousand Pounds Sterling a Year, was never so proud or so indolent as to lay aside the happy Talent which Nature had indulg'd him. The Earls of *Dorset* and *Roscommon*, the two Dukes of *Buckingham*, the Lord *Halifax* and so many other Noblemen, did not think the Reputation they obtain'd of very great Poets and illustrious Writers, any way derogatory to their Quality. They are more glorious for their Works than for their Titles. These cultivated the polite Arts with as much Assiduity, as tho' they had been their whole Dependance. They also have made Learning appear venerable in the Eyes of the Vulgar, who have need to be led in all Things by the Great; and who nevertheless fashion their Manners less after those of the Nobility (in *England* I mean) than in any other Country in the World.

LETTER XXII.

On Mr. Pope, and some other famous Poets.

I INTENDED to treat of Mr. *Prior*, one of the most amiable *English* Poets, whom you saw Plenipotentiary and Envoy Extraordinary at *Paris* in 1712. I also design'd to have given you some Idea of the Lord *Roscommon*'s and the Lord *Dorset*'s Muse; but I find that to do this I should be oblig'd to write a large Volume, and that after much Pains and Trouble you wou'd have but an imperfect Idea of all those Works. Poetry is a kind of Music, in which a Man should have some Knowledge before he pretends to judge of it. When I give you a Translation of some Passages from those foreign Poets, I only prick down,* and that imperfectly, their Music; but then I cannot express the Taste of their Harmony.

There is one *English* Poem especially which I should despair of ever making you understand, the Title whereof is *Hudibras*.* The Subject of it is the Civil War in the Time of the Grand Rebellion; and the Principles and Practice of the Puritans are therein ridicul'd. 'Tis *Don Quixot*, 'tis our *Satyre Menippée*[1] blended together. I never found so much Wit in one single Book as in that, which at the same Time is the most difficult to be translated. Who wou'd believe that a Work which paints in such lively and natural Colours the several Foibles and Follies of Mankind, and where we meet with more Sentiments than Words, should baffle the Endeavours of the ablest Translator? But the Reason of this is;

---

[1] A Species of Satyr in Prose and Verse written in *France* in 1594, against the Chiefs of the League at that Time. This Satyr which is also call'd *Catholicon d'Espagne*, was look'd upon as a Master-piece. *Rapin, Le Roi, Pithou, Passerat* and *Chrétien*, the greatest Wits of that Age, are the Authors of it; and 'twas entitled *Ménippée*, from *Menippus*, a cynical Philosopher, who had written Letters fill'd with sharp, satyrical Expressions, in Imitation of *Varro*, who compos'd Satyrs which he entitled *Satyræ Menippeæ*.

almost every Part of it alludes to particular Incidents. The Clergy are there made the principal Object of Ridicule, which is understood but by few among the Laity. To explain this a Commentary would be requisite, and *Humour* when explain'd is no longer Humour. Whoever sets up for a Commentator of smart Sayings and Repartees, is himself a Blockhead. This is the Reason why the Works of the ingenious Dean *Swift*, who has been call'd the *English Rabelais*, will never be well understood in *France*. This Gentleman has the Honour (in common with *Rabelais*) of being a Priest, and like him laughs at every Thing. But in my humble Opinion, the Title of the *English Rabelais* which is given the Dean, is highly derogatory to his Genius. The former has interspers'd his unaccountably-fantastic and unintelligible Book, with the most gay Strokes of Humour, but which at the same Time has a greater Proportion of Impertinence. He has been vastly lavish of Erudition, of Smut, and insipid Raillery. An agreeable Tale of two Pages is purchas'd at the Expence of whole Volumes of Nonsense. There are but few Persons, and those of a grotesque Taste, who pretend to understand, and to esteem this Work; for as to the rest of the Nation, they laugh at the pleasant and diverting Touches which are found in *Rabelais* and despise his Book. He is look'd upon as the Prince of Buffoons. The Readers are vex'd to think that a Man who was Master of so much Wit should have made so wretched a Use of it. He is an intoxicated Philosopher, who never writ but when he was in Liquor.

Dean *Swift* is *Rabelais* in his Senses, and frequenting the politest Company. The former indeed is not so gay as the latter, but then he possesses all the Delicacy, the Justness, the Choice, the good Taste, in all which Particulars our giggling rural Vicar *Rabelais* is wanting. The poetical Numbers of Dean *Swift* are of a singular and almost inimitable Taste; true Humour whether in Prose* or Verse, seems to be his peculiar Talent, but whoever is desirous of understanding him perfectly, must visit the Island in which he was born.

'Twill be much easier for you to form an Idea of Mr.

Pope's Works. He is in my Opinion the most elegant, the most correct Poet; and at the same Time the most harmonious (a Circumstance which redounds very much to the Honour of this Muse) that *England* ever gave Birth to. He has mellow'd the harsh Sounds of the *English* Trumpet to the soft Accents of the Flute. His Compositions may be easily translated, because they are vastly clear and perspicuous; besides, most of his Subjects are general, and relative to all Nations.

His *Essay on Criticism* will soon be known in *France*, by the Translation which *l'Abbé de Renel* has made of it.*

Here is an Extract from his Poem entitled the *Rape of the Lock*, which I just now translated with the Latitude I usually take on these Occasions; for once again, nothing can be more ridiculous than to translate a Poet literally.*

Umbriel, *à l'instant, vieil Gnome rechigné,*
Va d'une aîle pesante & d'un air renfrogné
Chercher en murmurant la Caverne profonde,
Où loin des doux raïons que répand l'œil du monde
La Déesse aux vapeurs a choisi son séjour,
Les tristes Aquilons y siflent à l'entour.
Et le soufle mal sain de leur aride haleine
Y porte aux environs la fievre & la migraine.
Sur un riche Sofa derriere un Paravent
Loin des flambeaux, du bruit, des parleurs & du vent,
La quinteuse Déesse incessamment repose,
Le cœur gros de chagrin, sans en savoir la cause.
N'aiant pensé jamais, l'esprit toûjours troublé,
L'œil chargé, le teint pâle, & l'hypocondre enflé.
La medisante Envie, est assise auprès d'elle,
Vieil spectre féminin, décrépite pucelle,
Avec un air devot déchirant son prochain,
Et chansonnant les Gens l'Evangile à la main.
Sur un lit plein de fleurs negligemment panchée
Une jeune Beauté non loin d'elle est couchée,
C'est l'Affectation qui grassaïe en parlant,
Ecoute sans entendre, & lorgne en regardant.
Qui rougit sans pudeur, & rit de tout sans joïe,

De cent maux différens prétend qu'elle est la proïe;
Et pleine de santé sous le rouge & le fard,
Se plaint avec molesse, & se pame avec Art.

Umbriel, *a dusky, melancholy Sprite*
As ever sullied the fair Face of Light,
Down to the central Earth, his proper Scene,
Repairs to search the gloomy Cave of Spleen.
Swift on his sooty Pinions flits the Gnome,
And in a Vapour reach'd the dismal Dome.
No chearful Breeze this sullen Region knows,
The dreaded East is all the Wind that blows.
Here, in a Grotto, shelter'd close from Air,
And screen'd in Shades from Day's detested Glare,
She sighs for ever on her pensive Bed,
Pain at her Side, and Megrim *at her Head,*
Two Handmaids wait the Throne: Alike in Place,
But diff'ring far in Figure and in Face,
Here stood Ill-nature *like an ancient Maid,*
Her wrinkled Form in black and white array'd;
With Store of Prayers for Mornings, Nights, and Noons,
Her Hand is fill'd; her Bosom with Lampoons.
There Affectation, *with a sickly Mein,*
Shows in her Cheek the Roses of eighteen,
Practis'd to lisp, and hang the Head aside,
Faints into Airs, and languishes with Pride;
On the Rich Quilt sinks with becoming Woe,
Wrapt in a Gown, for Sickness and for Show.

This Extract in the Original, (not in the faint Translation I have given you of it,) may be compar'd to the Description of *La Molesse* (Softness or Effeminacy) in *Boileau's Lutrin.*

Methinks I now have given you Specimens enough from the *English* Poets. I have made some transient mention of their Philosophers, but as for good Historians among them, I don't know of any; and indeed a *French* Man was forc'd to write their History.* Possibly the *English* Genius, which is either languid or impetuous, has not yet requir'd that unaffected Eloquence, that plain but majestic Air which History requires. Possibly too, the Spirit of Party which exhibits

Objects in a dim and confus'd Light, may have sunk the Credit of their Historians. One half of the Nation is always at Variance with the other half. I have met with People who assur'd me that the Duke of *Marlborough* was a Coward, and that Mr. *Pope* was a Fool; just as some Jesuits in *France* declare *Pascal* to have been a Man of little or no Genius; and some Jansenists affirm Father *Bourdaloüe* to have been a mere Babbler. The Jacobites consider *Mary* Queen of *Scots* as a pious Heroine, but those of an opposite Party look upon her as a Prostitute, an Adulteress, a Murtherer. Thus the *English* have Memorials of the several Reigns, but no such Thing as a History. There is indeed now living, one Mr. *Gordon*, (the Publick are oblig'd to him for a Translation of *Tacitus*) who is very capable of writing the History of his own Country, but *Rapin de Thoyras* got the Start of him. To conclude, in my Opinion, the *English* have not such good Historians as the *French*, have no such Thing as a real Tragedy, have several delightful Comedies, some wonderful Passages in certain of their Poems, and boast of Philosophers that are worthy of instructing Mankind. The *English* have reap'd very great Benefit from the Writers of our Nation, and therefore we ought, (since they have not scrupled to be in our Debt,) to borrow from them. Both the *English* and we came after the *Italians*, who have been our Instructors in all the Arts, and whom we have surpass'd in some. I cannot determine which of the three Nations ought to be honour'd with the Palm; but happy the Writer who could display their various Merits.

LETTER XXIII.

On the Regard that ought to be shown to Men of Letters.

NEITHER the *English*, nor any other People have Foundations establish'd in favour of the polite Arts like those in *France*. There are Universities in most Countries, but 'tis in *France* only that we meet with so beneficial an Encouragement for Astronomy, and all Parts of the Mathematicks, for Physick, for Researches into Antiquity, for Painting, Sculpture and Architecture. *Lewis* the Fourteenth has immortaliz'd his Name by these several Foundations, and this Immortality did not cost him two hundred thousand Livres a Year.

I must confess that one of the Things I very much wonder at, is, that as the Parliament of *Great-Britain* have promis'd a Reward of twenty thousand Pounds Sterling to any Person who may discover the Longitude, they should never have once thought to imitate *Lewis* the Fourteenth in his Munificence with regard to the Arts and Sciences.

Merit indeed meets in *England* with Rewards of another kind, which redound more to the Honour of the Nation. The *English* have so great a Veneration for exalted Talents, that a Man of Merit in their Country is always sure of making his Fortune. Mr. *Addison* in *France* would have been elected a Member of one of the Academies, and, by the Credit of some Women, might have obtain'd a yearly Pension of twelve hundred Livres; or else might have been imprison'd in the *Bastile*, upon Pretence that certain Strokes in his Tragedy of *Cato* had been discover'd, which glanc'd at the Porter of some Man in Power. Mr. *Addison* was rais'd to the Post of Secretary of State in *England*. Sir *Isaac Newton* was made Warden of the Royal Mint. Mr. *Congreve* had a considerable[1] Employment. Mr. *Prior* was Plenipoten-

---

[1] Secretary for *Jamaica*.

tiary. Dr. *Swift* is Dean of St. *Patrick* in *Dublin*, and is more rever'd in *Ireland* than the Primate himself. The Religion which Mr. *Pope* professes* excludes him indeed from Preferments of ev'ry kind, but then it did not prevent his gaining two hundred Thousand Livres by his excellent Translation of *Homer*. I my self saw a long Time in *France* the Author of *Rhadamistus*[2]* ready to perish for Hunger: And the Son of one of the greatest Men[3] our Country ever gave Birth to, and who was beginning to run the noble Career which his Father had set him, would have been reduc'd to the Extremes of Misery, had he not been patroniz'd by Monsieur *Fagon*.*

But the Circumstance which mostly encourages the Arts in *England*, is the great Veneration which is paid them. The Picture of the prime Minister hangs over the Chimney of his own Closet, but I have seen that of Mr. *Pope* in twenty Noblemens Houses. Sir *Isaac Newton* was rever'd in his Life-time, and had a due respect paid to him after his Death; the greatest Men in the Nation disputing who shou'd have the Honour of holding up his Pall. Go into *Westminster-Abbey*, and you'll find that what raises the Admiration of the Spectator is not the Mausoleums of the *English* Kings, but the Monuments which the Gratitude of the Nation has erected, to perpetuate the Memory of those illustrious Men who contributed to its Glory. We view their Statues in that Abbey in the same Manner, as those of *Sophocles*, *Plato* and other immortal Personages were view'd in *Athens*; and I am persuaded, that the bare Sight of those glorious Monuments has fir'd more than one Breast, and been the Occasion of their becoming great Men.

The *English* have even been reproach'd with paying too extravagant Honours to mere Merit, and censured for interring the celebrated Actress Mrs. *Oldfield* in *Westminster-Abbey*, with almost the same Pomp as Sir *Isaac Newton*. Some pretend that the *English* had paid her these great Funeral Honours, purposely to make us more strongly sensible of the Barbarity and Injustice which they object to us,

[2] Mr. *de Crebillon*.   [3] *Racine*.

for having buried *Mademoiselle le Couvreur** ignomini-
ously in the Fields.

But be assur'd from me, that the *English* were prompted
by no other Principle, in burying Mrs. *Oldfield* in *Westminster-Abbey*, than their good Sense. They are far from being
so ridiculous as to brand with Infamy an Art which has
immortaliz'd an *Euripides* and a *Sophocles*; or to exclude
from the Body of their Citizens a Sett of People whose
Business is to set off with the utmost Grace of Speech and
Action, those Pieces which the Nation is proud of.

Under the Reign of *Charles* the First, and in the Begin-
ning of the Civil Wars rais'd by a Number of rigid
Fanaticks, who at last were the Victims to it; a great many
Pieces were publish'd against Theatrical and other Shews,
which were attack'd with the greater Virulence, because that
Monarch and his Queen, Daughter to *Henry* the Fourth of
France, were passionately fond of them.

One Mr. *Prynne*,* a Man of most furiously scrupulous
Principles, who wou'd have thought himself damn'd had he
wore a Cassock instead of a short Cloak, and have been glad
to see one half of Mankind cut the other to Pieces for the
Glory of God, and the *Propaganda Fide*;* took it into his
Head to write a most wretched Satyr against some pretty
good Comedies, which were exhibited very innocently
every Night before their Majesties. He quoted the Authority of the Rabbis, and some Passages from St. *Bonaventure*,
to prove that the *Œdipus* of *Sophocles* was the Work of the
evil Spirit; that *Terence* was excommunicated *ipso facto*; and
added, that doubtless *Brutus*, who was a very severe
Jansenist, assassinated *Julius Cæsar*, for no other Reason,
but because he, who was *Pontifex Maximus*, presum'd to
write a Tragedy the Subject of which was *Œdipus*. Lastly, he
declar'd that all who frequented the Theatre were excommunicated, as they thereby renounc'd their Baptism. This
was casting the highest Insult on the King and all the Royal
Family; and as the *English* lov'd their Prince at that Time,
they cou'd not bear to hear a Writer talk of excommunicat-
ing him, tho' they themselves afterwards cut his Head off.
Prynne was summon'd to appear before the Star-Chamber;

his wonderful Book, from which Father *Le Brun** stole his, was sentenc'd to be burnt by the common Hangman, and himself to lose his Ears. His Tryal is now extant.

The *Italians* are far from attempting to cast a Blemish on the Opera, or to excommunicate Signior *Senesino* or Signora *Cuzzoni*.* With regard to my self, I cou'd presume to wish that the Magistrates wou'd suppress I know not what contemptible Pieces, written against the Stage. For when the *English* and *Italians* hear that we brand with the greatest Mark of Infamy an Art in which we excell; that we excommunicate Persons who receive Salaries from the King; that we condemn as impious a Spectacle exhibited in Convents and Monasteries; that we dishonour Sports in which *Lewis* the Fourteenth, and *Lewis* the Fifteenth perform'd as Actors; that we give the Title of the Devil's Works to Pieces which are receiv'd by Magistrates of the most severe Character, and represented before a virtuous Queen; when, I say, Foreigners are told of this insolent Conduct, this Contempt for the Royal Authority, and this Gothic Rusticity which some presume to call Christian Severity; what an Idea must they entertain of our Nation? And how will it be possible for 'em to conceive, either that our Laws give a Sanction to an Art which is declar'd infamous, or that some Persons dare to stamp with Infamy an Art which receives a Sanction from the Laws, is rewarded by Kings, cultivated and encourag'd by the greatest Men, and admir'd by whole Nations? And that Father *Le Brun*'s impertinent Libel against the Stage, is seen in a Bookseller's Shop, standing the very next to the immortal Labours of *Racine*, of *Corneille*, of *Moliere*, &c.

LETTER XXIV.

On the Royal Society and other Academies.

THE *English* had an Academy of Sciences many Years before us,* but then it is not under such prudent Regulations as ours, the only Reason of which very possibly is, because it was founded before the Academy of *Paris*; for had it been founded after, it would very probably have adopted some of the sage Laws of the former, and improv'd upon others.

Two Things, and those the most essential to Man, are wanting in the Royal Society of *London*, I mean Rewards and Laws. A Seat in the Academy at *Paris* is a small, but secure Fortune to a Geometrician or a Chymist; but this is so far from being the Case at *London*, that the several Members of the Royal Society are at a continual, tho' indeed small Expence. Any Man in *England* who declares himself a Lover of the Mathematicks and natural Philosophy, and expresses an Inclination to be a Member of the Royal Society, is immediately elected into it.[1] But in *France* 'tis not enough that a Man who aspires to the Honour of being a Member of the Academy, and of receiving the Royal Stipend, has a love for the Sciences; he must at the same Time be deeply skill'd in them; and is oblig'd to dispute the Seat with Competitors who are so much the more formidable as they are fir'd by a Principle of Glory, by Interest, by the Difficulty itself, and by that Inflexibility of Mind, which is generally found in those who devote themselves to that pertinacious Study, the Mathematicks.

The Academy of Sciences is prudently confin'd to the Study of Nature, and, indeed, this is a Field spacious enough

---

[1] The Reader will call to Mind that these Letters were written about 1728 or 30, since which Time the Names of the several Candidates are, by a Law of the Royal Society, posted up in it, in order that a Choice may be made of such Persons only as are qualified to be Members. The celebrated Mr. *de Fontenelle* had the Honour to pass thro' this *Ordeal*.

for fifty or threescore Persons to range in. That of *London* mixes indiscriminately Literature with Physicks: But methinks the founding an Academy merely for the polite Arts is more judicious, as it prevents Confusion, and the joining, in some Measure, of Heterogeneals, such as a Dissertation on the Head-dresses of the *Roman* Ladies with an hundred or more new Curves.

As there is very little Order and Regularity in the Royal Society, and not the least Encouragement; and that the Academy of *Paris* is on a quite different Foot, 'tis no wonder that our Transactions are drawn up in a more just and beautiful Manner than those of the *English*. Soldiers who are under a regular Discipline, and besides well paid, must necessarily, at last, perform more glorious Atchievements than others who are mere Voluntiers. It must indeed be confess'd that the Royal Society boast their *Newton*, but then he did not owe his Knowledge and Discoveries to that Body; so far from it, that the latter were intelligible to very few of his Fellow-Members. A Genius like that of Sir *Isaac* belong'd to all the Academies in the World, because all had a thousand Things to learn of him.

The celebrated Dean *Swift* form'd a Design, in the latter End of the late Queen's Reign, to found an Academy for the *English* Tongue upon the Model of that of the *French*. This Project* was promoted by the late Earl of *Oxford*, Lord High Treasurer, and much more by the Lord *Bolingbroke*, Secretary of State, who had the happy Talent of Speaking without Premeditation in the Parliament-house with as much Purity as Dean *Swift* writ in his Closet, and who would have been the Ornament and Protector of that Academy. Those only wou'd have been chosen Members of it, whose Works will last as long as the *English* Tongue, such as Dean *Swift*, Mr. *Prior*, whom we saw here invested with a publick Character, and whose Fame in *England* is equal to that of *La Fontaine* in *France*; Mr. *Pope* the English *Boileau*, Mr. *Congreve* who may be call'd their *Moliere*, and several other eminent Persons whose Names I have forgot; all these would have rais'd the Glory of that Body to a great Height even in it's Infancy. But Queen *Anne* being snatch'd suddenly from the World, the Whigs were resolv'd to ruin the Protectors of the intended Academy, a Circumstance that was of the most fatal Consequence to polite Literature. The Members of this Academy would have had a very great Advantage over those who first form'd that of the *French*, for *Swift, Prior, Congreve, Dryden, Pope, Addison, &c.* had fix'd the *English* Tongue by their Writings; whereas *Chapelain, Colletet, Cassaigne, Faret, Perrin, Cotin,* our first Academicians, were a Disgrace to their Country; and so much Ridicule is now attach'd to their very Names, that if an Author of some Genius in this Age had the Misfortune to be call'd *Chapelain* or *Cotin*, he would be under a Necessity of changing it.

One Circumstance, to which the *English* Academy should especially have attended, is, to have prescrib'd to themselves Occupations of a quite different kind from those with which our Academicians amuse themselves. A Wit of this Country ask'd me for the Memoirs of the *French* Academy. I answer'd, they have no Memoirs, but have printed threescore or fourscore Volumes in Quarto of Compliments. The Gentleman perus'd one or two of 'em, but without being able to understand the Style in which they were written, tho' he understood all our good Authors perfectly. All, says he, I see in these elegant Discourses is, that the Member elect having assur'd the Audience that his Predecessor was a great Man, that Cardinal *Richelieu* was a very great Man, that the Chancellor *Seguier* was a pretty great Man, that *Lewis* the Fourteenth was a more than great Man; the Director answers in the very same Strain, and adds, that the Member elect may also be a sort of great Man, and that himself, in Quality of Director, must also have some Share in this Greatness.

The Cause why all these academical Discourses have unhappily done so little Honour to this Body is evident enough. *Vitium est temporis potiùs quam hominis.* (The Fault is owing to the Age rather than to particular Persons.) It grew up insensibly into a Custom for every Academician to repeat these Elogiums at his Reception; 'twas laid down as a kind of Law, that the Publick should be indulg'd from

Time to Time the sullen Satisfaction of yawning over these Productions. If the Reason should afterwards be sought, why the greatest Genius's who have been incorporated into that Body have sometimes made the worst Speeches; I answer, that 'tis wholly owing to a strong Propension, the Gentlemen in Question had to shine, and to display a thread-bare, worn-out Subject in a new and uncommon Light. The Necessity of saying something, the Perplexity of having nothing to say, and a Desire of being witty, are three Circumstances which alone are capable of making even the greatest Writer ridiculous. These Gentlemen, not being able to strike out any new Thoughts, hunted after a new Play of Words, and deliver'd themselves without thinking at all; in like Manner as People who should seem to chew with great Eagerness, and make as tho' they were eating, at the same Time that they were just starv'd.

'Tis a Law in the *French* Academy, to publish all those Discourses by which only they are known, but they should rather make a Law never to print any of them.

But the Academy of the *Belles Lettres* have a more prudent and more useful Object, which is, to present the Publick with a Collection of Transactions that abound with curious Researches and Critiques. These Transactions are already esteem'd by Foreigners; and it were only to be wish'd, that some Subjects in them had been more thoroughly examin'd and that others had not been treated at all. As for Instance, we should have been very well satisfied, had they omitted I know not what Dissertation on the Prerogative of the Right Hand over the Left;* and some others, which tho' not publish'd under so ridiculous a Title, are yet written on Subjects that are almost as frivolous and silly.

The Academy of Sciences, in such of their Researches as are of a more difficult kind and a more sensible Use, embrace the Knowledge of Nature and the Improvements of the Arts. We may presume that such profound, such uninterrupted Pursuits as these, such exact Calculations, such refin'd discoveries, such extensive and exalted Views, will, at last, produce something that may prove of Advantage to the Universe. Hitherto, as we have observ'd together, the most useful Discoveries have been made in the most barbarous Times. One wou'd conclude, that the Business of the most enlightned Ages and the most learned Bodies, is, to argue and debate on Things which were invented by ignorant People. We know exactly the Angle which the Sail of a Ship is to make with the Keel, in order to its sailing better; and yet *Columbus* discover'd *America*, without having the least Idea of the Property of this Angle: However I am far from inferring from hence, that we are to confine our selves merely to a blind Practice, but happy it were, wou'd Naturalists and Geometricians unite, as much as possible, the Practice with the Theory.

Strange, but so it is, that those Things which reflect the greatest Honour on the human Mind, are frequently of the least Benefit to it! A Man who understands the four Fundamental Rules of Arithmetic, aided by a little good Sense, shall amass prodigious Wealth in Trade, shall become a Sir *Peter Delmé,* a Sir *Richard Hopkins*, a Sir *Gilbert Heathcot,** whilst a poor Algebraist spends his whole Life in searching for astonishing Properties and Relations in Numbers, which at the same time are of no manner of Use, and will not acquaint him with the Nature of Exchanges. This is very nearly the Case with most of the Arts; there is a certain Point, beyond which, all Researches serve to no other Purpose, than merely to delight an inquisitive Mind. Those ingenious and useless Truths may be compar'd to Stars, which, by being plac'd at too great a Distance, cannot afford us the least Light.

With regard to the *French* Academy, how great a Service would they do to Literature, to the Language, and the Nation, if, instead of publishing a set of Compliments annually, they would give us new Editions of the valuable Works written in the Age of *Lewis* the Fourteenth, purged from the several Errors of Diction which are crept into them. There are many of these Errors in *Corneille* and *Moliere*, but those in *La Fontaine* are very numerous. Such as could not be corrected, might at least be pointed out. By this Means, as all the *Europeans* read those Works, they would teach them our Language in its utmost Purity, which, by that Means, would be fix'd to a lasting Standard; and valuable *French* Books being then printed at the King's Expence, would prove one of the most glorious Monuments the Nation could boast. I have been told that *Boileau* formerly made this Proposal, and that it has since been revived by a Gentleman[1]* eminent for his Genius, his fine Sense, and just Taste for Criticism; but this Thought has met with the Fate of many other useful Projects, of being applauded and neglected.

---

[1] *L'Abbé de Rothelin* of the *French* Academy.

APPENDIX A.

Letter XXV, 'On Paschal's Thoughts concerning Religion, &c.'

The twenty-fifth letter first appeared in French, in the *Lettres philosophiques* (1734). Voltaire's decision to append his remarks on Pascal as an additional letter was taken some time between April and July in 1733 (compare letters D584 and D631), but the text of the *Letters concerning the English Nation* appeared as originally conceived. The twenty-fifth letter first appeared in English (by an unknown translator) in the 'Second Edition' of the *Letters concerning the English Nation* (London: Davis, 1741); it is this text which is reproduced here.

References in square brackets to the italicized passages of Pascal are to the 1963 Lafuma edition of Pascal's *Pensées*. The version of Pascal which is quoted here by Voltaire does not correspond precisely to the text of modern editions and translations; Voltaire is not—on this occasion—guilty of distorting his opponent's words (though this charge has often been made): the only text of Pascal available in Voltaire's time was the Port-Royal edition, and this differs significantly from the text of modern editions. Eighteenth-century English readers read Pascal in the translation of Basil Kennet, first published in 1704, and often reprinted; the English translator of Voltaire's twenty-fifth letter did not use Kennet, however, and preferred to translate Pascal anew.

The twenty-fifth letter contains scarcely a mention of England, and the question of how it relates to the remainder of the work is a vexed one. The English were greatly interested in Pascal (the second edition of Kennet's translation appeared in 1727, while Voltaire was in London), and this may be one of the causes which prompted Voltaire to write his 'Anti-Pascal'. It has been suggested by Roland Desné (see Select Bibliography) that the style of attack on Pascal in the twenty-fifth letter is reminiscent of English free-thinkers (Locke, Collins, Toland), with whom Voltaire deliberately wished to ally himself. To the extent that Pascal's Jansenism is presented through the optic of English free thought, the twenty-fifth letter can be said to be an 'English' letter.

*   *   *

I here send you the remarks which I made long since on Mr. *Paschal*'s thoughts. I beg you not to compare me, on this occasion, to *Hezekiah*, who would have had all *Solomon*'s works burnt. I revere Mr. *Paschal*'s genius and eloquence; but the more I revere them, the more firmly I am persuaded, that he himself would have corrected many of those thoughts, which were thrown by him upon paper, in the design of examining them afterwards; and I admire his genius at the same time that I combat his notions.

It appears to me that Mr. *Paschal*'s design, in general, was to exhibit mankind in an odious light. He exerts the utmost efforts of his pen, in order to make us all appear wicked and wretched. He writes against the human species in much the same strain as he wrote against the *Jesuits*. He ascribes, to the essence of our nature, things that are peculiar to some men only; and speaks injuriously, but at the same time eloquently, of mankind. I shall be so bold as to take up the pen, in defence of my fellow creatures, in opposition to this sublime misanthropist. I dare affirm, that we are neither so wretched, nor so wicked, as he declares us to be. 'Tis likewise my firm opinion, that had he executed, in the book he intended to write, the plan laid down by him in his thoughts, it would have been found a work full of eloquent false reasonings, and untruths deduc'd in a wonderful manner. I even think that the great number of books which have been written, of late years, to prove the truth of the Christian religion, so far from edifying the reader, will be found so many stumbling blocks. Do these authors pretend to know more of this matter than Christ and his Apostles? This is like surrounding an oak with reeds, to keep it from falling; but surely the latter may be rooted up without prejudicing the oak in any manner.

I have made a discretionary choice of some of *Paschal*'s thoughts, and annex'd the several answers to them. 'Tis your business to judge how I may have acquitted my self on this occasion.

I.   [L. 149]

The greatness and misery of man are so visible, that true religion must necessarily have taught us, that there are, inherently, in him, some mighty principle of greatness; and, at the same time, some mighty principle of misery; for true religion cannot but be perfectly acquainted with our nature; by which I mean, that it must know the utmost extent of its greatness and misery, and the reason of both: to true religion we also must address our selves, in order to account for the astonishing contrarieties which are found on that occasion.

This way of reasoning seems false and dangerous; for the fable of *Prometheus* and *Pandora*; the *Androgyni* of *Plato*, and the tenets of the people of *Siam*, &c. would account as well for these apparent contrarieties. The Christian religion would remain true, tho' no person should draw those ingenious conclusions from it, which can have no other effect than to shew the shining imagination of those who form them.

The sole view of the Christian religion, is to teach simplicity, humility and charity. Any one who should attempt to treat metaphysically of it, would only make it a source of numberless errors.

II. [L. 149]

Let any person examine on these heads the several religions in the world, and see whether any of them, except the Christian religion, satisfies the mind in such an enquiry. Will it be that taught by the philosophers, who propose to us, as the only good, the good inherent in our selves? But is this true good? Will this be found a remedy to our evils? Will the equalling man to the Deity cure the former of his presumption? On the other hand, have those who put us on a level with brutes, and confin'd all our blessings to those which the earth dispenses, thereby discover'd a true remedy for our lusts?

The philosophers never taught a religion, and their philosophy was not the subject to be combatted. No philosopher ever pretended to be inspir'd by the Almighty; for had he done this, he would no longer have acted in the character of a philosopher, but in that of a prophet. The question is not to enquire whether Jesus Christ ought to be preferr'd to *Aristotle*; but to prove that the religion of the former is the true one; and that those of *Mohammed*, of the heathens, and every other in the world, are false.

III. [L. 131]

And nevertheless, without this mystery, which of all others is the most incomprehensible, we are incomprehensible to ourselves. The intricacies of our condition are all conceal'd in the abyss of original sin; insomuch that man is more incomprehensible without this mystery, than this mystery is incomprehensible to man.

Can we call it reasoning to say, *That man would be incomprehensible, were it not for that incomprehensible mystery?* Why shou'd we go farther than the Scriptures? Does it not argue rashness to imagine, that they stand in need of a support, or can receive any from these philosophical ideas?

What answer would *Paschal* have made to one who should have spoke thus: I know, that the mystery of original sin is the object of faith, not of reason. I very well conceive what man is, without discovering any thing mysterious on that occasion. I perceive, that he comes into the world like other animals; that women of the most delicate constitutions have the hardest labours; that women, and the females among brutes, sometimes lose their lives on those occasions; that, sometimes, the construction of the organs of certain children is so disorder'd, that they pass their lives deprived of one or two senses, and without the enjoyment of the rational faculties; that those whose passions are most lively, are found to have the best constructed organs; that the principle of self-love is equally predominant in all men, and that they stand in no less need of 'em, than of the five senses; that God inspired us with this principle of self-love, for the preservation of our being; and gave us religion, to govern this self-love; that our ideas are just or inconsistent, dark or clear, according to the strength or weakness of our organs, or in proportion to our prejudices; that we depend entirely on the air which surrounds us, and the food we eat; and that there is nothing inconsistent or contradictory in all this.

Man is not an ænigma, as you figure him to yourself to be, merely to have the pleasure of unriddling it. Man seems to have his due place in the scale of beings; superior to brutes, whom he resembles, with regard to the organs; but inferior to other beings, to whom he very possibly may bear a resemblance, with respect to thought. Man is like every thing we see round us, a composition in which good and evil, pleasures and pains are found. He is inform'd with passions to rouze him to act; and indued with reason, to be as the director of his actions. If man was perfect, he would be God; and those contrarieties, which you call contradictions, are so many necessary ingredients to the composition of man, who is just what he ought to be.

IV. [L. 149]

Let us follow our own impulses, turn our eyes inward, and see whether we do not therein find the living characteristicks of those two natures.

*Is it possible for so great a number of contradictions to be found
united in one and the same subject? This duplicity in us is so
evident, that some have thence been induc'd to think, that men are
inform'd with two souls; those imagining it impossible for one
single subject, to exhibit such strange and sudden varieties: To
swell, one instant, with pride and self-conceit; and, the next, to sink
and tremble in all the horrors of a desponding condition.*

The diversity which is found in our wills, is not so many contradictions in nature, and man is not a single subject. He consists of a
numberless multitude of organs. If only one of these be ever so
little out of order, it must necessarily change all the impressions
made on the brain; and the animal must be inform'd with new
thoughts, and a new will. 'Tis very certain, that we are sometimes
dejected with sorrow, and at others, elated with pride; and this
must necessarily be the case, when we are in opposite situations.
An animal who is fed and fondled by his master, and another who
is put anatomically to a lingring death, feel very different sensations. 'Tis the same with regard to us; and that difference which is
found in man is so far from being contradictory, that it would be
contradictory for it not to be found. Those madmen who declar'd,
that we are inform'd with two souls, might, by a parity of reasoning, have ascrib'd to us thirty or forty; for that man, whose spirits
are strongly agitated, has, sometimes, thirty or forty ideas of the
same thing; and must necessarily be inform'd with such ideas,
according to the different faces under which that object appears to
him.

This pretended duplicity, in man, is an idea equally absurd and
metaphysical. 'Twou'd be equally just to assert, that the dog who
bites and fawns is double; that the hen who, for some time, takes
care of her chickens, and afterwards abandons them, is double; that
the mirrour, which represents different objects, is double; and that
the tree, which, at one time, is tufted with leaves, and, at another,
quite naked, is also double. I own indeed, that man is incomprehensible; but the whole compass of nature is so; and we do not find
a greater number of apparent contradictions in man, than in the
rest of the creation.

V.   [L. 418]

*The not laying a wager that God exists, is laying that he does not
exist. Which side will you take? Let us weigh the loss and gain, in
believing that God exists. If you win, you win all; if you lose, you
lose nothing: Lay therefore, without the least hesitation, that he*

exists. Yes, I must lay; but I possibly hazard too great a stake. Let us see: since there is an equal chance whether you win or lose, if you were to stake one life against two, you surely might venture the wager.

'Tis evidently false to assert, that, *The not laying a wager that God exists, is laying that he does not exist:* For certainly that man whose mind is in a state *of doubt, and is desirous of information*, does not lay on either side.

Besides, this article is somewhat indecent and childish. The idea of gaming, of losing or winning, is quite unsuitable to the dignity of the subject.

Farther, the interest I have to believe a thing, is no proof that such a thing exists. If you should say to me, I will give you the empire of the world, in case you will believe that I am in the right, I wish very sincerely, when such an offer is made me, that you are in the right: but I cannot believe this, till you have prov'd it to me. The first step you shou'd take (might it be objected to Mr. *Paschal*) wou'd be, to convince my reason. 'Tis doubtless my interest to believe that there is a God: but if, according to your system, God came but for so very few; if the number of the elect is so small, that we shudder at the bare reflection; and if I am unable, from my own impulse, to do any thing; be so good as to tell me what interest I can have in believing you? Is it not visibly my interest to believe the direct contrary? With what face can you talk to me of infinite bliss, to which scarce one man, among a million, has the least claim? If you are desirous of convincing me, take a different course; and don't one moment din my ears with gaming, staking, heads or tails; and, at another, terrify me by scattering thorns up and down the path which I ought, and am determined to tread. Your reasoning would only lead men to atheism, did not the voice of all nature proclaim the existence of a God, in a manner as forcible as those subtilties are weak.

VI.   [L. 573]

When I reflect on the blindness and misery of man, and the aston-ishing contrarieties which are seen in his nature: and when I behold the whole universe dumb; and man unenlightned, left to himself, and wandring, as it were, in this nook of the universe, without knowing who plac'd him there; the things he is come to do, and what will become of him after death: I step back, struck with horror, like a man who, when asleep, having been carried into a frightful, desert island, shou'd awake, not knowing where he is, nor how to get out of this island. Hence I wonder that mankind are not seiz'd with despair, every time they reflect on the wretchedness of their condition.

Whilst I was perusing this reflection, I receiv'd a letter from a friend who lives in a far distant country. His words are as follow.

'I am at this time exactly as when you left me; neither gayer nor more dejected, neither richer nor poorer; I enjoy perfect health, and am blest with all things that make life agreeable; undisturb'd by love, by avarice, by ambition, or by envy; and will venture to call my self, so long as these things last, a very happy man.'

A great many men are no less happy than my correspondent. 'Tis with man as with brutes. Here a dog shall eat and lie with his mistress; there, another plays the turn-spit, and is equally happy; a third runs mad, and is knock'd on the head. With regard to my self, when I take a view of *London* or *Paris*, I see no cause to plunge into the despair mention'd by Mr. *Paschal*. I see a city which does not resemble, in any manner, a desert island; but on the contrary, a populous, rich, and well govern'd place, where mankind are as happy as it is consistent with their nature to be. What man in his senses would attempt to hang himself, because he does not know in what manner God is seen face to face, nor is able to unravel the mystery of the Trinity? He might as justly sink with despair because he has not four feet and a pair of wings. Why should endeavours be us'd to make us reflect on our Being with horror? Our existence is not so wretched as some persons would make us believe it to be. To consider the universe as a dungeon, and all mankind as so many criminals carrying to execution, is the idea of a madman: to suppose the world to be a scene of delight, where nothing but pleasures are found, is the dream of a Sybarite; but to conclude that the earth, that mankind, and the brutes are just what they ought to be, is, in my opinion, thinking like a wise man.

VII. [L. 454]

The Jews *imagine, that God will not for ever leave other nations involv'd in this darkness; that a saviour or deliverer for all mankind, will come; that they are sent into the world to proclaim it; that they were created purposely to be the heralds of that mighty event; and to call upon all nations to unite with them, in expecting such a redeemer.*

The *Jews* have always been in expectation of a redeemer; but then 'tis a redeemer with regard to them, not for us; they expect a Messias who will bring the Christians in subjection to the *Jews*; whereas we expect the Messias will one day unite the *Jews* with the Christians. Their notions on this head are directly opposite to those entertain'd by us.

VIII.   [L. 451]

The law by which this people is govern'd, is, in all respects, the most ancient law in the world; the most perfect, and the only one which has ever been observ'd in a society or state, without any interruption. This Philo Judæus *shews in several places, as* Josephus *does admirably well against* Appion, *wherein he proves its antiquity to be so very remote, that even the word law was not known, in the most ancient governments, till above a thousand years afterwards; so that* Homer, *who speaks of so many nations, has never once mentioned the word. We may easily judge of the perfection of this law from the bare perusal of it, it appearing, that all things are there attended to, with so much wisdom, equity, and judgment, that the most ancient* Greek *and* Roman *legislators having some knowledge of the system in question, borrow'd their principal laws from it; as appears from the laws of the twelve tables, and from the other evidences exhibited by* Josephus *on that occasion.*

The asserting that the *Jewish* law justly boasts the greatest antiquity, is an absolute falshood, since the *Jews* before the time of *Moses* their lawgiver, liv'd in *Egypt*, a country the most renowned of any in the universe for its wise laws.

The other assertion is equally false, *viz.* that the word law was not known till after *Homer*, this poet mentioning the laws of *Minos*; and the word law is likewise found in *Hesiod*. And tho' the word law had not been specified even in *Hesiod* or *Homer*, that would be nothing to the purpose. There were kings and judges; consequently there were laws.

'Tis equally false when he affirms, that the *Greeks* and *Romans* borrow'd some laws from the *Jews*. This cou'd not be in the infancy of the *Roman* commonwealth, it not being possible for them to be then acquainted with the *Jews*; nor cou'd it be during its flourishing state, they, at that time, having those *Barbarians* in the utmost contempt; a circumstance known to the whole world.

IX.   [L. 452, L. 492]

The sincerity of this people is also wonderful. They preserve,
with the utmost affection and fidelity, the book wherein Moses
declares to them that they have always behav'd ungratefully
towards God, and that he knows they will be still more ungrateful
after his death; but that he appeals to heaven and earth, whether he
had not reproach'd them sufficiently for it: Finally, that God
incens'd at their transgressions, will disperse and scatter them
among all nations: That, as they had provok'd him to jealousy, by
serving gods which are no gods, he also will provoke them, by
calling a people who were not his people. Nevertheless the Jews
preserve at the hazard of their lives, this book, which reflects so
much dishonour on them in every respect; an instance of sincerity
that is not to be parallel'd; nor can its root be in nature.

Instances of this sincerity are met with every where, and the root
of it springs wholly from its nature. The pride of every individual
among the *Jews* prompts him to believe, that he does not owe his
ruin to his detestable politicks, his ignorance of the polite arts, and
his rusticity; but that the wrath of God punishes him. He finds
a pleasure in reflecting that it was necessary, before he cou'd
be humbled, to have recourse to miracles; and that those of his
persuasion, tho' punish'd by the Almighty, are yet his darling
people.

Shou'd a preacher go up into the pulpit, and address the *French*
in manner following: *you are a parcel of cowardly, ignorant fel-*
lows, and were beat at Hochstet *and* Ramillies, *merely because you*
did not know how to make a proper defence: the preacher, I say,
wou'd get his brains knock'd out. But shou'd he speak thus: 'You
are Catholicks, and for that reason belov'd by heaven. The enor-
mity of your sins had drawn down upon you the wrath of God,
who therefore gave you up to the hereticks at *Hochstet* and
Ramillies; but when you turned to the Lord, he gave his benedic-
tion to your courage at *Denain*.' Such a speech as this wou'd win
him the affection of his auditors.

X.   [L. 618]

If there is a God, he only must be lov'd, and not the creatures.

It is incumbent on man to love, and that with the utmost tenderness, the creatures: it is incumbent on him to love his country, his

wife, and his children; and this love is so inherent that the Almighty forces a man, spite of himself, to love them. To argue upon contrary principles wou'd be a barbarous way of reasoning.

XI. [L. 421]

We are born unjust, every man considering only to gratify himself, a circumstance which clashes with order in general. Man shou'd direct his views to the general good; self-tendency being the source of all the disorders which arise in war, polity, oeconomy, &c.

This is agreeable to order in general. It wou'd be as impossible for a society to be founded and support it self, without the principle of self-love, as for a person to attempt to get children when unenflam'd by lust; or to support his body by food, at a time that he has no appetite. 'Tis the self-love which is innate in us that aids the love of others; 'tis by our mutual wants that we are useful to the rest of mankind: 'Tis the foundation of all commerce; 'tis the bond which unites men eternally to each other. Had it not been for self-love, not a single art wou'd have been invented; nor a society even of ten persons, founded. This self-love with which nature has inspir'd every animal, makes him pay a regard to that of others. The law directs this principle, and religion refines it. The Almighty indeed might, if he had thought proper, have formed creatures whose only object shou'd be the good of others. Had this been the case, merchants would have traded to the *Indies* merely from a principle of love; and the mason wou'd have saw'd stone, with no other view but to serve his neighbour. But God has settled things upon another foot; for which reason we ought not to accuse the instinct he has giv'n us, but apply it to the several uses for which it is assign'd by him.

XII. [L. 502]

The hidden sense of the prophecies cou'd not lead men into error; and none but a people whose heart was so entirely carnal, cou'd have mistook the sense of them.

For when an abundance of blessings were promised, cou'd any thing but their lusts which applied them to the good things of this world, have prevented their interpreting them as meant of true and solid blessings?

Would it have been possible for the most sagacious people that ever liv'd to have understood them otherwise? They were slaves to the *Romans*; they expected a redeemer by whose aid they shou'd be victorious; and who would make *Jerusalem* formidable throughout the world. How was it possible for them to see with the eye of reason, that conqueror and that monarch in Christ, whom they beheld with their bodily eyes poor and crucified? How cou'd they understand, by the name of their chief city, a heavenly *Jerusalem*, since the immortality of the soul is not once mention'd in the decalogue? How cou'd a people, who adhered so scrupulously to their law, discover (unless enlightned from above) in the prophecies which were not their law, a God conceal'd beneath the form of a circumcis'd *Jew*, whose new religion, has destroyed and set in the most detestable light, circumcision and the sabbath, the sacred foundations on which the *Jewish* law is built? Had *Paschal* been born a *Jew*, he would have fallen into the same mistakes. Once again, let us worship God without attempting to pierce thro' the veil which hides his mysteries from us.

XIII.　　　　　　　[L. 261]

The time of Christ's first coming is foretold, but that of his second coming is not, and for this reason, because the first was to be private; but the second must be so open and conspicuous that even his enemies will be forc'd to acknowledge him.

The time of Christ's second coming was foretold in a still clearer manner than the first: In all probability it slipt Mr. *Paschal's* memory, that Christ in chap. xxi. of St. *Luke*, declares expressly thus.

'And when we shall see *Jerusalem* encompassed with armies, then know that the desolation thereof is nigh. – And there shall be signs in the sun, and in the moon, and in the stars; and upon the earth distress of nations, with perplexity, the sea and the waves roaring. For the powers of heaven will be shaken. – And then shall they see the son of man coming in a cloud with power and great glory.'

Have not we here a clear prophecy with regard to Christ's second coming? but if this be an event that is yet to come, it would argue great presumption in us to enquire of providence concerning it.

XIV.   [L. 287]

The Messias in the opinion of the carnal Jews, will be a powerful temporal prince; whereas the carnal Christians think he is come to exempt us from loving God, and to give us sacraments which, without our concurrence, shall operate all-powerfully upon us: but neither of these is the Christian or Jewish religion.

This article is rather a satyrical fling, than a Christian reflection. 'Tis plain that the *Jesuits* are level'd at here. But was any *Jesuit* ever known to assert, that Christ came into the world *to exempt us from loving God?* The controversy concerning loving God is a mere contest about words, like most of these scientifical quarrels whence such strong animosities, such fatal calamities, have sprung. There is another defect also in this article: I mean the author's supposing that the expectation of a Messias was considered by the *Jews* as an article of their religion, whereas it was only a consolatory reflection which prevail'd among them. The *Jews* hop'd a redeemer would come; but then they were not oblig'd to believe this, as an article of faith. Their whole religion was compriz'd in the book of the law; and the prophets were never consider'd by them as Lawgivers.

XV.   [L. 274]

In order for a due examination of the prophets we must understand them: for, if we believe they have but one meaning, 'tis certain the Messias is not yet come; but, if they have two meanings, he certainly came in Christ Jesus.

The Christian religion is so true, that it does not want the aid of doubtful proofs or evidences: but if any circumstance is capable of shaking the foundations of that holy, that rational religion, 'tis this opinion of Mr. *Paschal.* He asserts that ev'ry part of scripture bears a double meaning: but a person who should be so unhappy as to be an unbeliever, might speak thus to him: any man who delivers himself in such terms, that his words may bear a double interpretation, intends to impose upon mankind; and this double-dealing is always punish'd by the laws. How can you therefore without blushing admit those very things in God, for which mankind are detested and punished. Nay, in how contemptible a light do you consider, with what indignation do you treat, the oracles of the heathens, because they were always susceptible of a double interpretation? Might not we rather assert, that such prophecies, which relate directly to Christ, have but one meaning, like that of *Daniel*, of *Micah*, &c.? And could it not even be said, that the truth of religion would be proved, tho' we had never heard of the prophecies?

XVI.   [L. 308]

The infinite distance between the body and spirit points out the infinitely more infinite distance between spirit and love; this being supernatural.

We may reasonably suppose Mr. *Paschal* would never have introduc'd such wild stuff into his work, had he allow'd himself sufficient time for the composing it.

XVII.   [L. 236]

Such particulars as are most apparently weak, are found very strong by those who consider things in their proper light: for instance, the two genealogies given by St. Matthew *and St.* Luke. *'Tis manifest this was not done by confederacy.*

The editors of *Paschal*'s thoughts ought to have suppress'd this reflection, the bare explication of which would, perhaps, be of prejudice to religion. Of what use is it to declare that those genealogies, those fundamental points of religion, clash with one another, unless a method be pointed out to reconcile them? An antidote should have been administred at the same time with the poison. What an idea should we form to ourselves of a lawyer who was to say, my client contradicts himself? but these apparent weaknesses will be found of great strength, by those who view things in their proper light.

XVIII.   [L. 439]

Let no one, therefore, reproach us with want of light, since we ourselves declare this professedly; but let them acknowledge the truth of religion even in the gloom and obscurity of it; in the very little light we have in it; and in the indifference which we shew with regard to gaining light into it.

What odd characteristics of truth are here brought us by *Paschal*? Which then are the characteristics of falshood? How! wou'd it be enough for a man, who was desirous of being believed, to say, *I am*

obscure, I am unintelligible? 'Twould shew much more judgment
to present nothing but the light of faith to the eye, rather than such
abstruse touches of erudition.

XIX.   [L. 242]

If there was but one religion, the Almighty would be too manifest.

How! you say that if there was but one religion the Almighty
would be too manifest. You surely forget that you tell us, in every
page, that the time will come when there will be but one religion. According to your reasoning, the Almighty will then be too
manifest.

XX.   [L. 453]

*I affirm that the Jewish religion did not consist in any of these
things, but only in the love of God; and that God rejected and
condemn'd all other things.*

How! did God reject and condemn all those things, the performance of which he himself had so strictly, and so minutely, enjoined
the *Jews?* Is it not more just to assert, that the law of *Moses*
consisted in love and in worship? The reducing all things to the
love of God argues much less a love for God, than the hatred
which every *Jansenist* bears to his neighbour *Molinist.*

XXI.   [L. 634]

*The most important action in life, is the choice of a trade, and yet
chance determines on this occasion. 'Tis custom makes soldiers,
bricklayers, and such like.*

What is it should determine soldiers, bricklayers, and mechanics in
general, but the things we call chance or custom? 'Tis only with
respect to arts of genius that persons find a self-impulse; but as to
those trades or professions which all men are capable of exercising,
'tis extremely just and natural that custom should determine on
those occasions.

XXII.   [L. 47]

*Every man who examines his own thoughts will find they are
always busied in things past, and in those to come. We scarce ever*

reflect on the present; and if we ever do reflect on it, 'tis with no other design than to borrow lights from it, in order for our disposal of futurity. The present is never our aim: past and present are our means: futurity only is our object.

'Tis our duty, so far from complaining, to thank the author of nature, for informing us with that instinct which is for ever directing us to futurity. The most valuable treasure possess'd by man, is that hope which softens our cares; and which, whilst we are enjoying present pleasures, paints future ones in the imagination. If mankind were so unhappy as to employ their minds only on the time present, no person would sow, build, plant, or make the least provision in any respect; but would be in want of all things in the midst of this false enjoyment. Was it possible for so elevated a genius as Mr. *Paschal* to insist on the truth of so false a proposition? Nature has settled things on such a foot, that every man should enjoy the present, by supporting himself with food, by getting children, by listning to agreeable sounds, by employing his faculty of thinking and feeling; and that, at the instant of his quitting these several conditions, and even in the midst of them, he should reflect on the morrow, without which he would die for want to day.

XXIII. [L. 136]

But, examining this more attentively, I found that the total disregard of mankind with respect to the procuring themselves repose and tranquillity, and to the living inwardly, abstracted as it were from the world, springs from a cause which is but too real; I mean, from the natural infelicity of our weak, our mortal condition, which is so very wretched, that nothing is able to comfort us, at the time that we are not prevented by any thing from reflecting on it, and that we behold nothing but our selves.

This expression, *we behold nothing but our selves*, does not present any thing intelligible to the mind.

What would that man be, who should continue in a state of inactivity, and is supposed to contemplate himself? I affirm that this person would not only be a simpleton, quite useless to society; but I affirm that such a man cannot exist; for what should the man in question contemplate? His body, his feet, his hands, his five senses? He either must be an idiot, or he would make a proper use of these. Would there still remain his faculty of thinking for him to contemplate? But he cannot contemplate that faculty without exercising it. He either will think on nothing; will think on those ideas which are already present to his imagination, or form new ones: now, all his ideas must come from without. Thus is he necessarily employed, either about his senses, or about his ideas: consequently he, on this occasion, is either out of himself, or an idiot.

Once again, 'tis impossible for mankind to continue in that suppos'd lethargy; 'tis absurd to imagine it, and foolish to pretend to it. Man is born for action, as the fire tends upwards, and a stone downwards. Not to be employed, and not to exist, is one and the same thing with regard to man; the whole difference consists in his employments as they are either calm or tumultuous, dangerous or useful.

XXIV.   [L. 136]

Mankind are inform'd with a secret instinct, which prompts them to seek for diversion and employment from without, a circumstance arising from a sense they have of their perpetual misery; and they are inform'd with another instinct, arising from the greatness of their first nature, which teaches them that happiness is found no where but in repose.

As this secret instinct is the first principle, and the necessary foundation of society, it proceeds rather from the kindness of our Creator; and is an instrument of our felicity, rather than a sense of our misery. I know not how our first parents pass'd their time in the garden of *Eden*; but if each of them had made their own person the sole object of their respective thoughts, the propagation of mankind would have been extremely dubious. Is it not absurd to suppose, that they were indued with perfect senses, that is, with perfect instruments for action, merely that they might pass their whole lives in contemplation? And is it not whimsical, that thinking men should imagine that idleness ennobles, and that action degrades human nature?

XXV.   [L. 136]

When, therefore, Cineas told Pyrrhus (who propos'd to repose himself and enjoy his friends, after he shou'd have conquer'd a great part of the world) that he had better promote his own felicity, by enjoying that repose at the time they were speaking, rather than undergo such a series of fatigues in order for the obtaining it; it would, (I say) have been extremely difficult for Pyrrhus *to put this advice in execution; nor was it much more just and rational than the design of this ambitious youth. They both took it for granted, that it was possible for man to draw contentment solely from himself and from his present blessings, without filling the void of his heart with imaginary hopes, which is false; for* Pyrrhus *could not be happy, neither before nor after he had conquer'd the world.*

The example of *Cineas* does very well in *Boileau*'s satyrs, but not in a philosophical treatise; a wise king may be happy at home; and the exhibiting *Pyrrhus* as a madman, has nothing to do with the rest of mankind.

XXVI.   [L. 136]

We therefore ought to own, that man is so very unhappy, that he would grow tir'd with himself, without any foreign cause to make him so, merely from the state of his condition.

On the contrary, man is so happy in this particular; and we are so greatly obliged to the author of nature, that he has made uneasiness inseparable from inactivity, in order to force us, by that means, to be useful both to our neighbour and ourselves.

XXVII.   [L. 136]

How comes it to pass that this man, who lately lost his only son; and who, being involved in the most vexatious law-suits, was this morning almost in a despairing condition, seems now perfectly easy? You must not wonder at it. His eye is, at present, wholly employ'd in examining which way it will be possible for a stag, whom his hounds have been closely pursuing these six hours, to escape. Man, tho' ever so much oppress'd with grief, if we can but prevail upon him to engage in some diversion, is happy during that time.

Such a man acts very wisely, diversions being a more infallible remedy against grief, than the *Jesuit*'s bark in fevers. Let us not censure nature for this, who is ever at hand to indulge us any assistance.

XXVIII. [L. 434]

Let us figure to ourselves a considerable number of men bound in chains, and all sentenc'd to die; some of whom being daily executed in presence of the rest, those who survive see their own condition in that of their fellow prisoners; and gazing one upon another sorrowfully, and lost to all hopes, expect their turn to be next. This is an image of the condition of mankind.

This comparison is certainly false. A parcel of wretches bound in chains, who are executed one after another, are unhappy, not only because they suffer, but also because they feel what other men do not. The natural condition of man is not to be either chain'd or murther'd; but all men, like animals and plants, are sent into the world to grow, and live a certain period; to beget their like, and die. Satyrists may, as often as they please, exhibit man in his worst light; but if ever so little use be made of our reason, we shall own that, of all animals man is the most perfect, the happiest, and longest lived.

Instead therefore of wondring at, and complaining of the infelicity and shortness of life; we ought, on the contrary, to wonder that our happiness should be so great, and of so long duration, and congratulate our selves on that account. To reason only philosophically, I will venture to observe, that that man discovers great pride and temerity, who asserts that we ought, from our nature, to be in a better condition than we really are.

XXIX. [L. 449]

The sages among the heathens who declar'd that there is but one God, were persecuted; the Jews were hated, and the Christians still more so.

They were sometimes persecuted just as a man would be, who, in this age, should teach the worship of one God, independently from the establish'd worship. *Socrates* was not condemn'd for saying, *there is but one God*, but for inveighing against the outward worship of his country; and for stirring up against himself, and that very unseasonably, a set of powerful enemies. With regard to the *Jews*, they were hated, not because they believed only in one God, but because they bore a ridiculous hatred to other nations; because they were a set of barbarians, who cruelly butcher'd their conquer'd enemies; and because this grovelling, this superstitious, and ignorant people, who were utter strangers to the polite arts and trades, had a contempt for the most civiliz'd and refin'd nations. As to the Christians, the heathens bore an aversion to them, because they endeavour'd to destroy their religion and government, in which they succeeded at last; in like manner as the protestants have got possession of those very countries, where during many years they were persecuted and butcher'd.

XXX. [L. 680]

There are great faults in Montagne. *He is fill'd with obscene words. This is quite bad. His notions, with regard to self-murder, are horrible.*

Montagne speaks in quality of a Philosopher, not as a Christian. He gives us the arguments *pro* and *con* with respect to suicide. To speak philosophically, what injury does that man do to society, who quits it when he can be of no longer service to it? An ancient man has got the stone, and is in inexpressible torture. His friends tell him, if you don't get yourself cut, you'll die soon; but if you undergo the operation, you may doat and slaver on a year longer, a heavy burthen to yourself, and to all about you. I'll suppose, that the tortur'd creature, on hearing this, takes the resolution not to be any longer troublesom to any one. This is pretty nearly the case exhibited by *Montagne*.

XXXI. [L. 782]

How many stars have been discover'd by telescopes, which were hid from the philosophers of former ages? The scriptures were boldly impeach'd concerning what is there said, in so many places, with regard to the vast number of stars. We know, say those, that there are 1022.

'Tis certain, that the sacred writers, in matters relating to physics, always adapted themselves to the receiv'd notions. Thus they suppose the earth to be immovable, the sun to travel, &c. 'Tis not, in any manner, from astronomical refinement, that they assert the stars to be numberless; but merely to suit themselves to vulgar capacities. And indeed, tho' our sight discovers but 1022 stars, or thereabouts; nevertheless, when we look attentively on the sky, the dazzled eye imagines it then sees a numberless multitude. The sacred authors therefore express themselves agreeably to this vulgar notion; their compositions not being left to mankind, in the design of making them naturalists. And 'tis highly probable, that God did not reveal to *Habakkuk*, to *Baruch*, or to *Micah*, that an *Englishman*, nam'd *Flamstead*, wou'd, one day, insert in his catalogue upwards of 7000 stars, discover'd by the assistance of telescopes.

XXXII. [L. 81]

Can we call it courage in a dying man, to defy, in his weakness and agony, a God omnipotent and eternal?

Such a case never happen'd; and no one but a creature out of his senses, and quite raving, could say, *I believe in God*, and *defy him*.

XXXIII. [L. 822]

I willingly credit those histories, the witnesses to which let themselves be cut to pieces.

The difficulty is not only to know, whether we ought to give credit to witnesses, who die in defence of their testimony, as so many enthusiasts have done; but likewise, whether such witnesses really lost their lives on that account; whether their testimony has been transmitted to us; whether they lived in the countries where 'tis related they died. How comes it to pass, that *Josephus*, who was born at the time of Christ's death; *Josephus*, who hated *Herod*; *Josephus*, who was but faintly attach'd to the *Jewish* principles, does not once mention any of these particulars? This is what Mr. *Paschal* would have unravell'd with success, as so many eloquent writers have done, since his death.

XXXIV. [L. 83]

There are two extremes in the sciences, which are contiguous: The first is, the natural ignorance in which all men are born. The other extreme is, that to which great souls attain, who, after having acquir'd all that it is possible for man to know, find they know nothing; and meet in that very point of ignorance whence they set out.

This is mere sophistry; and its falsity consists in the word *ignorance*, which is taken in two different senses. One who can neither read nor write, is an ignorant person; but a mathematician, tho' he be unacquainted with the occult principles of nature, is not so ignorant, as when he first began to learn to read. Though Sir *Isaac Newton* was not able to give the reason why a man can move his arm at pleasure, this did not make him less knowing in other particulars. A person, who is ignorant of the *Hebrew* language, but skilled in the *Latin* is learned, in comparison of another, who understands no tongue but his own.

XXXV. [L. 132]

A man cannot be call'd happy, because diversions are capable of giving him pleasure; diversions coming from without, and therefore are dependent; and consequently, they may be disturb'd by a thousand accidents, which form so many unavoidable afflictions.

That man is actually happy, who enjoys pleasure; and this pleasure can arise no otherwise than from without. All our sensations, and ideas, can result only from outward objects; in like manner as we can nourish our bodies no otherwise than by taking in foreign substances, in order for their being chang'd into our own.

XXXVI. [L. 518]

The extremes of genius are said to border upon folly, no less than the extremes of imperfection. Mediocrity only is consider's as good.

'Tis not the extremes of genius, but the extreme vivacity and volubility of genius, which are said to border upon folly; the extremes of genius, are extreme justness, extreme delicacy, extreme extent, which are diametrically opposite to folly.

An extreme *defect of genius*, is the want of conception, an absolute vacuity with regard to ideas; 'tis not folly but stupidity. Folly is a disorder in the organs, which makes us perceive several objects too quick; fixes the imagination on a single one, with too great intenseness and violence. Neither is it mediocrity that is consider'd as good; but 'tis the keeping clear of the two opposite vices; 'tis what we call a just medium, not mediocrity.

XXXVII. [L. 889]

If our condition was truly happy, it would not be proper to divert us from thinking on it.

The direct state of our condition is, to reflect on those outward objects to which we bear a necessary relation. 'Tis false to say, that it is possible for a man to be diverted from thinking on the condition of human nature; for to what object soever he applies his thoughts, he applies them to something which is necessarily united to human nature; and, once again, for a man to reflect or think on himself, abstractedly from natural things, is to think on nothing; I say, on nothing at all, a circumstance of which I desire the reader to take notice.

People, so far from preventing a man from thinking on his condition, are ever entertaining him with the pleasures of it. With a scholar, fame and erudition are made the topicks of conversation; and, with a prince, matters relating to his grandeur. Pleasure is the subject with which all persons are entertain'd.

XXXVIII. [L. 705]

The same accidents, the same uneasinesses, and passions, are found in persons of the most exalted condition, and in those of the lowest: But some are at the top of the wheel, and others near the centre; consequently the latter are less agitated by the same motion.

'Tis false to assert, that those in a low condition are less agitated than such as are in exalted stations; on the contrary, their grief is more poignant, as they can have less relief. Of an hundred persons who lay violent hands on themselves in *London*, ninety are mean persons, and scarce one of high rank. The comparison of the wheel is ingenious, but false.

XXXIX. [L. 778]

Mankind are not taught to be honest, tho' they are taught every thing else; and yet there is nothing in which they pride themselves so much, as in honesty. Thus it appears, that the only particular they boast a knowledge in, is the very thing which they are not taught.

Persons are taught how to become honest men, otherwise few would be so. Should a father permit his child, during his infancy, to pocket every thing that came in his way; at fifteen, he'd take up a pistol and go upon the road. Should he be prais'd for telling a lye, he'd turn out a knight of the post; and was he to be pamper'd in lust, he'd certainly become an errant debauchee. Mankind are taught all things; virtue, religion.

XL. [L. 780]

How stupid was it in Montagne, *to draw his own picture; and this, not occasionally, and in opposition to his own maxims, as every one will fail in doing; but agreeably to his own maxims, and as his first and principal object: for, to vent trifles merely by chance, and thro' frailty, is a common evil; but to vent them designedly, and such as those in question, is intolerable.*

How delightful a design was that of *Montagne*, in drawing so natural a picture of himself! For mankind was the original he copied; and how trifling was it in *Nicole, Mallebranche*, and *Paschal*, to attempt to depretiate *Montagne*!

XLI. [L. 734]

When I consider'd, whence it should come to pass, that people give so much credit to such numbers of Quacks, who boast their being possessed of Nostrums, so as frequently to entrust their lives in their hands, I imagin'd that the true cause of this is, there being such things as true medicines in the world; for it wou'd be impossible that there should be so many spurious ones, or so much credit given to them, if there were none genuine. Had there never been any such, and that all diseases in general had been incurable, 'tis impossible mankind cou'd have imagin'd that there are any in nature; and still more, that so many multitudes of people should have given credit to those who boasted their being possessed of such medicines. Was a person to pretend, that he had got a secret which wou'd preserve people from the grave, no one would believe him, because there have been no examples of this. But as a great number of medicines have been found genuine, from the experience of the greatest men, this circumstance won the belief of mankind. For, as the thing could not be denied in general, because some particular effects have been found true; the vulgar, who are not able to find out, among these particular effects, which are the true ones, therefore give credit to them all. In like manner, the reason why so many false effects of the Moon are believed, is, because there are some true ones, such as the ebbing and flowing of the sea.

Thus it appears to me as evidently, that the sole reason why there are so many false miracles, false revelations, and witchcrafts, is, because there are true ones.

In my opinion, mankind are not oblig'd, necessarily, in order for their crediting what is false, to be acquainted with what is true.

People ascrib'd a thousand false influences to the Moon, before the least true relation, to the ebbing and flowing of the sea, was thought on. The first man who found himself sick, easily gave credit to the first quack he met with. No one ever saw a hobgoblin, or wizard, and yet many believ'd there were such beings: No man was ever an eye-witness to the transmutation of metals, and yet many have been ruin'd by their believing what is call'd the Philosopher's stone. Did the *Greeks*, the *Romans*, and the *Heathens*, give credit to the false miracles, of which they had numberless multitudes, for no other reason, but because they had been spectators of true ones?

XLII. [L. 697]

The harbour is a rule to mariners; but where shall we find such a point in morality?

In the single maxim following, admitted by all nations: 'Do, as you would be done by.'

XLIII. [L. 29]

Ferox gens nullam esse vitam sine armis putat: *These prefer death to the living in peace, whilst others prefer death to war. Every opinion may be prefer'd to life, the love of which appears so strong and natural.*

This is spoke, by *Tacitus*, of the *Catalans*. But there is no people, of whom it has been, and may be, said, *They prefer death to war.*

XLIV. [L. 510]

The more genius and capacity a person has, he finds the greater number of persons who are originals in their way. The vulgar cannot perceive any difference between man and man.

Very few men can justly boast an original character; most squaring their conduct, their thinking and feeling, accordingly as they are influenc'd by education. Nothing is so uncommon as a genius who strikes out a new path for himself to walk in. But among the croud of men who travel on in company, each of them has some little difference in his gait, which is perceived by those only who have a piercing eye.

XLV.   [L. 511]

There therefore are two kinds of genius; the one, to penetrate, in a strong and lively manner, into consequences and principles, and this we call a just turn of thinking; the other, the comprehending a great number of principles without confounding them, and this we call a mind turn'd for geometry.

I am of opinion that we now give the name of a mind turn'd for geometry, to a man of a methodical and consequential turn of thinking.

XLVI.   [L. 138]

Death is more easy to be borne without reflecting on it, than the reflection on death when out of danger.

We cannot say that a man bears death easily or uneasily, when he does not reflect at all upon it. He who has no sensation, bears nothing.

XLVII.   [L. 109]

We imagine that all mankind have a like perception of those objects which present themselves to them, but this is a random conjecture, since we have no proof of it. I plainly find that the same words are applied on the same occasions; and that every time two men see, for instance, snow, they both express the sight of this same object by the same words, both saying that it is white; and, from this conformity with regard to the application, people draw a strong conjecture, with respect to the conformity of the idea; and yet this is not demonstration, tho' great odds might be laid in favour of the affirmative.

White, among the several colours, shou'd not have been brought as a proof on this occasion. White, which is an assemblage of all the rays in general, appears shining in the eye of every one; dazzles a little when gaz'd upon for some time; and has the same effect on all eyes: but we might say, that perhaps all eyes do not perceive colours in the same manner.

XLVIII.   [L. 530]

All our reasoning reduces it self to this, viz. its yielding to sensation.

Our reasoning must yield to sensation in matters of taste, not in those of erudition.

XLIX. [L. 534]

Such as judge of a work by rule, are, with respect to other men, like those who have a watch, in comparison of such as have none. One man shall say, we have been here these two hours: and another, we have been here but three quarters of an hour. I look on my watch, and say to the former, you are tir'd; and to the latter, you think the time very short.

In works of taste, in musick, poetry, and painting, taste serves as a watch; and that man who judges of them only by rule, judges wrong.

L. [L. 49]

Cæsar, in my opinion, was too old to set about the conquest of the world. This was an amusement that suited Alexander, *he being a young man whose impetuosity it was difficult to check: but* Julius Cæsar *shou'd have been more compos'd.*

'Tis vulgarly suppos'd, that *Alexander* and *Julius Cæsar* left their respective countries with a design to go and conquer the earth, but this is far from being the case. *Alexander* succeeded his father as Generalissimo of the united forces of *Greece*; and was appointed chief of the enterprize, which the *Greeks* form'd, to revenge the injurious treatment they had met with from the *Persian* monarch. He defeated the common enemy; and continu'd his conquests as far as *India*, because *Darius*'s kingdom extended so far; in like manner as the Duke of *Marlborough*, had he not been stopp'd by Marshal *Villars*, wou'd have march'd to *Lyons*.

With regard to *Julius Cæsar*, he was one of the chief personages of the *Roman* commonwealth. He quarrel'd with *Pompey* as the *Jansenists* do with the *Molinists*; on which occasion they endeavour'd to cut one anothers' throats. But a single battle, in which less than ten thousand men fell, decided their contest at once.

By the way, Mr. *Pascal*'s reflection may, possibly, be false in every respect. It was necessary, that *Julius Cæsar* shou'd have liv'd to the age he did, in order for him to get the better of all the intrigues which were form'd against him; and 'tis surprizing that

Alexander, when so young, shou'd have renounc'd pleasures, for the sake of engaging in so laborious and painful a war.

LI.   [L. 794]

'Tis whimsical enough to consider, that there shou'd be men in the world (thieves for instance,) who having bid defiance to all the laws of God and man, form to themselves a set of laws, to which they pay the most implicit obedience.

The reflecting on this is more useful than whimsical; it proving, that no society of men can subsist a single day without rules or laws.

LII.   [L. 678]

Man is neither an angel nor a brute: and the misfortune is, that he who attempts to act the angel, plays the brute.

The man who endeavours to destroy the passions, instead of regulating them, attempts to act the angel.

LIII.   [L. 685]

A horse does not endeavour to make himself admir'd by his companion. We indeed perceive those beasts fir'd with some kind of emulation, when running a race; but this is of no farther consequence, for when they are got together in the stable, that horse which is less agreeably shap'd than the other, will not, on that account, yield up his oats to him. But 'tis different with mankind: their virtue is not satisfied with itself; and they are not contented unless they can reap such a benefit from it as may be disadvantageous to others.

One man, because he is less handsome than another, will not give up his bread to him for that reason; but the stronger dispossesses the weaker of it. Among brutes and among men the strong prey upon the feeble.

LIV.   [L. 199]

If man was to begin by studying himself, he would find how difficult it is for him to proceed farther. How will it be possible for a part to know the whole? He perhaps will aspire to acquaint himself, at least, with those parts to which he himself bears a proportion. But all the parts of the world bear such a relation one to the other, and are so connected, that I am of opinion 'tis impossible to know one without the other, and without the whole.

It would not be proper to divert man from searching after those things which may be of advantage to him, from this reflection, that it is impossible for him to know all things.

> *Non possis oculo quantum contendere linceus;*
> *Non tamen idcircò contemnas lippus inungi.*
> HORAT. Epist. I. Lib. i.

That is,

> Yours cannot be as good as *Lynceus'* eyes:
> What then! when sore must I fit cures despise?
> CREECH.*

We are acquainted with a great number of truths, and have discover'd a multitude of useful inventions. Let us be easy, tho' we do not know the relation which may be between a spider and *Saturn*'s ring; and continue to examine those things which are within the sphere of our comprehension.

LV. [L. 765]

If thunder always fell on vallies, poets, and those who are able to reason only on things of this nature, would be at a loss for proofs.

A simile or comparison is no proof either in verse or prose. In poetry it serves as an embellishment; and in prose, it illustrates things, and makes them strike more sensibly upon us. Such poets as have compar'd the misfortunes of persons in exalted stations, to thunder breaking upon mountains, would draw quite opposite comparisons, if the contrary happen'd in nature.

LVI. [L. 199]

To this frame and composition of mind and body are owing, that most philosophers have confounded the ideas of things; and ascribed, to the body, things which relate only to the mind; and, to the mind, such as suit the body only.

If we knew what it is in which the mind consists, we then might justly complain of philosophers, for ascribing such things to it as are quite foreign; but we are not acquainted either with the mind or body. We have not the least idea of the one; and our ideas, with regard to the other, are vastly imperfect: consequently we are not able to settle their respective limits.

LVII.　　　　　　　　　　[L. 586]

As we say poetical beauty, we likewise ought to say geometrical and medicinal beauty; and yet we don't say so, the reason of which is, we know very well what is the object of geometry, and what is the object of physick; but we do not know what that is in which the charm or beauty consists, which is the object of poetry. We do not know what this natural model, which we ought to imitate, is; and, for want of this knowledge, certain odd terms have been invented, as golden age, miracle of our time, fatal laurel, beautiful star, &c. *and this jargon is called poetical beauty. But any man who shall figure to himself a woman dress'd after this model, will see a pretty maid quite cover'd with looking glasses, and in tinsel chains.*

This is absolutely false. We ought not to say geometrical beauty, nor medicinal beauty, because a theorem and a purge do not affect the senses in an agreeable manner; and because we give the name of beauty to those things only which charm the senses, as music, painting, eloquence, poetry, regular architecture, &c. The reason given by Mr. *Pascal* is equally false. We very well know what it is that forms the object of poetry. It consists in painting with strength, clearness, delicacy and harmony: Poetry is harmonious eloquence. Mr. *Paschal* must have had very little taste, to say that *fatal laurel, beautiful star*, and such like stuff, are poetical beauties: and the editors of his *Thoughts* must have been very little conversant in polite literature, otherwise they would not have printed a reflection so unworthy of its illustrious author.

I shall not send you the rest of my remarks on Mr. *Paschal*'s thoughts, as this would lead me into too tedious enquiries. 'Tis enough for me to have imagin'd that I discover'd several errors, arising from inattention, in so great a genius: and 'tis some consolation to one so much confin'd and limited as mine, to be firmly persuaded, that the greatest men fall into mistakes, as well as the vulgar.

APPENDIX B.

Extracts from Voltaire's *An Essay upon the Civil Wars of France and also upon the Epick Poetry of the European Nations from Homer down to Milton*

This volume, published in London in 1727, marks Voltaire's début as an English writer. The two essays were designed to prepare the way for the long-awaited publication the following year of *La Henriade*, but they also look forward to his next work in English, the *Letters concerning the English Nation*. It is clear from the 'Advertisement to the Reader' which prefaces the volume that Voltaire is planning a book about the English, and that already at this early stage he is distancing himself from established models of travel-writing about England. The second essay, on epic poetry, gives separate consideration to seven poets, and devotes the longest section of all to Milton. Voltaire's enthusiasm for a poet he can only recently have read in English (the first French translation of *Paradise Lost* appeared in 1729) anticipates the *Letters* (XVIII–XXII) on other English writers which Voltaire wrote soon after, also in English, and at a time when he was becoming increasingly prominent in London's literary world.

* * *

ADVERTISEMENT TO THE READER.

It has the Appearance of too great a Presumption in a Traveller, who hath been but eighteen Months in England *to attempt to write in a Language, which he cannot pronounce at all, and which he hardly understands in Conversation. But I have done what we do every Day at School, where we write* Latin *and* Greek, *tho' surely we pronounce them both very pitifully, and should understand neither of them if they were uttered to us with the right* Roman *or* Greek *Pronunciation.*

I look upon the English *Language as a learned one, which deserves to be the Object of our Application in* France, *as the* French *Tongue is thought a kind of Accomplishment in* England.

Besides, I did not learn English *for my Private Satisfaction and Improvement only, but out of a kind of Duty.*

I am ordered to give an Account of my Journey into England.
*Such an Undertaking can no more be attempted without under-
standing the Language, than a Scheme of Astronomy could be laid
without the help of Mathematicks. And I have not a Mind to
imitate the late Mr.* Sorbieres,* *who having staid three Months in
this Country without knowing any Thing, either of its Manners or
of its Language, thought fit to print a Relation which proved but a
dull scurrilous Satyr upon a Nation he knew nothing of.*

Our European *Travellers for the most Part are satyrical upon
their neighboring Countries, and bestow large Praises upon the*
Persians *and* Chineses; *it being too natural to revile those who
stand in Competition with us, and to extol those who being far
remote from us, are out of the reach of Envy.*

*The true Aim of a Relation is to instruct Men, not to gratify their
Malice. We should be busied chiefly in giving faithful Accounts of
all the useful Things and of the extraordinary Persons, whom to
know, and to imitate would be a Benefit to our Countrymen. A
Traveller who writes in that Spirit, is a Merchant of a nobler Kind,
who imports into his native Country the Arts and Virtues of other
Nations.*

I will leave to others the Care of describing with Accuracy, Paul's
Church, *the* Monument, Westminster, Stonehenge, *&c. I consider*
England *in another View; it strikes my Eyes as it is the Land which
hath produced a* Newton, *a* Locke, *a* Tillotson, *a* Milton, *a* Boyle,
*and many great Men either dead or alive, whose Glory in War, in
State-Affairs, or in Letters, will not be confined to the Bounds of
this Island.*

*Whosoever had the Honour and the Happiness to be acquainted
with any of them, and will do me the Favour to let me know some
notable (tho' perhaps not enough known) Passages of their Lives,
will confer an Obligation not only upon me, but upon the Publick.*

*Likewise if there are any new Inventions or Undertakings,
which have obtained or deserved Success, I shall be obliged to those
who will be so kind as to give me an Information of that Nature.
And shall either quote my Authors, or observe a religious Silence,
according as they think it proper.*

*As to this present Essay, it is intended as a kind of Preface or
Introduction to the* Henriade, *which is almost entirely printed,
nothing being wanting but the printing of the Cuts which I must
recommend here as particular Master-Pieces of Art in their Kind:
'tis the only Beauty in the Book, that I can answer for.*

*   *   *

MILTON.

Milton is the last in *Europe* who wrote an *Epick* Poem, for I wave all those whose Attempts have been unsuccessful, my Intention being not to descant on the many who have contended for the Prize, but to speak only of the very few who have gain'd it in their respective Countries.

Milton, as he was travelling through *Italy* in his Youth, saw at *Florence* a Comedy call'd *Adamo*, writ by one *Andreino* a Player, and dedicated to *Mary de Medicis* Queen of *France*. The Subject of the Play was the *Fall of Man*; the Actors, God, the Devils, the Angels, *Adam*, *Eve*, the Serpent, Death, and the Seven Mortal Sins. That Topick so improper for a Drama, but so suitable to the absurd Genius of the *Italian* Stage, (as it was at that Time) was handled in a Manner intirely conformable to the Extravagance of the Design. The Scene opens with a Chorus of Angels, and a Cherubim thus speaks for the Rest: 'Let the Rainbow be the Fiddlestick of the Fiddle of the Heavens, let the Planets be the Notes of our Musick, let Time beat carefully the Measure, and the Winds make the Sharps, &c.' Thus the Play begins, and every Scene rises above the last in Profusion of Impertinence.

Milton pierc'd through the Absurdity of that Performance to the hidden Majesty of the Subject, which being altogether unfit for the Stage, yet might be (for the Genius of *Milton*, and for his only) the Foundation of an *Epick* Poem.

He took from that ridiculous Trifle the first Hint of the noblest Work, which human Imagination hath ever attempted, and which he executed more than twenty Years after.

In the like Manner, *Pythagoras* ow'd the Invention of Musick to the Noise of the Hammer of a Blacksmith. And thus in our Days Sir *Isaak Newton* walking in his Gardens had the first Thought of his System of Gravitation, upon seeing an Apple falling from a Tree.*

If the Difference of Genius between Nation and Nation, ever appear'd in its full Light, 'tis in *Milton's* Paradise lost.

The *French* answer with a scornful Smile, when they are told there is in *England* an *Epick* Poem, the Subject whereof is the Devil fighting against God, and *Adam* and *Eve* eating an Apple at the Persuasion of a Snake. As that Topick hath afforded nothing among them, but some lively Lampoons, for which that Nation is so famous; they cannot imagine it possible to build an *Epick* Poem upon the subject of their Ballads. And indeed such an Error ought to be excused; for if we consider with what Freedom the politest

Part of Mankind throughout all *Europe*, both Catholicks and Protestants, are wont to ridicule in Conversation those consecrated Histories; nay, if those who have the highest Respect for the Mysteries of the Christian Religion, and who are struck with Awe at some Parts of it, yet cannot forbear now and then making free with the *Devil*, the *Serpent*, the Frailty of our first Parents, the Rib which *Adam* was robb'd of, and the like; it seems a very hard Task for a profane Poet to endeavour to remove those Shadows of Ridicule, to reconcile together what is Divine and what looks absurd, and to command a Respect that the sacred Writers could hardly obtain from our frivolous Minds.

What *Milton* so boldly undertook, he perform'd with a superior Strength of Judgement, and with an Imagination productive of Beauties not dream'd of before him. The Meaness (if there is any) of some Parts of the Subject is lost in the Immensity of the Poetical Invention. There is something above the reach of human Forces to have attempted the Creation without Bombast, to have describ'd the Gluttony and Curiosity of a Woman without Flatness, to have brought Probability and Reason amidst the Hurry of imaginary Things belonging to another World, and as far remote from the Limits of our Notions as they are from our Earth; in short to force the Reader to say, 'If God, if the Angels, if Satan would speak, I believe they would speak as they do in *Milton*.'

I have often admir'd how barren the Subject appears, and how fruitful it grows under his Hands.

The *Paradise Lost* is the only Poem wherein are to be found in a perfect Degree that Uniformity which satisfies the Mind and that Variety which pleases the Imagination. All its Episodes being necessary Lines which aim at the Centre of a perfect Circle. Where is the Nation who would not be pleas'd with the Interview of *Adam* and the *Angel*? With the Mountain of Vision, with the bold Strokes which make up the Relentless, undaunted, and sly Character of Satan? But above all with that sublime Wisdom which *Milton* exerts, whenever he dares to describe God, and to make him speak? He seems indeed to draw the Picture of the Almighty, as like as human Nature can reach to, through the mortal Dust in which we are clouded.

The *Heathens* always, the *Jews* often, and our Christian Priests sometimes, represent God as a Tyrant infinitely powerful. But the God of *Milton* is always a Creator, a Father, and a Judge, nor is his Vengeance jarring with his Mercy, nor his Predeterminations repugnant to the Liberty of Man. These are the Pictures which lift up indeed the Soul of the Reader. *Milton* in that Point as well as in many others is as far above the ancient Poets as the Christian Religion is above the *Heathen* Fables.

But he hath especially an indisputable Claim to the unanimous Admiration of Mankind, when he descends from those high Flights to the natural Description of human Things. It is observable that in all other Poems Love is represented as a Vice, in *Milton* only 'tis a Virtue. The Pictures he draws of it, are naked as the Persons he speaks of, and as venerable. He removes with a chaste Hand the Veil which covers everywhere else the enjoyments of that Passion. There is Softness, Tenderness and Warmth without Lasciviousness; the Poet transports himself and us, into that State of innocent Happiness in which *Adam* and *Eve* continued for a short Time: He soars not above human, but above corrupt Nature, and as there is no Instance of such Love, there is none of such Poetry.

How then it came to pass that the *Paradise Lost* had been so long neglected, (nay almost unknown) in *England*, (till the Lord *Sommers* in some Measure *taught Mankind to admire it*,) is a Thing which I cannot reconcile, *neither* with the Temper, *nor* with the Genius of the *English* Nation.

The Duke of *Buckingham* in his Art of Poetry gives the Preference to *Spencer*. It is reported in the Life of the Lord *Rochester*, that he had no Notion of a better Poet than *Cowley*.

Mr. *Dryden's* Judgement on *Milton* is still more unaccountable. He hath bestow'd some Verses upon him, in which he puts him upon a Level with, nay above *Virgil* and *Homer;*

> The Force of Nature could not further go,
> To make a third she join'd the former two.

The same Mr. *Dryden* in his Preface upon his Translation of the *Æneid*, ranks *Milton* with *Chapellain* and *Lemoine* the most impertinent Poets who ever scribbled. How he could extol him so much in his Verses, and debase him so low in his Prose, is a Riddle which, being a Foreigner, I cannot understand.

In short one would be apt to think that Milton has not obtained his true Reputation till Mr. *Adisson*, the best Critick as well as the best Writer of his Age, pointed out the most hidden Beauties of the *Paradise Lost*, and settled forever its Reputation.

It is an easy and a pleasant Task to take Notice of the many Beauties of *Milton* which I call universal: But 'tis a ticklish Undertaking to point out what would be reputed a Fault in any other Country.

I am very far from thinking that one Nation ought to judge of its Productions by the Standard of another, nor do I presume that the *French* (for Example) who have no *Epick* Poets, have any Right to give Laws on *Epick* Poetry.

But I fancy many *English* Readers, who are acquainted with the *French* language, will not be displeas'd to have some Notion of the Taste of that Country: And I hope they are too just either to submit to it, or despise it barely upon the Score of its being foreign to them.

Would each Nation attend a little more than they do, to the Taste and the Manners of their respective Neighbours, perhaps a general good Taste might diffuse itself through all *Europe* from such an intercourse of Learning, and from that useful Exchange of Observations. The *English* Stage, for Example, might be clear'd of mangled Carcasses, and the Style of their tragick Authors, come down from their forced Metaphorical Bombast to a nearer Imitation of Nature. The *French* would learn from the *English* to animate their Tragedies with more Action, and would contract now and then their long Speeches into shorter and warmer Sentiments.

The *Spaniards* would introduce in their Plays more Pictures of human Life, more Characters and Manners, and not puzzle themselves always in the Entanglements of confus'd Adventures, more romantick than natural. The *Italian* in Point of Tragedy would catch the Flame from the *English*, and all the Rest from the *French*. In Point of Comedy, they would learn from Mr. *Congreve* and some other Authors, to prefer Wit and Humour to Buffoonery.

To proceed in that View, I'll venture to say that none of the *French* Criticks could like the Excursions which *Milton* makes sometimes beyond the strict Limits of his Subject. They lay down for a Rule that an Author himself ought never to appear in his Poem; and his own Thoughts, his own Sentiments must be spoken by the Actors he introduces. Many judicious Men in *England* comply with that Opinion, and Mr. *Adisson* favours it. I beg Leave in this place to hazard a Reflection of my own, which I submit to the Reader's Judgement.

Milton breaks the Thread of his Narration in two Manners. The first consists of two or three kinds of Prologues, which he premises at the Beginning of some Books. In one Place he expatiates upon his own Blindness; in another he compares his Subject and prefers it to that of the *Iliad*, and to the common Topicks of War, which were thought before him the only Subject fit for *Epick* Poetry; and he adds that he hopes to soar as high as all his Predecessors, unless the cold Climate of *England damps his Wings*.

His other Way of interrupting his Narration, is by some Observations which he intersperses now and then upon some great Incident, or some interesting Circumstance. Of that Kind is his Digression on Love in the fourth Book;

> *Whatever* Hippocrites *austerely talk*
> *Defaming as impure, what God declares*
> *Pure, and commands to some, leaves free to all.*
> *Our Maker bids increase, who bids abstain*
> *But our Destroyer foe to God and Men?*
> *Hail wedded Love, &c.*

As to the first of these two Heads, I cannot but own that an Author is generally guilty of an impardonable Self-love, when he lays aside his Subject to descant on his own Person; but that human Frailty is to be forgiven in *Milton*; nay, I am pleas'd with it. He gratifies the Curiosity, it raises in me about his Person, when I admire the Author, I desire to know something of the Man, and he whom all Readers would be glad to know, is allow'd to speak of himself. But this however is a very dangerous Example for a Genius of an inferior Order, and is only to be justified by Success.

As to the second Point I am so far from looking on that Liberty as a Fault, that I think it to be a great Beauty. For if Morality is the aim of Poetry, I do not apprehend why the Poet should be forbidden to intersperse his Descriptions with moral Sentences and useful Reflexions, provided he scatters them with a sparing Hand, and in proper Places either when he wants Personages to utter those Thoughts, or when their Character does not permit them to speak in the Behalf of Virtue.

'Tis strange that *Homer* is commended by the Criticks for his comparing *Ajax* to an Ass pelted away with Stones by some Children, *Ulysses* to a Pudding, the Council-board of *Priam* to Grashoppers. 'Tis strange, I say, that they defend so clamorously those Similes tho' never so foreign to the Purpose, and will not allow the natural Reflexions, the noble Digressions of *Milton* tho' never so closely link'd to the Subject.

I will not dwell upon some small Errors of *Milton*, which are obvious to every Reader, I mean some few Contradictions and those frequent Glances at the *Heathen* Mythology, which Fault by the by is so much the more unexcusable in him, by his having premis'd in his first Book that those Divinities were but Devils worshipp'd under different Names, which ought to have been a sufficient Caution to him not to speak of the Rape of *Proserpine*, of the Wedding of *Juno* and *Jupiter*, &c. as Matters of Fact.

I lay aside likewise his preposterous and aukward Jests, his Puns, his too familiar Expressions so inconsistent with the Elevation of his Genius, and of his Subject.

To come to more essential Points and more *liable* to be debated. I dare affirm that the Contrivance of the *Pandaemonium* would have been entirely disapprov'd of by Criticks like *Boyleau*, *Racine*, &c.

That Seat built for the Parliament of the Devils, seems very preposterous: Since Satan hath summon'd them altogether, and harangu'd them just before in an ample Field. The Council was necessary; but where it was to be held, 'twas very indifferent. The Poet seems to delight in building his *Pandaemonium* in *Doric* Order with Freeze and Cornice, and a Roof of Gold. Such a Contrivance savours more of the wild Fancy of our Father *le Moine*, then of the serious spirit of *Milton*. But when afterwards the Devils turn dwarfs to fill their Places in the House, as if it was impracticable to build a Room large enough to contain them in their natural Size; it is an idle Story which would match the most extravagant Tales. And to crown all, Satan and the chief Lords preserving their own monstrous Forms, while the rabble of the Devils shrink into Pigmees, heightens the Ridicule of the whole Contrivance to an unexpressible Degree. Methinks the true Criterion for discerning what is really ridiculous in an *Epick* Poem, is to examine if the same Thing would not fit exactly the Mock heroick. Then I dare say that no-thing is so adapted to that ludicrous way of Writing as the Metamorphosis of the Devils into Dwarfs.

The Fiction of *Death* and *Sin* seems to have in it some great Beauties and many gross Defects. In order to canvass this Matter with Order. We must first lay down that such shadowy Beings, as *Death*, *Sin*, *Chaos*, are intolerable when they are not allegorical. For Fiction is nothing but Truth in Disguise. It must be granted too, that an Allegory must be short, decent and noble. For an Allegory carried too far or too low, is like a beautiful Woman who wears always a Mask. An Allegory is a long Metaphor; and to speak too long in metaphor's must be tiresom, because unnatural. This being premis'd, I must say that in general those Fictions, those imaginary beings, are more agreeable to the Nature of *Milton's* Poem, than to any other; because he hath but two natural Persons for his Actors, I mean *Adam* and *Eve*. A great Part of the Action lies in imaginary Worlds, and must *of course* admit of imaginary Beings.

Then *Sin* springing out of the Head of Satan, seems a beautiful Allegory of Pride, which is look'd upon as the first Offence committed against God. But I question if *Satan*, getting his Daughter with Child, is an Invention to be approv'd off. I am afraid that Fiction is but a meer Quibble; for if Sin was of a masculine Gender in *English, as it is in all the other Languages*, that whole Affair Drops, and the Fiction vanishes away. But suppose we are not so nice, and we allow *Satan* to be in Love with *Sin, because this Word is made feminine in* English (as Death passes also for masculine) what a horrid and loathsome Idea does *Milton* present to the Mind, in this Fiction? *Sin* brings forth Death, this Monster inflam'd with Lust and Rage, lies with his Mother, as she had done with her Father. From that new Commerce, springs a Swarm of Serpents, which creep in and out of their Mother's Womb, and gnaw and tear the Bowels they are born from.

Let such a Picture be never so beautifully drawn, let the Allegory be never so obvious, and so clear, still it will be intolerable, on the Account of its Foulness. That Complication of Horrors, that Mixture of Incest, that Heap of Monsters, that Loathsomeness so far fetch'd, cannot but shock a Reader of delicate Taste.

But what is more intolerable, there are Parts in that Fiction, which bearing no Allegory at all, have no Manner of Excuse. There is no Meaning in the Communication between Death and Sin, 'tis distasteful without any Purpose; or if any Allegory lies under it, the filthy Abomination of the Thing is certainly more obvious than the Allegory.

I see with Admiration, *Sin*, the *Portress* of Hell, opening the Gates of the Abiss, but unable to shut them again; that is really beautiful, because 'tis true. But what signifies Satan and Death quarrelling together, grinning at one another, and ready to fight?

The Fiction of *Chaos*, *Night*, and *Discord*, is rather a Picture, than an Allegory; and for ought I know, deserves to be approv'd, because it strikes the Reader with Awe, not with Horror.

I know the Bridge built by Death and Sin, would be dislik'd in *France*. The nice Criticks of that Country would urge against that Fiction, that it seems too common, and that it is useless; for Men's Souls want no paved Way, to be thrown into Hell, after their Separation from the Body.

They would laugh justly at the Paradise of Fools, at the Hermits, Fryars, Cowles, Beads, Indulgences, Bulls, Reliques, toss'd by the Winds, at St. *Peter's* waiting with his Keys at the Wicket of Heaven. And surely the most passionate Admirers of *Milton*, could not vindicate those low comical Imaginations, which belong by Right to *Ariosto*.

Now the sublimest of all the Fictions calls me to examine it. I mean the War in Heaven. The Earl of *Roscommon*, and Mr. *Addison* (whose Judgement seems either to guide, or to justify the Opinion of his Countrymen) admire chiefly that Part of the Poem. They bestow all the Skill of their Criticism and the Strength of their Eloquence, to set off that favourite Part. I may affirm, that the very Things they admire, would not be tolerated by the *French* Criticks. The Reader will perhaps see with Pleasure, *in what consists so strange a Difference*, and what may be the Ground of it.

First, they would assert, that a War in Heaven being an imaginary Thing, which lies out of the Reach of our Nature, should be contracted in two or three Pages, rather than lengthen'd out into two Books; because we are naturally impatient of removing from us the Objects which are not adapted to our Senses.

According to that Rule, they would maintain that 'tis an idle Task to give the Reader the full Character of the Leaders of that War, and to describe *Raphael*, *Michael*, *Abdiel*, *Moloch*, and *Nisroth*, as *Homer* paints *Ajax*, *Diomede*, and *Hector*.

For what avails it to draw at length the Picture of these Beings, so utterly Strangers to the Reader, that he cannot be affected any Way towards them; by the same Reason, the long Speeches of these imaginary Warriors, either before the Battle or in the Middle of the Action, their mutual Insults, seem an injudicious Imitation of *Homer*.

The aforesaid Criticks would not bear with the Angels plucking up the Mountains, with their Woods, their Waters, and their Rocks, and flinging them on the Heads of their Enemies. Such a Contrivance (they would say) is the more puerile, the more it aims at Greatness. Angels arm'd with Mountains in Heaven, resemble too much the Dipsodes in *Rabelais*, who wore an Armour of *Portland* Stone six Foot thick.

The Artillery seems of the same Kind, yet more trifling, because more useless.

To what Purpose are these Engines brought in? Since they cannot wound the Enemies, but only remove them from their Places, and make them tumble down: Indeed (if the Expression may be forgiven) 'tis to play at Nine-Pins. And the very Thing which is so dreadfully great on Earth, becomes very low and ridiculous in Heaven.

I cannot omit here, the visible Contradiction which reigns in that Episode. God sends his faithful Angels to fight, to conquer and to punish the Rebels. *Go* (*says He, to* Michael *and* Gabriel)

> *... And to the Brow of Heaven*
> *Pursuing, drive them out from God and Bliss,*
> *Into their Place of Punishment, the Gulph*
> *Of Tartarus, which ready opens wide*
> *His fiery Chaos to receive their Fall.*

How does it come to pass, after such a positive Order, that the Battle hangs doubtful? And why did God the Father command *Gabriel* and *Raphael*, to do what He executes afterwards by his Son only.

I leave it to the Readers, to pronounce, if these Observations are right, or ill-grounded, and if they are carried too far. But in case these Exceptions are just, the severest Critick must however confess there are Perfections enough in *Milton*, to attone for all his Defects.

I must beg leave to conclude this Article on Milton with two Observations.

His Hero (I mean *Adam*, his first Personage) is unhappy. That demonstrates against all the Criticks, that a very good Poem may end unfortunately, in Spight of all their pretended Rules. Secondly, the *Paradise Lost* ends compleatly. The Thread of the Fable is spun out to the last. *Milton* and *Tasso* have been careful of not stopping short and abruptly. The one does not abandon *Adam* and *Eve*, till they are driven out of *Eden*. The other does not conclude, before *Jerusalem* is taken. *Homer* and *Virgil* took a contrary Way, the *Iliad* ends with the Death of *Hector*, the *Æneid*, with that of *Turnus*: The Tribe of Commentators have upon that enacted a Law, that a House ought never to be finish'd, because *Homer* and *Virgil* did not compleat their own; but if *Homer* had taken *Troy*, and *Virgil* married *Lavinia* to *Æneas*, the Criticks would have laid down a Rule just the contrary.

APPENDIX C.

Extract from Oliver Goldsmith's *Memoirs of M. de Voltaire*

Oliver Goldsmith's *Memoirs of M. de Voltaire* were published in monthly instalments during 1761 in the *Lady's Magazine*. The work remained unfinished, but the account of Voltaire in England, reproduced here, is important, since Goldsmith almost certainly gleaned information from people who had met Voltaire; Edward Young, in particular, is known to have been a close acquaintance of Voltaire's, and as an old man he was in touch with Goldsmith. The quotation from Voltaire's play *Brutus* is of particular interest. In the preface to his French tragedy, Voltaire states that he had completed one act in English before leaving England, and that he subsequently rewrote the whole in French. No manuscript survives of the act composed in English, and the speech quoted here— if it is genuine, as it seems to be—is the sole surviving fragment of an otherwise lost text.

*   *   *

England, about this time, was coming into repute thro' Europe, as the land of philosophers. Newton, Locke, and others began to attract the attention of the curious, and drew hither a concourse of learned men from every part of Europe. Not our learning alone, but our politics also, began to be regarded with admiration: a government in which subordination and liberty were blended in such just proportions was now generally studied as the finest model of civil society. This was an inducement sufficient to make Voltaire pay a visit to this land of philosophers and of liberty.

In the year 1720* Mr. Voltaire came over to England. A previous acquaintance with Atterbury, bishop of Rochester, and the lord Bolingbroke, was sufficient to introduce him among the polite, and his fame as a poet got him the acquaintance of the learned, in a country where foreigners generally find but a cool reception. He only wanted introduction, his own merit was enough to procure the rest. As a companion no man ever exceeded him when he pleased to lead the conversation, which however was not always the case. In company which he either disliked or despised, few could be more reserved than he; but when he was warmed in discourse, and had got over a hesitating manner which sometimes he was subject to, it was rapture to hear him. His meagre visage seemed insensibly to gather beauty, every muscle in it had meaning, and his eye beamed with unusual brightness. The person who writes this memoir, who had the honour and the pleasure of being his acquaintance, remembers to have seen him in a select company of wits of both sexes at Paris, when the subject happened to turn upon English taste and learning. Fontenelle, who was of the party, and who being unacquainted with the language or authors of the country he undertook to condemn, with a spirit truly vulgar began to revile both. Diderot, who liked the English, and knew something of their literary pretensions, attempted to vindicate their poetry and learning, but with unequal abilities. The company, quickly perceived that Fontenelle was superior in the dispute, and were surprised at the silence which Voltaire had preserved all the former part of the night, particularly as the conversation happened to turn upon one of his favourite topics. Fontenelle continued his triumph till about twelve o'clock, when Voltaire appeared at last rouz'd from his reverie. His whole frame seemed animated. He began his defence with the utmost elegance mixed with spirit, and now and then let fall the finest strokes of raillery upon his antagonist; and his harangue lasted till three in the morning. I must confess, that, whether from national partiality, or from the elegant sensibility of his manner, I never was so much charmed, nor did I ever remember so absolute a victory as he gained in this dispute. But to return: upon his arrival in England, his first care was to learn so much of the language as might enable him to mix in conversation and study more thoroughly the genius of the people. Foreigners are unanimous in allowing the English language to be the most difficult to learn of any in Europe. Some have spent years in the study to no purpose: but such was the application, and such the memory of our poet, that in six weeks he was able to speak it with tolerable propriety. In short his conduct in this particular was such as may serve for a model to future travellers. The French who before visited this island, were never at the trouble of attaining our language, but contented with barely describing the buildings and palaces of the kingdom, and transcribing a character of the people from former travellers, who were themselves unacquainted with our national peculiarities. Accordingly we find few of their books in which the English are not characterized as morose, melancholly, excessive lovers of pudding, and haters of mankind. This stupid account has been continued down from Scaliger to Muralt, while the virtues and vices which were peculiar to the country were wholly unknown. Voltaire quickly perceived that pride seemed to be our characteristic quality; a source from whence we derived our excellencies as well as our defects. He perceived that the only way to understand the English was to learn their language, adopt their manners, and even to applaud their oddities. With this view, when sufficiently initiated into our language, he joined in companies of every rank, lords, poets and artizans were successively visited; and he attained at the same time a proficiency in our language, laws and government, and thorough insight into our national character. Before him, our reputation for learning had for some time been established in Europe; but then we were regarded as entirely destitute of taste, and our men of wit, known not even by name among the literati. He was the first foreigner who saw the amazing irregular beauties of Shakespear, gave Milton the character he deserved, spoke of every English poet with some degree of applause, and opened a new page of beauty to the eyes of his astonished countrymen. It is to him we owe that our language has taken place of the Italian among the polite, and that even ladies are taught to admire Milton, Pope and Otway. The greatest part of our poet's time, during a residence of two years in England, was spent at Wandsworth, the seat of his excellency Sir Everard Falkener. With this gentleman he had contracted an intimacy at Paris: and as Sir Everard had insisted upon his company before he left France, he now could not refuse. Here he spent his time in that tranquility and learned ease which are so grateful to men of speculation; had leisure to examine the difference between our government and that of which he was born a subject; and to improve, by our example, his natural passion for liberty. He was resolved however to give some lasting testimony of that love which he had for freedom and which has ever made one of the strongest features in his character. The elder Brutus, condemning his own son in its cause, seemed a fine subject for this purpose, and naturally suited to the British theatre. The first act of this play he accordingly wrote in English, and communicated it to his friends for their approbation. It was somewhat surprising to find a stranger, who had resided in the country but one year, attempt so arduous an undertaking; but still more so to find him skilled in the beauties and force of our language. The reader may be pleased to see how he wrote in English: he makes Brutus, in the second scene of the first act, thus vindicate the cause of freedom.

'*Brutus*. Alledge not ties, his (*Tarquin*'s) crimes have broke them all. The Gods themselves, whom he has offended, have declared against him. Which of our rights has he not trod upon? True, we have sworn to be his subjects, but we have not sworn to be his slaves. You say you've seen our senate in humble suppliance pay him here their vows. Even here himself has sworn to be our father, and make the people happy in his guidance. Broke from his oaths, we are let loose from ours; since he has transgressed our laws, his the rebellion, Rome is free from guilt.'

This tragedy he afterwards completed in French; and at Paris it met with the fate he had foreseen. No piece was ever translated into a greater number of foreign languages, more liked by strangers, or more decried at home. He dedicates it to my lord Bolingbroke; and, as the dedication contains a fine parrallel between the English and French theatres, I shall beg leave to translate some part of it here.

'As it was too venturous an innovation, my lord, to attempt to write a tragedy in French without rhyme, and take such liberties as are allowed in England and Italy, I was at least determined to transplant those beauties from the English stage which I thought not incompatible with French regularity. Certain it is the English theatre is extremely defective. I have heard yourself say there was scarce a perfect tragedy in the language, but to compensate this, you have several scenes which are admirable. Almost all your tragic writers have been likewise deficient in that regularity and simplicity of plot, that propriety of diction, that elegance of stile, and those hidden strokes of art, for which we are remarkable since the times of Corneille. However your most irregular pieces have a peculiar merit; they excell in action, while ours are frequently tedious declamations, and at best conversation rather than a picture of passion. Our excessive delicacy often puts us upon making an uninteresting recital of what should rather be represented to the eyes of the spectator. Our poets are afraid to hazard any thing new before an audience composed of such as turn all that is not the *fashion* into ridicule.

'The inconvenience of our theatre also is another cause that our representations frequently appear dry and unentertaining. The spectators being allowed to sit on the stage, destroy almost all propriety of Action. For this reason, those decorations which are so much recommended by the antients can be but very rarely introduced. Thus it happens that the actors can never pass from one apartment into another without being seen by the audience, and all theatrical illusion must consequently be destroyed.

'How could we, for instance, introduce the ghost of Pompey, or the genius of Brutus, into the midst of a parcel of young fellows crowded upon the theatre, and who only stand there to laugh at all that is transacted? How could we, as the late Mr. Addison has done, have the body of Marcus born in upon the stage before his father? If he should hazard a representation of this nature, the whole pit would rise against the poet, and the ladies themselves would be apt to hide their faces.

'With what pleasure have I seen at London your tragedy of Julius Cæsar, which, though an hundred and fifty years old, still continues the delight of the people. I do not here attempt to defend the barbarous irregularity with which it abounds. What surprizes is, that there are not more in a work written in an age of ignorance, by a man who understood not Latin, and who had no other master but a happy genius. The piece is faulty; but, amidst such a number still, with what rapture do we see Brutus, with his dagger stained with the blood of Cæsar, harranguing the people.

'The French would never suffer a chorus composed of plebeians and artizans to appear upon the theatre; nor would they permit the body of Cæsar to be exposed, or the people excited from the rostrum. Custom, the queen of this world, changes at pleasure the taste of nations, and turns the sources of joy often into objects of disgust.

'The Greeks have exhibited objects upon their stage that would be equally disgusting to a French audience. Hippolitus, bruised by his fall, comes to count his wounds, and to pour forth the most lamentable cries. Philoctetes appears with his wound open, and the black gore streaming from it. Œdipus, covered with the blood which flowed from the sockets of his eyes, complains both of gods and men. In a word, many of the Greek tragedies abound with exaggeration.

'I am not ignorant that both the Greeks and the English have frequently erred, in producing what is shocking instead of what should be terrible, the disgusting and the incredible for what should have been tragic and marvellous. The art of writing was in its infancy at Athens in the time of Æschylus, and at London in the time of Shakespear. However, both the one and the other, with all their faults, frequently abound with a fine pathetic, and strike us with beauties beyond the reach of art to imitate. Those Frenchmen, who, only acquainted with translations or common report, pretend to censure either, somewhat resemble the blind man who should assert that the rose is destitute of beauty, because he perceives the thorns by the touch.

'But, though sometimes the two nations of which I am speaking transcend the bounds of propriety, and present us with objects of affright instead of terror, we, on the other hand, as scrupulous as they are rash, stop short of beauty for fear of being carried beyond it; and seldom arrive at the pathetic, for fear of transgressing its bounds.

'I am by no means for having the theatre become a place of carnage as we often find in Shakespear, and his successors, who, destitute of his genius, have only imitated his faults; but still I insist, that there are numberless incidents which may at present appear shocking to a French spectator, which, if set off with elegance of diction and propriety of representation, would be capable of giving a pleasure beyond what we can at present conceive.'

This gives us a tolerably just representation of the state in which Voltaire found the French theatre. His Œdipus was wrote in this dry manner, where most of the terrible incidents were delivered in cold recitation and not represented before the spectator. But, by observing our tragedies, like a skillful artist, he joined their fire to French correctness, and formed a manner peculiarly his own.

In studies of this nature he spent his time at Wandsworth, still employed either in improving himself in our language, or borrowing its beauties to transplant into his own. His hours of dissipation were generally spent among our poets, Congreve, Pope, Young, &c. or among such of our nobility as were remarkable either for arts or arms, as Peterborrow, Oxford, and Walpole. He was frequently heard to say, that Peterborrow had taught him the art of despising riches, Walpole the art of acquiring them, but Harley alone the secret of being contented.

The first time he visited Mr. Congreve, he met with a reception very different from what he had expected. The English dramatist, grown rich by means of his profession, affected to despise it, and assured Voltaire, that he chose rather to be regarded as a gentleman than a poet. This was a meanness which somewhat disgusted the Frenchman, particularly as he himself owed all his reputation to his excellence in poetry; he therefore informed Mr. Congreve, that his fame as a writer was the only inducement he had to see him; and though he could condescend to desire the acquaintance of a man of wit and learning, he was above soliciting the company of any private gentleman whatsoever.* The reflection of another, upon this occasion was, that he certainly is below the profession who presumes to think himself above it.

Mr. Voltaire has often told his friends, that he never observed in himself such a succession of opposite passions as he experienced upon his first interview with Mr. Pope. When he first entered the room, and perceived our poor melancholy English poet, naturally deformed, and wasted as he was with sickness and study, he could not help regarding him with the utmost compassion. But, when Pope began to speak, and to reason upon moral obligations, and dress the most delicate sentiments in the most charming diction, Voltaire's pity began to be changed into admiration, and at last even into envy. It is not uncommon with him to assert, that no man ever pleased him so much in serious conversation, nor any whose sentiments mended so much upon recollection.

There is a story commonly told of his being in company with Dr. Young and some others, when the conversation happened to turn upon Milton's Paradise. He displayed, as the story goes, all his critical skill in condemning the allegorical personages which Milton has introduced into his poem, and this with the utmost vivacity and unbounded freedom of speech. Upon which Young, regarding him with a fixed eye, spoke the following epigram.

> So very witty, wicked, and so thin;
> Fit emblem sure of Milton, death, and sin.

However, I only mention this to shew what trifles are generally ascribed to men when once grown famous. The wretchedness of the epigram will readily convince those who have any pretensions to taste, that Dr. Young could never have been the author: probably some blockhead made the verses first, and the story after.

Among the number of those who either patronized him or enrolled themselves in the number of his friends, was the dutchess of Marlborough. She found infinite pleasure in the agreeable vivacity of his conversation; but mistook his levity for want of principle. Such a man seemed to her the properest person to digest the memoirs of her life; which, even so early as this, she had an inclination of publishing. She proposed the task accordingly to him, and he readily undertook to oblige her. But when she shewed him her materials, and began to dictate the use she would have them turned to, Voltaire appeared no longer the good natured complying creature which she took him for. He found some characters were to be blackened without just grounds, some of her actions to be vindicated that deserved censure, and a mistress to be exposed to whom she owed infinite obligations. Our poet accordingly remonstrated with her grace, and seemed to intimate the inconsistency of such a conduct with gratitude and justice; he gravely assured her, that the publication of secrets which were communicated under the seal of friendship, would give the world no high opinion of her morals. He was thus continuing his discourse, when the dutchess, quite in a passion, snatched the papers out of his hands: I thought, said she, the man had sense, but I find him at bottom either a fool or a philosopher.

He was but two years in England, as has been hinted already; yet it is somewhat strange to think, how much he either wrote published or studied during so short a residence. He gave amongst his friends a criticism he had wrote in English upon Milton, which he concludes in this manner. 'It requires reach of thought to discover the defects of Milton; his excellencies lie obvious to every capacity; he attones for a few faults by a thousand beauties; and, like satan, the hero of his own poem, even when fallen he wears the appearance of majesty.'

But the performance upon which he founds his most lasting share of fame was published in this country. The French language had hitherto been deemed unsusceptible of the true epic dignity. Several unsuccessful attempts by Ronsard, Chapelaine and others had made critics despair of ever seeing an heroic poem in the language; and some writers had laid it down as actually impossible. Voltaire, who seemed to be born to encounter difficulty, undertook the task, and that at an age when pleasure is apt to silence the voice of ambition. This poem, which is now well known by the name of the Henriade, was first published under the title of the League. He began it in the Bastille, enlarged and corrected it for several years afterwards, and had some thoughts of publishing it in France. Upon shewing the manuscript to Fontenelle his friend, he was by him advised to retrench several passages which seemed to be written with too warm a spirit of liberty under such a government as theirs: but Voltaire, who considered those very passages as the greatest beauties of his work, was resolved the poem should make its first appearance in a country in love with liberty, and ready to praise every performance written in its defence. With this view he brought the work over with him to England, and offered it in the usual manner to a bookseller in order to be published. The bookseller, as some pretend, either unacquainted with its value, or willing to impose upon a stranger, offered him but a trifle for the manuscript, and would print only such a number as he thought proper. These were terms with which the author chose not to comply; and, considering the number and the rank of his friends, he was resolved to publish it by subscription. A subscription was opened accordingly, and quickly filled with persons of the first rank and eminence, not only of Great-Britain, but of Europe in general. A condition of the proposals was, that the subscribers should have their books a month before it was published in the ordinary manner in London. In this situation were things when an unforeseen accident called our poet out of the kingdom, being sent for by M. D'Argenson, prime Minister of France, in order to become the king's historiographer. Voltaire was therefore obliged to return with reluctance home, leaving to his bookseller the care of satisfying the subscribers. Voltaire however affirms that the bookseller, considering that there was no great difference between reading a book a month sooner or later, was resolved to indulge the curiosity of the public first, and gratify the subscribers after. As by this means the profits accruing from the sale, which were to be his own, would be greatly encreased. The reader may judge for himself whether this is not the true reason why the subscribers to the Henriade had not the work till a month after it was first published in London; and not against the author but his bookseller should their censure be levelled. It cannot be conceived what a number of enemies this raised Voltaire; for all imputed to him that meanness of which those who are of his acquaintance know him to be utterly incapable. A neglect, indeed, he was guilty of, in leaving no friend to see justice done to the public. This may be said of our poet's character in general, that he has frequently been guilty of indiscretions, but never of meanness. A mind employed in the contemplation of great virtues is sometimes guilty of trifling absurdities, *quas aut incuria fudit, aut humana parum cavit natura.** An honest man may sometimes unite with such as will render his actions suspected, but then it is the fault of good minds to be too credulous, and, instead of condemning such a man of falshood, we should pity his good nature.

The poem was dedicated to Queen Caroline, for which she made the author a present of her picture valued at two hundred guineas. The dedication breaths a spirit which at once characterizes the poet, the philosopher, and the man of virtue; and some prefer it even to any part of the succeeding performance. It must be confessed the Henriade has its faults; its incidents in general do not sufficiently interest or surprize; it seldom rises to the sublime, though it never falls into flatness. The moral reflections return too frequently, and retard that speed which is one of the greatest beauties of narration. However, with all its faults, the French regard it as the first epic poem in their language, and though (national partiality laid aside) it sinks infinitely below Milton; yet it will be sufficient to gain the author immortality.

Upon his return home, he found his fame greatly encreased, the prime minister of France himself being proud of ranking among the number of his friends. Scarce a country of Europe from which the learned did not send him their acknowledgements for the pleasure and instruction they had received from his last perform-ance. The king of France used frequently to entreat the pleasure of his company, for he found in him one who had learned from the English to treat monarchs with an honest freedom, and who dis-dained those mean submissions which at once render kings proud and miserable.

(*Collected Works of Oliver Goldsmith*, 5 vols.
(Oxford: Clarendon Press, 1966), iii. 246–56)

APPENDIX D.

Original anecdote of Voltaire and a Quaker

This article was first published in *The Yorkshireman*, a Quaker journal, in 1833. It affords us a curious glimpse of Voltaire in action among the English; the incident described clearly inspired the fictive encounter of Letter I.

*   *   *

Original anecdote of Voltaire and a Quaker.

I have received from an old friend and schoolfellow the following anecdote for publication. The Reader, who may have informed himself heretofore, respecting the character to which it relates, will be ready probably, with my friend, to pronounce it 'characteristic and curious.' It is a fact familiar to members of our society, that *Voltaire*, after some intercourse with us in this country, thought proper to write in disparagement of the quaker system, and that he was replied to by our friend Josiah Martin, in a publication which is still extant. *Ed.*

'Edward Higginson's Account of a Conversation with Voltaire.

—Some time in the year 1724, Francis de Voltaire boarded a while with a scarlet dyer nigh the ['Friends'] School at Half-farthing, in the parish of Wandsworth, kept then by John Huweidt, with whom I had served about half my time. Voltaire desired to be improved in the English tongue: and in discourse [with the master] chanced to fall on the subject of water baptism [which was treated between them] till, for want of understanding each other, they were so set, they could proceed no further: when Voltaire inquired whether he had never an *usher* [who] understood Latin. There was one; but as he was not of our profession my master thought him not suitable, therefore sent for me into the parlour, and Voltaire rehearsed their conference, desiring, if he missed, my master would put him right—but he had not. Then he began with me: and as they had been engaged for some time, there was the less for me to advance. I then mentioned Paul's assertion in the 17th ver. i. ch. I Cor. [For Christ sent me not to baptise, but to preach the gospel] which seemed so strange, that in a violent passion he said, I lied—

which I put up patiently, till he, becoming cooler, desired to know why I would impose upon a stranger. I said I had not imposed at all, but justly repeated the Apostle's words as they stood in our bibles. He replied, our bible was falsely translated, and done by heretics. I desired to know whether he would be set down by *Beza*, or *Castalio*. He styled them also heretics: I answered, I did presume he did not conceive that Paul's own handwriting was extant: he replied he did not. I then queried what he *would* be set down by—would he by the Greek. To this he assented, and thereon I fetched my Greek Testament, of Mattaire's edition in twelves, and referred him thereto: at the sight of which he was as much surprised as he was before enraged, desiring to know what our English clergy would object to this [text]. I said, their general reply was, that Paul meant 'not principally, or chiefly': Voltaire observed, they might in the same way elude all the rest of the book.

'Some short time after, Voltaire being at the Earl Temple's seat in Fulham, with *Pope*, and others such, in their conversation fell on the subject of water baptism—Voltaire assuming the part of the quaker—and at length [he] came to mention that assertion of Paul. *They* questioned there being any such assertion in all his writings: on which was a large wager [laid] as near as I remember of £500, and Voltaire not retaining where it was, had one of the Earl's horses and came over the ferry from Fulham to Putney, and rode to Half-farthing; and alighting in the yard desired our man to lead the horse about, being warm. Coming to my master, he asked for his little usher as he called me. When I came, he desired me to give him in writing the place where Paul said, "he was not sent to baptize"—which I presently did. Then courteously taking his leave, he mounted and rode back—[and, of course, won his wager!]

'During his stay at the Scarlet dyers in Wandsworth, I had to wait on him several times, and hear him read, in the *Spectators* chiefly. At other times he would translate the Epistle of Robert Barclay; commending the same [Barclay *wrote* it in the Latin] so far as to acknowledge it to be the finest or purest Church Latin he knew. In his translating his Epistle to king Charles II, instead of using the word thou or thee [for *tu or te* in the text] he *would* write *you*—which made it, to my ear, sound harsh.

'He seemed so taken with me, as to offer to buy out the remainder of my time. I told him, I expected my master would be very exorbitant in his demand. He said, Let his demand be what it might, he would give it him on condition I would yield to be his companion, keeping the same company—and [I] should always in every respect fare as he fared, wearing my clothes like his and of equal value: telling me then plainly, he was a Deist; adding, so were most of the noblemen in France and England; deriding the account given by the four Evangelists concerning the birth of Christ, and his miracles, &c. so far, that I desired him to desist; for I could not bear to hear my Saviour so reviled and spoken against. Whereupon he seemed under a disappointment, and left me with some reluctance.'

(*The Yorkshireman, a Religious and Literary Journal*, II
(Pontefract, 1833), i. 167–9)

EXPLANATORY NOTES

Johnson = Samuel Johnson, *A Dictionary of the English Language* (1755).

5 *The present Work*: the Preface was written by Nicolas Thiriot, who, being in London, saw this book through the press on Voltaire's behalf (see D584, D631). They were old friends, having known each other since 1714, when they worked in the same law practice. (Thiriot also spells his name 'Thieriot', but Thiriot better represents the pronunciation; Voltaire sometimes spells it 'Tiriot').

the other Compositions of its Author: by the time of the publication of the *Letters* in 1733, Voltaire was well known to London's reading-public. The following of his works had all been recently published in London: the *Essay upon the Civil Wars of France and upon Epick Poetry*, Voltaire's first work in English, in 1727, and reprinted in 1728 (twice) and 1731; *La Henriade* (the first French edition), in 1728, in a quarto edition followed in the same year by three octavo editions; a translation of *La Henriade* into English blank verse, in 1732; and, also in 1732, an English translation, frequently reprinted, of *The History of Charles XII*, only a year after the work's first publication in France.

6 *about 1731*: these dates are incorrect; Voltaire returned to France from England in the autumn of 1728.

will be found entertaining: Voltaire caused a sentence to be excised here; see Note on the Text (p. xxxi).

7 *that Letter here*: 'A Letter concerning the Burning of Altena', omitted from this edition, is an answer to some published criticisms of Voltaire's *Histoire de Charles XII*.

9 *I made a visit*: the 'I' who speaks is not of course Voltaire, but Voltaire's glove-puppet; but there are parallels between the adventures of the invented narrator and visits made to Quakers by the real Voltaire, in particular to Andrew Pitt in Hampstead, and to Edward Higginson in Wandsworth (see Appendix D).

9 *beaver*: 'A hat of the best kind; so called from being made of the fur of beaver' (Johnson).

thou art a stranger: the use of the second person singular 'thou' and its related forms, already rare in the sixteenth century, was completely lost in standard English of the eighteenth, except among Quakers. In his *Brief Account of the Rise and Progress of the People, call'd Quakers* (1694), William Penn explains this practice—and anticipates the humour which Voltaire would extract from it: '[The Quakers] also used the plain Language of *Thee* and *Thou*, to a single Person, what ever was his Degree among Men. And indeed the Wisdom of God, was much seen in bringing forth this People, in so plain an Appearance. For it was a *Close* and *Distinguishing Test* upon the Spirits of those they came among; shewing their Insides, and what predominated, notwithstanding their high and great Profession of Religion. This among the rest sounded so harsh to many of them, and they took it so ill, that they would say, *Thou me, thou my dog! If thou thou'st me, I'll thou thy Teeth down thy Throat*: forgetting the Language *they use to God* in their own Prayers, and the common Stile of the Scriptures, and that it is an absolute and essential Propriety of Speech. And what good, alas! had their Religion done them, who were so sensibly toucht with Indignation for the Use of this *Plain*, *Honest* and *True* Speech?' (William Penn, *A Collection of the Works* (London, 1726), i. 869).

11 *specious*: 'Plausible; superficially, not solidly right; striking at first view' (Johnson).

in the gospel: Josiah Martin objects to this presentation of the Quaker viewpoint in *A Letter from One of the People call'd Quakers to Francis de Voltaire, occasioned by his Remarks on that People in his Letters concerning the English Nation* (London, 1741), 2–3.

the Exposition of our Faith written by Robert Barclay: *Theologiae vere christianae apologia* (1675); Voltaire draws on this work for a number of details in this and subsequent letters.

14 *the monument*: this column was both a memorial to the Fire of London and a celebration of religious intolerance. It bore the following inscription (erased on the accession of James II, recut after the Revolution in the reign of William III, and erased again only in 1831): 'This Pillar was set up in perpetual

Remembrance of the most dreadful Burning of this Protestant City, begun and carried on by the Treachery and Malice of the Popish faction, in the beginning of September, 1666, in order to the effecting their horrid Plot for the extirpating the Protestant Religion and English Liberties and to introduce Popery and Slavery.' Hence the lines of Pope, a Catholic, in his *Epistle to Bathurst* (vv. 339–40): 'Where London's column, pointing at the skies, Like a tall bully, lifts the head, and lyes; . . .'

14 *such a babbling*: 'Thou hast describ'd the Man's Way of Speaking and Preaching very unfairly, if not in a very wanton and ludicrous manner' (Josiah Martin, *A Letter*, 3).

15 *assur'd that he is inspir'd by the Lord*: in practice, it was not this simple, as Voltaire well knew; the London newspapers of 1727–8 reported the story—which would have made a good Voltairean *conte*—of an unfortunate Quaker who had had to be imprisoned by his brethren on account of the intemperate spontaneity of his contributions to meetings.

Malbranche's doctrine: a reference to Malebranche's *Recherche de la vérité* (1674–5), first translated into English in 1694.

17 *for God's sake*: Josiah Martin rejects this anecdote: 'In thy *third* Letter the Philosopher is quite lost in the Historian; for what thou hast related of *George Fox* is very little of it true' (*A Letter*, 13).

18 *Dove non si chiavava*: 'where there was no fornicating'. A succession of editors have found here a reference to the conclave and have mistranslated the Italian as 'where there was no locking in'; this happy confusion between religion and sex would have pleased Voltaire.

19 *Quakers*: this is the explanation given by Barclay; it is not, however, universally accepted.

Oliver: Oliver Cromwell.

20 '*Thou hast tasted*': Voltaire himself has translated Barclay's Latin into English; it is accurate, though the passage has been slightly abridged.

21 *in good health*: 'That is unlikely to be true, being contrary to the *Quakers* manner of Address to a Father' (Josiah Martin, *A Letter*, 27).

22 *Philosophical Romance*: a scathing reference to Descartes's *Les Principes de la philosophie* (1647).

24 *the laws made against Nonconformists*: James II issued a Declaration of Indulgence in 1687 which aimed (but failed) to supersede the Test and Corporation Acts (1673 and 1661 respectively) which guaranteed to Anglican communicants a monopoly of power, both locally and nationally.

26 *many mansions*: John 14: 2. Addison and Steele had already had fun with this idea: 'Every Nation is distinguished by Productions that are peculiar to it. *Great Britain* is particularly fruitful in Religions, that shoot up and flourish in this Climate more than in any other. We are so famous Abroad for our great variety of Sects and Opinions, that an ingenious Friend of mine, who is lately returned from his Travels, assures me, there is a Show at this Time *carried* up and down in *Germany*, which represents all the Religions of *Great Britain* in Wax-work' (*The Tatler*, No. 257, 1710).

the establish'd church: a further allusion to the Test and Corporation Acts which discriminated against Catholics and Dissenters. Voltaire mentions, but plays down, the fact of legal discrimination against non-Anglicans: it has no part in his idealized picture of a tolerant state.

Guelphs and Gibelins: the quarrels of the Guelphs (usually supporting the Pope) and the Ghibellines (usually supporting the Holy Roman Emperor) lasted from the eleventh to the fourteenth century.

27 *the earl of Oxford and the lord Bolingbroke*: Robert Harley, first Earl of Oxford, and Henry St John, Viscount Bolingbroke, were leading Tory ministers in the reign of Anne.

jure divino: 'by divine right'.

a book: the *Dissertation sur la validité des ordinations des Anglais et sur la succession des évêques de l'Eglise anglicane* (1723). The author, Pierre François Le Courayer, was excommunicated on account of his defence of this work, and in 1728 he emigrated to England where he spent the rest of his long life; the University of Oxford conferred on him the honorary degree of Doctor of Divinity in 1732.

The lord B——: Bolingbroke.

28 *as Rabelais says*: 'He is, by the Virtue of God, an arrant Heretick, a resolute formal Heretick; I say, a rooted combustible Heretick, one as fit to burn as the little wooden Clock at

Rochel. His soul goeth to thirty thousand Carts-full of Devils' (*The Third Book of . . . Pantagruel*, chap. 22, translated by
Sir Thomas Urquhart, 1693).

29 *Alexander*: when Alexander the Great asked Diogenes what
he could do for him, Diogenes suggested Alexander get out of
his light.

Cato: Cato 'the Censor', well known from Plutarch, was
famously austere and puritanical.

30 *Royal-Exchange*: see Introduction (pp. xviii–xix).

31 *Arians or Socinians*: believers in two varieties of heresy concerning the Trinity. They question the divinity of Christ
and—in the case of the Socinians, who are more extreme than
the Arians—conceive him as the highest form of man; their
views seem to overlap with, though they are distinct from,
those of the Deists. The anti-Trinitarians were perceived as
posing a direct challenge to the Church of England, and they
had been debarred from the provisions of the 1689 Act of
Toleration. Athanasius in the fourth century had proposed
the interpretation of the Trinity (the 'Athanasian Creed')
which in later centuries became the standard teaching of the
Roman Catholic Church.

Dr. Clark: Samuel Clarke, an outstanding Anglican theologian and the most articulate exponent of the Latitudinarian
view that the essential truths of Christianity could be recon-
ciled with the new science of Newton and the new philosophy
of Locke.

32 *the Christian religion*: the two books are first, *A Discourse
concerning the Being and Attributes of God* (1705–6), originally given as the Boyle Lectures, and directed against both
Deism and atheism, and secondly, *The Verity and Certitude
of Natural and Revealed Religion* (1705).

a work: *The Scripture Doctrine of the Trinity* (1712), Clarke's
most controversial work, revived discussion of Arianism.

in case: 'If it should happen; upon the supposition that: a
form of speech now little used' (Johnson).

Sir Isaac Newton, Dr. Clark, Mr. Locke, Mr. Le Clerc &c:
Clarke knew Newton well, and had translated his *Opticks*
into Latin; Locke's *The Reasonableness of Christianity* (1695)
expresses views consonant with those of Clarke; and Jean

Leclerc, at one time a Unitarian minister in Amsterdam, popularized Locke's thought in various continental journals which he edited. By grouping these thinkers in this way, Voltaire identifies the latent connection between Newtonian science and anti-Trinitarian theology. These theological and scientific debates overlie the political divisions of the period (and politics will be the theme of the following letters), between Tory/High Church and Whig/Low Church. Larry Stewart writes that 'the emergence of a popular Newtonianism in the early eighteenth century meant that natural philosophy was injected with political and social ideology: the Newtonians were increasingly identified with the rise of a Whig oligarchy and with the difficult adjustments which followed the Revolution of 1687–89. It was thus not merely a political or intellectual revolution: for Newton and many of his enthusiastic followers, it was both' ('Samuel Clarke, Newtonianism, and the factions of post-Revolutionary England', *Journal of the History of Ideas*, 42 (1981), 53–4).

32 *Cardinal de Retz*: active in the troubles of the *Fronde* in the mid-seventeenth century; see the following letter.

33 *the old Romans*: the comparison between Britain and Rome was commonplace in contemporary English political writing; see, for example, *The Craftsman*, Nos. 4 (16 Dec. 1726) and 37 (14 Apr. 1727). The idea of London as a modern Rome influenced painters like Canaletto, who, during his stay in England (1746–55), produced many powerful images of the capital.

   Mr. Shippen: William Shippen, a Tory MP and prominent Jacobite.

   (*doubtless very unjustly*): the remark is ironic—Walpole's control of Parliament through patronage was ruthless. *The Knight and the Prelate* is a ballad of 1734:

   In the Island of Britain I sing of a K . . . t,
   Much fam'd for dispensing his favour aright,
   No Merit could he but what's palpable see,
   And he judg'd of Men's Worth by the Weight of their Fee.

   See also Introduction, pp. xxi–xxii.

   Flamen: a priest serving a particular Roman deity.

34 *interested motives*: the remark is highly ingenuous.

35 *Guises*: a powerful Catholic family, at the height of their influence during the reigns of Charles IX (1560–74) and Henry III (1574–89).

Rochefoucault's Memoirs: La Rochefoucauld, now best remembered as the author of *Maximes*, fought in the Fronde and published his *Mémoires* (1664), translated into English in 1684.

36 ... *Henry the fourth*: Emperor Henry VII, who died in 1313, was allegedly poisoned by a priest, Montepulciano, who had given him communion; Henry III was assassinated in 1589 by Jacques Clément, a young Dominican friar; and his successor, Henry IV, was assassinated in 1610 by François Ravaillac, a Catholic fanatic: Voltaire's examples are hand-picked to demonstrate the price of priestcraft.

38 *The priests ... among them*: looking back from the vantage-point of the French Revolution, Thomas Paine declares in *Rights of Man* (1791–2) that Voltaire's 'forte lay in exposing and ridiculing the superstitions which priestcraft united with statecraft had interwoven with governments'.

40 *a greater Tyranny*: this does not make sense; the clause ought to read 'because it removed a greater tyranny'. The error results from a mistranslation from the French (see Note on the Text, pp. xxix–xxx).

the Commons since become so formidable: this view is expressed in other political writings of the period, for example, in those of Swift and Bolingbroke.

42 *1723*: an error for 1726.

Lord Townshend: a leading minister under George I.

43 *a Factor in Aleppo*: Nathaniel Harley, brother of Robert, lived in Aleppo (in northern Syria) for twenty-five years. Such a long stay was quite exceptional, however; nor was his employment as menial as Voltaire implies—he was, in modern terms, an international financier. Johnson defines *factor* as 'one who transacts business for another'.

with sovereign Contempt: the proposition that the English, unlike the French, did not look down upon 'Traders' is questionable; one disgruntled member of the heavily taxed landed classes complained in 1733 about 'a Set of *broccado'd* Tradesmen cloathed in Purple and fine Linnen, and faring sumptu-

ously every Day, raising to themselves immense Wealth, so as
to marry their Daughters to the first Rank, and to leave to
their Sons such Estates as to enable them to live to the same
Degree' (*The Landed Interest consider'd [. . .] by a Yeoman of
Kent* (London: Roberts, 1733), 35).

44 *Yest*: an alternative spelling of 'yeast' (Johnson).

46 *Bassa*: 'A title of honour and command among the Turks; the
viceroy of a province; the general of an army' (Johnson).

Queen of England: Caroline, wife of George II, who became
queen in 1727; *La Henriade*, published in 1728, is dedicated to
her. Lady Mary Wortley Montagu wrote from Adrianople
(present-day Edirne) to Sarah Chiswell on 1 April 1717 describing in detail the practice of inoculation: 'You may
beleive [*sic*]', she concludes, 'I am very well satisfy'd of the
safety of the Experiment since I intend to try it on my dear
little Son. I am Patriot enough to take pains to bring this
usefull invention into fashion in England, and I should not fail
to write to some of our Doctors very particularly about it if I
knew any one of 'em that I thought had Virtue enough to
destroy such a considerable branch of their Revenue for the
good of Mankind' (*The Complete Letters*, ed. R. Halsband,
vol. I (Oxford, 1965), 339).

Father Courayer: see note on 'a book' above, p. 177.

Dr. Clark and Mr. Leibnitz: a reference to the correspondence between Clarke and Leibniz carried on under the spon-
sorship of Caroline, and published in a bilingual French and
English edition in 1717. The debate was triggered by
Leibniz's remark, in a letter to Caroline, that Newtonian
physics had led to a decline of natural religion in England;
against Leibniz, Clarke defended the Newtonian notion of
'absolute space'; his underlying purpose was to demonstrate
the crucial presence of God in the Newtonian universe.

47 *their Beauty*: the practice of inoculation was more controversial in England than Voltaire suggests, and there was initial
opposition from both churchmen and doctors. One pam-
phleteer writes that: 'Posterity perhaps will scarcely be
brought to believe, that an Experiment practiced only by a
few *Ignorant Women*, amongst an illiterate and unthinking
People, shou'd on a sudden, and upon a slender Experience,
so far obtain in one of the Politest Nations in the World, as to
be receiv'd into the *Royal Palace*' (William Wagstaffe, *A Let-*

ter to Dr. Freind; shewing the Danger and Uncertainty of Inoculating the Small Pox, second edn. (London, 1722), 5–6); a French translation of this pamphlet appeared in 1722. It was only much later, in the mid-1760s, that inoculation began to be used in programmes of mass treatment. Lady Mary also published anonymously in 1722 an article entitled 'A Plain Account of the Innoculating of the Small Pox by a Turkey Merchant' (in *Essays and Poems*, ed. R. Halsband and I. Grundy (Oxford, 1977), 95–7).

49 *Warriors and Ministers of State shall come in their order*: they never do. This remark recalls the reference in the 'Advertisement to the Reader' (Appendix B) to the 'many great Men whose Glory in War, in State-Affairs will not be confined to the Bounds of this Island'. The intention to include letters on these topics was evidently abandoned at a later stage.

50 *in the opposite Party*: Voltaire made a last-minute change to this sentence; see Note on the Text (p. xxxi).

51 *impertinent*: '1. Of no relation to the matter in hand; of no weight. 2. Importunate; intrusive; meddling. 3. Foolish; trifling' (Johnson).

a parte rei: *universalia a parte rei*, a term used by Scholastic philosophers to describe universals as objective realities independent of the intellect.

52 *one of their greatest Philosophers*: Anaxagoras (mentioned by name in the next chapter), who wrote that: 'The sun, the moon and all the stars are red-hot stones which the rotation of the aither carries round with it' (*The Presocratic Philosophers*, trans. G. S. Kirk and J. E. Raven (Cambridge, 1971), 391).

53 *Thuanus*: Jacques-Auguste de Thou, author of a 138-volume history of the second half of the sixteenth century, *Historiarum sui temporis libri* (1604–20); his comments on the Reformation and the Wars of Religion earned the displeasure of Rome—and doubtless, therefore, the favour of Voltaire.

Fustian: 'a high swelling kind of writing made up of heterogeneous parts, or of words and ideas ill associated; bombast' (Johnson).

55 *the cherubic Doctor*: the first four titles in this list are names genuinely attributed to the scholastic philosophers identified in the footnotes. The seriousness of the list is punctured however by the final 'cherubic Doctor', the fictitious author of a

nonsense work in Rabelais's Library of Saint-Victor: 'Muddisnowt Doctoris cherubici de origine roughfootedarum et wryneckedorum ritibus libre septem' (*Pantagruel*, chap. 7, trans. Sir Thomas Urquhart (1653)). This allusion to Rabelais's celebrated satire of old-fashioned learning reinforces Voltaire's polemic, and provides it with a pedigree (notwithstanding the criticisms of Rabelais which Voltaire makes in Letter XXII).

55 *living wholly in God*: a mistranslation from Voltaire's French (see Note on the Text, p. xxx). The sense is '. . . did not doubt that we saw everything in God'.

57 '. . . *thinks or not*': this, the only direct quotation of Locke in the book, is from the section which started the famous 'thinking matter' controversy. Voltaire has truncated the sentence so as to avoid all reference to God. The phrase as quoted here has been translated word for word from the French translation of the *Essay* by Pierre Coste. Locke's original sentence in full is as follows: 'We have the *Ideas* of *Matter* and *Thinking*, but possibly shall never be able to know, whether any mere material Being ['whether Matter' in the first edition] thinks, or no; it being impossible for us, by the contemplation of our own *Ideas*, without revelation, to discover, whether Omnipotency has not given to some Systems of Matter fitly disposed, a power to perceive and think, or else joined and fixed to Matter so disposed, a thinking immaterial Substance: It being, in respect of our Notions, not much more remote from our Comprehension to conceive, that GOD can, if he pleases, superadd to Matter *a Faculty of Thinking*, than that he should superadd to it *another Substance, with a Faculty of Thinking*; since we know not wherein Thinking consists, nor to what sort of Substances the Almighty has been pleased to give that Power, which cannot be in any created Being, but merely by the good pleasure and Bounty of the Creator' (*An Essay concerning Human Understanding*, iv. 3. 6).

Faith and Revelation: this is ingenuous in the extreme. John W. Yolton writes that 'Voltaire was aware of the extensive reaction in England to Locke's suggestion. He was correct also in his remark about the issue for Locke being philosophical, not a challenge to faith and revelation, although that was not how it was interpreted. Locke made that suggestion as a conceptual point related to the limitations of our knowledge of soul and body, but his British readers did not examine the suggestion, as Voltaire urged, "calmly and impartially". Many French readers of Locke, and of Locke filtered through Voltaire, reacted similarly' (*Locke and French Materialism* (Oxford, 1991), 40).

57 *his Dispute with Mr. Locke*: Edward Stillingfleet, Bishop of Worcester, attacked Locke's *Essay*, as did others, for containing latent anti-Trinitarian ideas and so lending weight to the Deism of John Toland's *Christianity not Mysterious* (1696). Voltaire tells us that Stillingfleet lost the argument; but only after he has shown us how Locke's philosophy may be used to undermine the religious orthodoxy.

60 *... in their Countries*: Voltaire plays down the theological and political controversies surrounding Locke. Anthony Collins and John Toland, known in their own time as Deists, might now be termed pantheistic materialists; Margaret C. Jacob describes them as being 'at the intellectual heart of the radical Whig "college"' (*The Radical Enlightenment: Pantheists, Freemasons and Republicans* (London, 1981), 151). Voltaire casually mentions their names in this heterogeneous list but nowhere in the *Letters* does he discuss their ideas. Their beliefs were based on a 'radical' or atheistic interpretation of the new science (Descartes, Newton, Locke), and they were opposed by more moderate thinkers like Clarke. Locke's *The Reasonableness of Christianity* (1695) 'did not go so far as the deists were to wish, but it deployed some arguments that could be construed in their favour. Toland claimed that his *Christianity not mysterious* was a precocious pupil of Locke's own work, a claim which Locke strained to deny but which made his own moderate position much more difficult to maintain with any conviction' (John Redwood, *Reason, Ridicule and Religion: The Age of Enlightenment in England, 1660–1750* (London, 1976), 101–2).

65 *Schotten... Format*: Descartes's *Géométrie* first appeared with the *Discours de la méthode* in 1637 and was later published separately; Frans van Schooten published a Latin translation of the work together with a commentary (1659); his contemporary Pierre de Fermat was described by Pascal as 'le plus grand géomètre de toute l'Europe'.

66 *Rohault's little Work*: Jacques Rohault's *Traité de physique* (1671), translated into English in 1716.

69 *some Fruits fall from a Tree*: Voltaire was the first person to

relate this anecdote, in the *Essay on Epic Poetry* (1727), where he specifies the fruit in question as 'an Apple'; in the *Eléments de la philosophie de Newton* (1738) he tells the story again, adding that he heard it from Mrs Conduitt, Newton's niece.

70 *Mr. Picart*: Jean Picard, a seventeenth-century French astronomer.

Feet (of Paris): the French *pied de roi* measured 0.324 metres, as opposed to the *pied anglais*, which measured 0.305 metres.

73 *Mr. Whiston*: William Whiston succeeded Newton in 1703 as Lucasian Professor of Mathematics in Cambridge; his essay *The Cause of the Deluge Demonstrated* (1714) was mocked by Swift.

Elogium of Sir Isaac Newton: Fontenelle's *Eloge de Monsieur le Chevalier Neuton* (1728) was translated into English in the year of its appearance.

75 *Procedes huc, & non amplius*: a misquotation of Job 38: 11.

76 *Antonio de Dominis*: Italian theologian and physicist, who in 1611 published the first explanation of the rainbow as the refraction of light in raindrops.

80 *Dr. Wallis*: Revd John Wallis, Savilian Professor of Geometry at Oxford, best known for his *Arithmetica Infinitorum* (1655).

Lord Brounker: Viscount Brouncker, a mathematician and first president of the Royal Society.

81 *Mr. Perrault*: the seventeenth-century French doctor and architect Claude Perrault (brother of the author Charles Perrault).

another Work: *The Chronology of the Ancient Kingdoms Amended* (1728). Newton here assumes—as surely Voltaire did not—the complete accuracy of the Book of Genesis, and he follows Archbishop Ussher who in 1650 fixed the date of creation at 8 a.m. on Saturday, 22 October, 4004 BC.

87 *Othello*: the three plays of Shakespeare cited here, *Othello*, *Hamlet*, and *Julius Caesar*, were all performed at either Drury Lane or Lincoln's Inn Fields between September and December 1726, at the time when Voltaire was discovering Shakespeare (and learning English).

88 *Sophs*: Soph, 'A young man who has been two years at the university' (Johnson); cf. American *sophomore*.

90 *in a servile Manner*: Voltaire underlines the tendentious nature of his rendering of Hamlet's soliloquy (III, i). The references to 'cruel gods' and to 'the hypocrisy of our lying priests' have little to do with Shakespeare, and everything to do with Voltaire's campaign against the Church.

91 *The Passage ... as follows*: from Dryden's heroic tragedy *Aureng-Zebe* (produced and published in 1676), IV. i; Voltaire may have seen the work when it was performed at Drury Lane in 1727.

93 *some Letters ... French Nations*: Voltaire alludes to the work which is an immediate predecessor of his own, Béat de Muralt's *Lettres sur les Anglais et les Français* (1725); the work is anecdotal, more concerned with English food (good oysters), women (bad teeth), and opera (indifferent music) than with English religion, politics, and philosophy.

Misantrope: *The Plain-Dealer*, first performed probably in 1676, and published in 1677; the work was highly praised by Dryden.

95 *School for married Women*: *The Country Wife*, published and probably first acted in 1675.

Earth ... on thee: Voltaire apparently quotes from memory. The full text of the 'Epitaph on Sir John Vanbrugh, Architect of Blenheim Palace', by Abel Evans (1679–1737), is:

> Under this stone, Reader, survey
> Dead Sir John Vanbrugh's house of clay.
> Lie heavy on him, Earth! for he
> Laid many heavy loads on thee!

96 *Buononcini*: Giovanni Bononcini, an Italian opera composer, who between 1720 and 1732 lived in London, where he was the famous rival of Handel.

97 *If you ... every Night*: in other words, do as Voltaire did.

99 *an English Nobleman*: Lord Hervey, later a prominent Whig politician in Walpole's administration; Voltaire knew him in England, and they corresponded long after Voltaire's return to France. It was Lady Hervey who stimulated Voltaire to write his only love poem in English:

> H ... y would you know the passion
> You have kindled in my breast?
> Trifling is the inclination
> That by words can be expressed.

> In my silence see the lover;
> True love is by silence known;
> In my eyes you'll best discover
> All the power of your own.

99 *his Lordship's Verses . . . in our Tongue*: this is the only occasion on which Voltaire provides a translation without the original. Is Voltaire playing a joke on Hervey? The translation, as elsewhere, is highly tendentious, and without the English original for comparison, the reader is led to attribute the anti-clerical satire to Hervey rather than to his translator. The poem, written in 1729 by Lord Hervey from Italy to his wife in England, was long thought lost or even fictitious; the full text is reproduced in *Lord Hervey and His Friends* (London, 1950), edited by the Earl of Ilchester, pp. 35–6, 283–7; the extract translated by Voltaire is found in his English *Notebooks* (i. 238), which in addition contain a first draft of his translation into French (i. 101). The relevant section of the original poem is as follows (*Lord Hervey and His Friends*, 283):

> Throughout all Italy beside,
> What does one find but want and pride?
> Farces of superstitious folly,
> Decay, distress and melancholy,
> The havoc of despotic pow'r,
> A country rich, its' [*sic*] owners poor,
> Unpeopled towns, and lands untill'd,
> Bodies uncloath'd and mouths unfill'd.
> The nobles miserably great,
> In painted domes, and empty state,
> Too proud to work, too poor to eat.
> No arts the meaner sort employ,
> They nought improve, nor ought enjoy.
> Each clown from mis'ry grows a Saint,
> He prays from idleness, and fasts from want.

101 *mention of him*: in the *Memoirs of the Life of the Right Honourable John late Earl of Rochester, written by Monsieur St. Evremont*, included in the third edition of Rochester's *Works* (1709).

Boileau . . . Satyr on Man: Boileau's *Satire VIII*, vv. 55–60, 65–6.

102 *Oldham a little alter'd*: John Oldham, a poet, educated at St
Edmund Hall, Oxford. Famous for his savage *Satires upon the
Jesuits* (1681)—which Voltaire must have liked—and for his
'imitations' or free translations of such classical authors as
Horace and Juvenal. In these imitations, the Latin original was
often printed on the facing page, or at the end of the poem—
exactly as Voltaire does here with his own 'imitations'. The
present quotation (omitted from both French versions of the
text) is taken from 'The Eighth Satyr of Monsieur Boileau,
Imitated' (1683), but is significantly abridged. The passage in
full is as follows (*The Poems of John Oldham*, ed. H. F.
Brooks and R. Selden (Oxford, 1987), p. 164, vv. 70–90.):

> Yet, pleas'd with idle whimsies of his brain,
> And puft with pride, this haughty thing would fain
> Be thought himself the only stay and prop,
> That holds the mighty frame of Nature up:
> The Skies and Stars his properties must seem,
> And turn-spit Angels tread the spheres for him:
> Of all the Creatures he's the Lord (he cries)
> More absolute, than the *French* King of his.
> *And who is there* (say you) *that dares deny*
> *So own'd a truth?* That may be, Sir, do I.
> But to omit the controversie here,
> Whether, if met, the Passenger and Bear,
> This or the other stands in greater fear:
> Or, if an Act of Parliament should pass
> That all the *Irish* wolves should quit the place,
> They'd strait obey the Statutes high command,
> And at a minutes warning rid the Land:
> This boasted Monarch of the world, that aws
> The Creatures here, and with his beck gives laws;
> This titular King, who thus pretends to be
> The Lord of all, how many Lords has he?

Brooks and Selden comment that in Oldham's rendering of
Boileau, 'the demeaning expressions are thicker-sown than in
the French. The comparison is instructive. Boileau's satire
obeys a canon of dignity from which, within that neo-classical
limit, one of its merits, an urbane "keeping", derives. One of
the merits of Oldham's is in being under less restraint, and
enjoying, therefore, a greater alacrity in sinking. His pejora-
tive vocabulary is extended in its lower range. And Boileau

could never have dropped, even once, into burlesque, as Oldham does when he describes as "turn-spit Angels" the intelligences that rule the spheres' (p. lxi). This last phrase is precisely one of those which Voltaire has censored in the passage he quotes.

102 *Rochester ... Satyr against Man*: *A Satyr against Reason and Mankind*, vv.72, 75–95. Voltaire carefully selects a passage which allows him to lambaste pedantic metaphysicians more preoccupied with futile fact than with action. Rochester's 'An Allusion to Horace' is often cited as the first 'imitation' in English of a classical author; 'A Satyr against Mankind', first published in 1679, draws in part on Boileau's eighth satire, and so anticipates the imitation by Oldham from which Voltaire has just quoted.

103 *Voiture*: Vincent Voiture, an original member of the Académie française, was a prominent *salon* poet in the 1630s and 1640s; his *Lettres* had a formative influence on the 'classical' French language of the following generation—and also on the studiedly casual style of Voltaire's own *Letters concerning the English Nation*. Voiture's *Letters* appeared in English translation in 1657, and again in 1696, in a version by Dryden and Dennis which was reprinted several times in the early eighteenth century.

104 *Bristol Stones*: 'A kind of soft diamond found in a rock near the city of Bristol' (Johnson).

in this Manner: 'Upon the late storme, and of the death of his Highnesse ensuing the same', vv. 1–10, 31–4 (1658/59). Voltaire's rendering of Waller is notably tamer and less impetuous than the original. The intention, in part, is to demonstrate the superiority of French classical taste.

105 *Bayle's Dictionary*: Voltaire is mistaken; the anecdote is found not in Bayle but in the collection of anecdotes of Gilles Ménage known as the *Menagiana* (1693).

107 *prick down*: *to prick*, 'to mark a tune' (Johnson).

Hudibras: mock-heroic poem by Samuel Butler (1662-63-77); the first great satire to turn the fanaticism of the Commonwealth into farce.

108 *true Humour ... in Prose*: there is curiously no mention anywhere in the book of *Gulliver's Travels*, despite the fact that Voltaire read the work with enthusiasm, and wrote from

London only a week after its publication urging his friend Thiriot to translate the book into French (D308, D310, D315).

109 *Essay on Criticism . . . made of it*: the *Essai sur la critique* was published in Paris in June 1730; this letter was apparently written not long before that date. Du Resnel's only other poetic production was a translation of Pope's *Essay on Man* (1737). Many years later, Voltaire would claim in a letter (D15481) that he had written half of Du Resnel's verse himself, so they may have collaborated on the translation of the *Essay on Criticism*.

to translate a Poet literally: *The Rape of the Lock*, iv. 13–36 (1712, enlarged 1714). Voltaire does not, of course, try to be literal. The following translation begins straightforwardly, but the final third is clearly twisted in the direction of anti-clerical satire.

110 *a French Man . . . their History*: the thirteen-volume *Histoire d'Angleterre* (1724–35) was begun by Paul Rapin de Thoyras, and finished after his death by David Durand; the work influenced Montesquieu. Rapin de Thoyras was also the author of a *Dissertation sur les Whigs et les Torys* (1717).

113 *The Religion which Mr. Pope professes*: he was a Roman Catholic, and therefore debarred from local and national office by the Corporation and Test Acts, and subject to double taxes.

the Author of Rhadamistus: Prosper Jolyot de Crébillon, known as Crébillon *père*, the pre-eminent French dramatist of the first decade of the century, and Voltaire's only eighteenth-century rival as a tragedian (Montesquieu preferred the tragedies of Crébillon). The two dramatists began a spectacular and long-lasting feud in 1741.

Fagon: Louis XIV's physician.

114 *Mademoiselle le Couvreur*: Adrienne Lecouvreur, a famous French actress who died in 1730 (the same year as Anne Oldfield) and was refused Christian burial in Paris; Voltaire wrote a poem on her death.

Mr. Prynne: William Prynne, a Puritan pedant, educated at Oriel College, Oxford. His *Histrio-mastix: The Players Scourge . . . wherein it is largely evidenced by divers arguments . . . that popular stage-playes . . . are sinfull, heathenish, lewde, ungodly spectacles* (1632) runs to over a thousand pages. He is also the author of umpteen pamphlets, against men who wore their hair long, against women who wore their hair short, against anyone who wore cosmetics. So spectacular is his fanaticism that he is given an article to himself in Bayle's *Dictionnaire*.

114 *Propaganda Fide*: 'propagation of the faith'.

115 *Le Brun*: Pierre Le Brun, *Discours sur la comédie, où l'on voit la réponse au théologien qui la défend* (1694, and reprinted 1731).

   Signior Senesino or Signora Cuzzoni: Senesino, an alto castrato, and Cuzzoni, a soprano, were two of the star performers of Italian opera in London in the 1720s and early 1730s; Handel wrote especially for them the roles of Caesar and Cleopatra in *Giulio Cesare* (1724).

116 *many Years before us*: the Royal Society was founded in 1660, the Académie des Sciences in 1666.

117 *This Project*: Swift, *A Proposal for Correcting, Improving, and Ascertaining the English Tongue* (1712).

119 *the Right hand over the Left*: if this learned paper had not existed, Voltaire would have had to invent it. There was no need, however, as Henri Morin published 'Des privilèges de la main droite' in the *Mémoires de l'Académie des Inscriptions et Belles-Lettres* in 1723, just too soon to be influenced by his colleague in the Academy of Lagado who 'had been Eight Years upon a Project for extracting Sun-Beams out of Cucumbers' (*Gulliver's Travels*).

120 *Delmé . . . Hopkins . . . Heathcot*: Sir Peter Delmé (d. 1728), a director and later governor of the Bank of England, and immensely wealthy (in 1724 his investments amounted to over £400,000); he was the brother-in-law of Everard Fawkener, and a subscriber to the first edition of *La Henriade*. Sir Richard Hopkins (d. 1736), a director and, from 1733, sub-governor of the South Sea Company. Sir Gilbert Heathcote (d. 1733), one of the founders, and later governor, of the Bank of England, and reputedly the richest commoner in England (he was worth £700,000 at his death). Heathcote is said to be the prototype of Sir Andrew Freeport in *The Spectator*; Pope alludes to his stinginess in the *Dunciad* (ii. 251–2) and in the *Epistle to Bathurst* (103–4): 'The grave Sir Gilbert holds it for a rule, | That "every man in want is knave or fool".'

121 *a Gentleman*: the abbé de Rothelin, whom Voltaire consulted in 1733 about the acceptability of the *Letters* for publication (see D559 and D570); Rothelin was not (as is often claimed) a royal censor: Voltaire approached him simply as a highly placed friend.

149 *Creech*: Thomas Creech's translations of Horace were first published in 1684.

152 *Mr. Sorbieres*: Samuel Sorbière, *Relation d'un voyage en Angleterre* (Paris, 1664), translated into English in 1709.

153 *an Apple falling from a Tree*: compare Letter XV, p. 69.

162 *In the year 1720*: the correct date is 1726.

167 *whatsoever*: compare Letter XIX, p. 96.

170 *quas . . . natura*: 'due either to carelessness or to human negligence' (Horace, *Ars poetica*, 352–3).

The Oxford World's Classics Website

www.worldsclassics.co.uk

- Browse the full range of Oxford World's Classics online

- Sign up for our monthly e-alert to receive information on new titles

- Read extracts from the Introductions

- Listen to our editors and translators talk about the world's greatest literature with our Oxford World's Classics audio guides

- Join the conversation, follow us on Twitter at OWC_Oxford

- Teachers and lecturers can order inspection copies quickly and simply via our website

www.worldsclassics.co.uk

American Literature

British and Irish Literature

Children's Literature

Classics and Ancient Literature

Colonial Literature

Eastern Literature

European Literature

Gothic Literature

History

Medieval Literature

Oxford English Drama

Poetry

Philosophy

Politics

Religion

The Oxford Shakespeare

A complete list of Oxford World's Classics, including Authors in Context, Oxford English Drama, and the Oxford Shakespeare, is available in the UK from the Marketing Services Department, Oxford University Press, Great Clarendon Street, Oxford OX2 6DP, or visit the website at www.oup.com/uk/worldsclassics.

In the USA, visit www.oup.com/us/owc for a complete title list.

Oxford World's Classics are available from all good bookshops. In case of difficulty, customers in the UK should contact Oxford University Press Bookshop, 116 High Street, Oxford OX1 4BR.